How To Pass

Spoken English For Industry and Commerce

Threshold Level

Student's Book

How to Pass
Spoken English for Industry and Commerce
Threshold Level

Published in 1996

© Copyright Logophon Lehrmittel Verlag GmbH

All rights reserved. No part of this publication may be reproduced, stored in a retrieval system, or transmitted in any form or by any means, electronic, photocopying, recording or otherwise, without prior permission of the publisher.

Das Werk ist in allen seinen Teilen urheberrechtlich geschützt. Jede Verwendung ist ohne Zustimmung des Verlags unzulässig. Das gilt insbesondere für Vervielfältigungen, Übersetzungen, Mikroverfilmung und die Einspeicherung in und Verarbeitung durch elektronische Systeme.

ISBN 3-922514-34-0

Published by:	Logophon Lehrmittel Verlag GmbH
Verlag:	Alte Gärtnerei 2, 55128 Mainz
Illustrations by:	Hsiang-Shan Kung-Scherer
Layout by:	Lynne M Evans

Printed and bound in Slovakia.

Accompanying Material to this book:

How to Pass Spoken English for Industry and Commerce Threshold Level
Teacher's Book ISBN 3-922514-40-5

How to Pass Spoken English for Industry and Commerce Threshold Level
Student's Cassette ISBN 3-922514-41-3

How to Pass Spoken English for Industry and Commerce Threshold Level
Picture Book ISBN 3-922514-42-1

Acknowledgements

The authors would like to thank all those who have helped in writing this book.

Special thanks to the LCCIEB, especially Liam Swords, Dawn Postans and Rupert Jones-Parry.

Special thanks also to Jean Pierre Jouteux and Gabi Schaub at Logophon.

Many thanks especially to Lucy Davison, John Davison, Nicky Westgate and John Green.

Thanks also to Wilf Curry, Safeway, Chollerford Garage, Lloyds Bank, Humshaugh Surgery, Saxon Financial Advice, Fourstones Paper Mill, Tynedale Council, The Globe Inn, Woodlands Post Office, Hexham General Hospital, London Transport Museum, European Language Skills, Stakis Coylumbridge, The Scotsman Communications Ltd and Camelot Group plc.

Thanks also to the following: Dr John McCollum, Joy McCollum, Dick Shotton, John Davison, Mike Saxon, Hazel Saxon, Kevin Allan, Scott Swan, Joan Swan, Maggie Wardle, Pat Egglestone, Hilary Stewart, Joy Taylor and Brit, Winifried Carr, Dorothy Wilson, George Robertson, Joanne McEwan.

Threshold Examination

From the LCCIEB brochure "Languages for Industry and Commerce":
"The examination lasts for 30 minutes and there are five sections: A, B, C, D and E."

Section A (5 minutes)

Greeting and warm-up introductory conversation

The examiner will greet, welcome and settle the candidate in as friendly a way as possible, then slowly describe the tasks of the examination in order (about 2 minutes). The examiner will then ask the candidate about work, study, family, interests, travel, future career or any other topics that may naturally occur in the course of the conversation. The conversation will be kept largely factual since section E will afford the opportunities for the expression of opinions and attitudes.

The purpose of this section is to give candidates a chance to warm up and express themselves before the more structured tasks begin and to give the examiner information about the candidate to guide the selection of topics in section E.

Section B (5 minutes)

Picture sequence

The examiner will show the candidate a sequence of pictures showing a series of events and will ask the candidate to describe what is happening over the whole sequence, then ask questions requiring the candidate to relate the events in time and modify the verb accordingly, eg 'What happened then?' 'What is he going to do?' 'What had she done before that?' 'What was happening while...?' 'What do you think she will do next?, etc

The purpose of this section is to test a candidate's ability to handle time expressions and verb tenses.

Section C (10 minutes)

Pathfinding on the basis of a taped announcement

A short announcement on a tape will be played twice and candidates shown a map, diagram, etc on which they are required to show that they can locate places and carry out instructions given in the announcement, eg advertising bargains at a particular place in a department store; change of a platform, etc at a railway station; school notices on tannoy, etc. The announcement will often include time references, so that candidates have to get themselves to the right place at the right time.

The purpose of this section is to ensure that candidates can understand recorded messages, public announcements, etc and use them along with plans, maps, diagrams, etc to find their way in an unfamiliar environment.

Section D (5 minutes)

Reading and reacting

Candidates will be shown *either* a headline, advertisement, press appeal, etc; *or* a picture/diagram of some machine or article in everyday use, with the parts labelled where necessary, and brief instructions on its use, eg a ticket machine, telephone, luggage storage locker, automatic cash dispenser, etc. Candidates have to show they understand the message by carrying out instructions, eg completing a form, inserting a coin, pressing a button, etc. Where required, they have to talk their way out of any problems by eliciting or providing more information in conversation with the examiner.

The purpose of this section is to ensure that candidates can carry out or interpret instructions given visually in relation to some display, machine or other data presented in graphic form.

Section E (5 minutes)

Attitudinal conversation

The examiner will have a general conversation with the candidate to encourage the expression of attitudes on matters of personal history and common concern, eg likes/dislikes, right/wrong, agreement/disagreement, beautiful/ugly, fair/unfair, good/bad, against/in favour, etc. Candidates should express themselves freely and give their opinions.

The purpose of this section is to test whether candidates can express opinions and attitudes in every day matters and to give candidates a chance to project their personal identity through language.

Introduction

This Series of books is for candidates preparing for the four levels of the Spoken English For Industry and Commerce (SEFIC) examinations. It takes the learner from beginner to advanced level in approximately 480 hours.

This book prepares candidates for the second level (Threshold) SEFIC exam and is divided into 60 Units, each Unit providing approximately 2 hours of classroom teaching. At the end of each Unit there is a list of new language items divided into vocabulary and structures with room for students to paraphrase or translate. Students are encouraged to prepare each Unit by looking up the new vocabulary before the lesson. Every tenth Unit is a revision Unit which consolidates the vocabulary and structures presented in the previous nine Units.

The syllabus is a thematic content-based syllabus which emphasises the process of learning and employs task-based activities. Learners are encouraged to use the subject language to discuss their own experience and knowledge relating to the themes and to express opinions about the subject matter. Language is not treated as a subject which one can learn/acquire per se, but rather as a means of receiving and giving information about another subject, ie as a means of communication.

The themes cover **personal information** (identity, character, appearance), **house and home** (type, place, costs, furniture, rooms), **environment** (town, country, weather), **travel and transport** (public transport, private vehicles, directions), **food and drink** (mealtime, restaurant, tastes, values), **shops and shopping** (weights, measures, prices, goods), **services** (telephone, bank, post office, garage), **health and hygiene** (body, states, illness, medicine), **perception and bodily movement** (feeling, seeing, handling), **work** (place, wages, duties, boss, colleagues), **education** (school, teachers, subjects, exams, future), **foreign languages** (aims, problems, skills), **leisure** (entertainment, hobbies, sport), **human relations** (friends, clubs, contacts), and **current affairs** (news, scandal, society). The speech acts and functions learned are those required to elicit and express factual information about the themes covered and which enable students to get things done (suasion). Thus, *expressing factual information about the environment* describes such language as "It's cold", "There are 3 restaurants in this town", "This town is boring/dirty". Similarly, *getting things done in connection with food and drink* would include such language as "A packet of ..., please", "Can I have a..., please", "Can I have the bill, please?"

This level is accompanied by: a Teacher's book, containing teaching notes, tapescripts and answers to exercises; a Picture book, including full-colour photographs and a cassette containing all the listening material from the Units.

By the end of this level students should be able to cope in temporary contact with foreign language speakers in everyday situations, whether as visitors to the foreign country or with visitors to their own country.

How to Pass
Spoken English for Industry and Commerce
Threshold Level

CONTENTS

				parts of exam practised				
Theme	Unit	Page	Title	A	B	C	D	E
HOUSE AND HOME	1	1-4	Where do you live?	✓		✓		
	2	5-8	Lifestyle	✓		✓		
	3	9-12	What's he doing?	✓	✓			
	4	13-16	Would you like to live in this house?	✓		✓	✓	✓
	5	17-20	Do you have a computer?	✓			✓	
ENVIRONMENT AND WEATHER	6	21-26	Life in the country is too quiet for me.	✓	✓			✓
	7	27-30	What's the weather like?	✓		✓		
	8	31-34	How do you get from the library to the golf club?	✓		✓		✓
	9	35-38	Have you ever been sailing?	✓			✓	
	10	39-42	**REVISION**					
TRAVEL AND TRANSPORT	11	43-46	Have you ever travelled on the London Underground?	✓		✓	✓	
	12	47-52	What's the best holiday you've ever had?	✓	✓		✓	
	13	53-56	Has flight JG971 from Tokyo arrived yet?	✓		✓	✓	
	14	57-60	When's the next train to Corbridge?	✓		✓	✓	
	15	61-64	I think that cars are the safest way to travel.	✓				✓
FOOD AND DRINK	16	65-68	Going Shopping	✓		✓		
	17	69-72	Eating Out	✓		✓	✓	
	18	73-76	Eating In	✓			✓	✓
	19	77-80	A pint of beer please.	✓		✓	✓	
	20	81-84	**REVISION**					
SHOPS AND SHOPPING	21	85-88	Rubbish and Recycling	✓				✓
	22	89-92	Where can you buy a safety pin?	✓		✓		
	23	93-96	How many metres are there in a kilometre?	✓		✓	✓	
	24	97-102	At the Supermarket		✓	✓	✓	✓
	25	103-106	Which department is it in?	✓		✓	✓	✓
SERVICES	26	107-112	What's the code for Cork?	✓	✓		✓	
	27	113-118	Do you have a driving licence?	✓	✓			✓
	28	119-124	Who do you bank with?	✓	✓	✓	✓	✓
	29	125-128	Where's the nearest car park?	✓		✓	✓	
	30	129-132	**REVISION**					

How to Pass
Spoken English for Industry and Commerce
Threshold Level

CONTENTS

Theme	Unit	Page	Title	A	B	C	D	E
HEALTH AND HYGIENE	31	133-138	I've got a headache.	✓	✓	✓		
	32	139-142	Rescue at Sea	✓		✓		✓
	33	143-146	Do you live a healthy life?	✓				✓
	34	147-150	Do you have medical insurance?	✓		✓	✓	✓
WORK	35	151-156	What do you do for a living?	✓	✓			
	36	157-160	Applying for a job.	✓		✓	✓	
	37	161-164	Who do you work for?	✓		✓	✓	
	38	165-170	What happens to your waste paper?	✓	✓			
	39	171-174	At Work	✓			✓	✓
	40	175-178	**REVISION**					
EDUCATION AND LANGUAGES	41	179-182	What was your favourite subject at school?	✓		✓	✓	✓
	42	183-188	How long have you been learning English?	✓		✓	✓	✓
	43	189-192	Why are you learning English?	✓			✓	
	44	193-196	I don't have time to learn vocabulary.	✓			✓	✓
LEISURE TIME	45	197-200	What do you do in your spare time?	✓				✓
	46	201-206	Going Swimming	✓	✓		✓	
	47	207-212	What's On?	✓		✓	✓	
	48	213-216	Where did you go on holiday last year?	✓		✓	✓	
	49	217-220	What's the best book you've ever read?	✓		✓		✓
	50	221-224	**REVISION**					
CURRENT AFFAIRS	51	225-228	Which newspaper do you read and why?	✓		✓	✓	✓
	52	229-232	What would you do if you won £20 million?	✓		✓		✓
	53	233-236	What was on the news last night?	✓				
	54	237-240	Young French student requires rented accommodation.	✓		✓		✓
	55	241-244	Are you free on Tuesday afternoon?			✓	✓	
	56	245-250	She's going to type a letter.	✓	✓	✓	✓	✓
EXAM PREPARATION	57	251-256	**Exam Practice 1**	✓	✓	✓	✓	✓
	58	257-262	**Exam Practice 2**	✓	✓	✓	✓	✓
	59	263-268	**Exam Practice 3**	✓	✓	✓	✓	✓
	60	269-274	**Exam Practice 4**	✓	✓	✓	✓	✓

parts of exam practised

UNIT 1

Where do you live?

1 a Listen to your teacher.

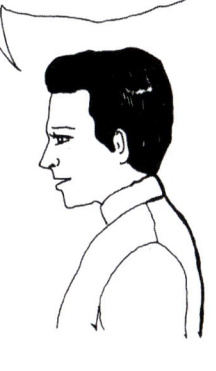

My name's Alison. I live in Sheffield.

What's your name? Where do you live?

b Ask 5 neighbours.

c Write 5 sentences about your neighbours.

eg   Alison lives in Sheffield.

1 _____
2 _____
3 _____
4 _____
5 _____

d Match the pictures and the words.

_d_ block of flats
___ semi-detached house
___ bungalow
___ detached house
___ terraced house

Check with your neighbour.

e Listen to the cassette and fill in the following.

Listen again and check.

		block of flats	semi-detached house	bungalow	detached house	terraced house	Kelso	Portsmouth	Cambridge	Sheffield	Dover
1	Alison	✓								✓	
2	Dave										
3	Sally										
4	Andy										
5	Chris										

f Fill in the following.

What kind of house do you live in? _____.

g Ask 5 neighbours.

Unit 1

2 a Put the words in the right space.

> bedroom   bathroom   hall   dining room
> living room   study   kitchen

After work, I go home by bus. When I arrive home, I open my front door and go into the _____ where I take my coat and shoes off. Then I go into the _____ where I have a wash, and then I go into the bedroom where I change my clothes. After that I go into the _____ and prepare something to eat for my children. They come home at 5 o'clock and we eat dinner together in the _____. After dinner we go into the _____ where we watch TV and relax. The children go to their bedrooms when they want to go to sleep and I normally go to my _____ so I can do some work. When I'm tired I go into my _____, get into bed and go to sleep.

Check with your neighbour.

b Which rooms do you have? ....

Fill in the column marked 'you'.

(✓ = yes / x = no)

	you	your neighbour
bedroom	....	....
living room	....	....
bathroom	....	....
study	....	....
hall	....	....
kitchen	....	....
dining room	....	....

c Ask your neighbour ....

eg *Do you have a bedroom?*
Yes I do. / No I don't.

d Fill in the following.

I have _____ but my neighbour doesn't.

My neighbour has _____ but I don't.

We both have _____.

Neither of us have _____.

e Ask your neighbour.

1 Which room do you sleep in?
2 Which room do you eat in?
3 Which room do you watch TV in?
4 Which room do you work in?
5 Which room do you change your clothes in?

f Can you name 3 things you both have in your rooms?

3 a Match the pictures and the words.

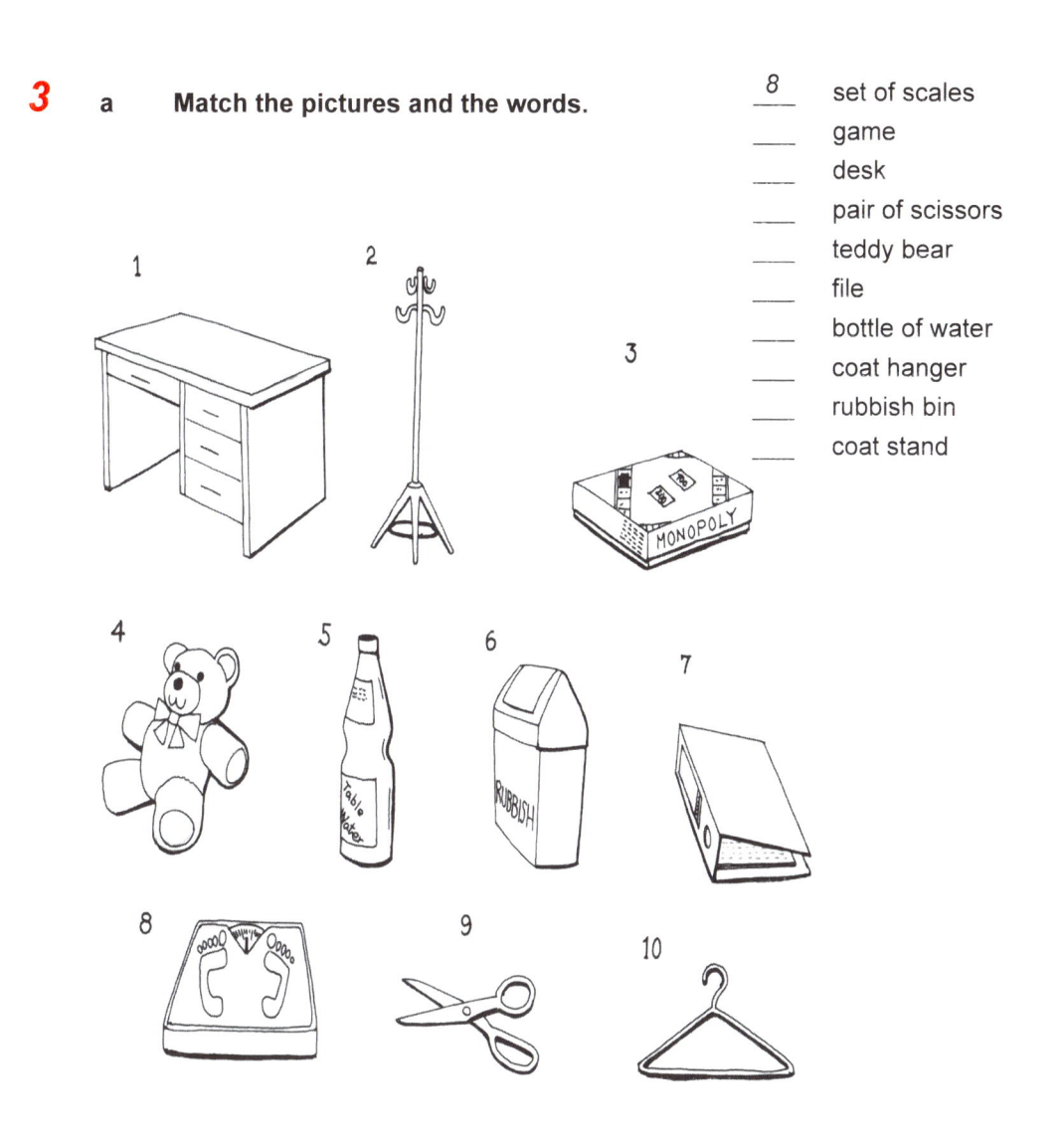

_8_	set of scales
___	game
___	desk
___	pair of scissors
___	teddy bear
___	file
___	bottle of water
___	coat hanger
___	rubbish bin
___	coat stand

1 desk 2 coat stand 3 game (Monopoly)
4 teddy bear 5 bottle of water 6 rubbish bin 7 file
8 set of scales 9 pair of scissors 10 coat hanger

b Ask your neighbour.

eg *What's number 1? It's a desk.*

c Fill in the following about yourself ......

eg *Which room is your desk in?*
It's in my study.

	you	your neighbour
set of scales	....	....
game	....	....
desk	....	....
pair of scissors	....	....
teddy bear	....	....
file	....	....
bottle of water	....	....
coat hanger	....	....
rubbish bin	....	....
coat stand	....	....

d Ask your neighbour and fill in the rooms ....

4 a Translate the following.

Vocabulary

block of flats _____

semi-detached house _____

bungalow _____

detached house _____

terraced house _____

bedroom _____

living room _____

bathroom _____

study _____

hall _____

kitchen _____

dining room _____

set of scales _____

game _____

desk _____

pair of scissors _____

teddy bear _____

file _____

bottle of water _____

coat hanger _____

rubbish bin _____

coat stand _____

Structures

What's your name? _____

My name's Alison _____

Where do you live? _____

I live in Sheffield. _____

Alison lives in Sheffield. _____

What kind of house do you live in? _____

I live in a flat. _____

Do you have a bedroom? _____

Yes I do. _____

No I don't. _____

I have a study but my neighbour doesn't. _____

My neighbour has 3 bedrooms but I don't. _____

We both have a kitchen and a bathroom. _____

Neither of us have a hall. _____

What's number 1? _____

It's a desk. _____

Which room is your desk in? _____

It's in my study. _____

UNIT 2

Lifestyle

Roger Regular's Diary

Mon Work 9am - 5pm
Tues Work 9am - 5pm
Wed Work 9am - 5pm
Thur Work 9am - 5pm
Fri Work 9am - 5pm
Sat Relax
Sun Relax

1 a Listen to the cassette and fill in the missing information.

I have a very regular lifestyle. I work _____ days a week from _____ to _____. I always get up at _____ when my alarm clock goes off. At _____ I have breakfast and at _____ I leave home. It takes _____ minutes to get to work so I normally arrive at _____. I make a cup of coffee and then I start work at _____. In the morning I read the post, write letters and make phone calls. I have lunch from _____ to _____. After lunch I have meetings and see people. I go home at _____. In the evening I have dinner and read a newspaper. It's normally about _____ when I go to bed.

Listen again and check.

b Tell your neighbour about Roger.

eg *He has a very regular lifestyle. He works...*

c Answer these questions about Roger.

1 How many days a week does Roger work? _____ .
2 What time does he get up? _____ .
3 What does he do in the office in the morning? _____ .
4 What does he do in the afternoon? _____ .
5 What time does he go to bed? _____ .

Check with your neighbour.

d Here are some answers. Can you write the questions?

1 _____ ? He has breakfast at 8.00am.
2 _____ ? He leaves home at 8.15am.
3 _____ ? He has meetings and sees people.
4 _____ ? He finishes work at 5.00pm.
5 _____ ? He has dinner and reads a newspaper.

Check with your neighbour.

Edward Exciting's Diary

Mon	?	Thur	?
Tues	?	Fri	?
Wed	?	Sat	?
		Sun	?

2 a   Read this information about Edward.

I don't have a regular lifestyle. I start work at different times. I sometimes work at the weekend. I don't normally have lunch unless I have a business lunch. I have a company car because I travel a lot in my job. I work in different places and I often stay in hotels. I go to bed when I'm tired.

b   Tell your neighbour about Edward.

eg   *He doesn't have a regular lifestyle. He starts work...*

c   Fill in the following.

eg   *I don't have a regular lifestyle. He doesn't have a regular lifestyle.*

1   I don't have breakfast. _____ .

2   _____ . He doesn't have a company car.

3   I don't travel a lot in my job. _____ .

4   _____ . He doesn't often stay in hotels.

5   I don't work on Sundays. _____ .

Check with your neighbour.

d   Answer these questions about Edward using "Yes he does." or "No he doesn't."

eg   *Does Edward have a regular lifestyle? No he doesn't.*

1   Does Edward start work at different times? _____ .

2   Does he normally have lunch? _____ .

3   Does he have a company car? _____ .

4   Does he travel a lot in his job? _____ .

5   Does he go home every night? _____ .

Check with your neighbour.

3   a   **Now write about yourself using "Yes I do." or "No I don't."**

eg   *Do you always get up at the same time? Yes I do.*

1   Do you always have breakfast at the same time? _____ .
2   Do you always start work at the same time? _____ .
3   Do you always work in the same place? _____ .
4   Do you always have lunch at the same time? _____ .
5   Do you always go to bed at the same time? _____ .

b   **Ask your neighbour the same questions.**

c   **Fill in the following about yourself using the words in the box below.**

| always | normally | often | sometimes | rarely | never |

eg   *I always get up at the same time.*

1   I _____ have breakfast at the same time.
2   I _____ start work at the same time.
3   I _____ work in the same place.
4   I _____ have lunch at the same time.
5   I _____ go to bed at the same time.

d   **Tell your neighbour about yourself.**

e   **Fill in this chart about yourself.**

		you	your neighbour
1	How many days a week do you work?		
2	Do you sometimes work at weekends?		
3	How long does it take to get to work?		
4	How long do you have for lunch?		
5	What time do you have breakfast?		
6	What time do you have lunch?		
7	Do you watch TV in the evenings?		
8	Do you have a company car?		
9	Do you travel a lot in your job?		
10	What time do you go to bed?		

f   **Ask your neighbour the questions**

g   **Tell your teacher about your neighbour.**

h   **Write 5 sentences about yourself.**

eg   *I never work at weekends.*

1 _____ .
2 _____ .
3 _____ .
4 _____ .
5 _____ .

4 a Translate the following.

Vocabulary

lifestyle _____
regular _____
alarm clock _____
go off _____
take _____
read the post _____
write letters _____
make phone calls _____
have meetings _____
see people _____
in the morning _____
after lunch _____
in the afternoon _____
in the evening _____
at different times _____
unless _____
business lunch _____
company car _____
travel _____
always _____
normally _____
often _____
sometimes _____
rarely _____
never _____

Structures

I have a very regular lifestyle. _____
He has a very regular lifestyle. _____
What time does he have breakfast? _____
He has breakfast at 8.00am. _____
I don't have a regular lifestyle. _____
He doesn't have a regular lifestyle. _____
Does he have a regular lifestyle? _____
Yes he does. _____
No he doesn't. _____
Do you always get up at the same time? _____
Yes I do. _____
No I don't _____
I always get up at the same time. _____
I never work at weekends. _____

UNIT 3

What's he doing?

1   a   Match the sentences and the pictures.

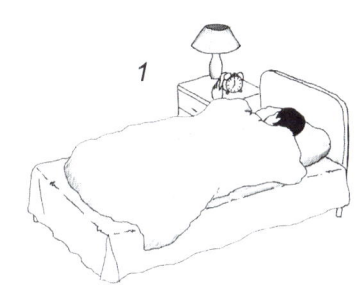

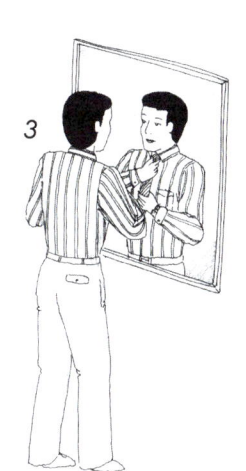

a	It's 7 o'clock in the morning and Jeremy is lying in bed. `1`
b	He's washing his face.
c	He's looking in the mirror.
d	He's eating breakfast.
e	He's leaning over the wash basin.
f	His alarm clock's ringing and he's trying to switch it off.
g	He's getting dressed.
h	He's holding a bowl in his left hand.
i	He's putting his jacket on.
j	He's unlocking the car.
k	He's coming downstairs.

Check with your neighbour.

b   Ask your neighbour about Jeremy.

eg   What's he doing in picture 1?   He's lying in bed.

c   Answer the questions using "Yes he is." or "No he isn't."

eg   Is he unlocking the car in picture 1?   No he isn't.

1   Is he washing his face in picture 3? _____.
2   Is he wearing a jacket in picture 2? _____.
3   Is he eating breakfast in picture 4? _____.
4   Is he coming downstairs in picture 5? _____.
5   Is he putting his jacket on in picture 3? _____.

Check with your neighbour.

Unit 3

2

a   **Describe the people in the picture to your neighbour.**

eg   *Tony has short dark hair and glasses.*

Tony   *Deborah*   *Joe*

Sally   *Roger*   *Amanda*

b   **Make up 5 questions about the people.**

eg   *What's Tony doing?*

1 _____ ?
2 _____ ?
3 _____ ?
4 _____ ?
5 _____ ?

Check with your teacher and then ask your neighbour your questions.

eg   *What's Tony doing? He's drinking coffee.*

c   **Fill in the following using "is" or "isn't".**

eg   *Tony isn't typing a letter.*

1   Joe _____ writing.
2   Roger _____ smoking.
3   Deborah _____ typing.
4   Sally _____ watching TV.
5   Amanda _____ smoking.

Check with your teacher

d   **Close your book. Tell your neighbour what Tony, Deborah, Joe, Sally, Roger and Amanda are doing.**

e   **Look around the class. Ask your neighbour what the other students are doing.**

3 a **Put the words in the right place.**

sandals	waistcoat	shoes	shirt	glasses	skirt
dress	tie	suit	jacket	trousers	
shorts	scarf	brooch	T-shirt	socks	necklace
blouse	boots	bracelet	earrings	pullover	
Tony	**Deborah**	**Joe**	**Sally**	**Roger**	**Amanda**

Check with your teacher.

b Write 5 questions about the people.

eg *What's Tony wearing?*

1 _____ ?

2 _____ ?

3 _____ ?

4 _____ ?

5 _____ ?

c Ask your neighbour.

eg *What's Tony wearing? He's wearing shorts, sandals, a T-shirt and glasses.*

d Look around the class. Ask your neighbour what other students are wearing.

e Answer these questions.

1 What are you wearing? _____ .

2 What is your neighbour wearing? _____ .

3 What is your teacher wearing? _____ .

f Look around your class. Describe somebody to your neighbour.

eg *She's wearing a blue dress, shoes, a brooch and earrings, and she's talking to the teacher. Who is it?*

g Look around your class. Ask your neighbour questions like these.

eg *Who's wearing a white T-shirt? What's the teacher doing?*

4 a Translate the following.

Vocabulary

lie _____	sandals _____
wash his face _____	waistcoat _____
mirror _____	shoes _____
wear _____	shirt _____
lean over _____	glasses _____
wash basin _____	skirt _____
ring _____	dress _____
try _____	tie _____
switch off _____	jacket _____
get dressed _____	trousers _____
hold _____	shorts _____
bowl _____	scarf _____
put on _____	brooch _____
unlock _____	T-shirt _____
come downstairs _____	socks _____
drink _____	necklace _____
smoke _____	blouse _____
talk _____	boots _____
write _____	bracelet _____
watch TV _____	suit _____
eat _____	earrings _____
type _____	pullover _____

Structures

What's he doing in picture 1? _____
He's lying in bed. _____
Is he unlocking the car in picture 1? _____
Yes he is. _____
No he isn't. _____
Tony has short dark hair and glasses. _____
What's Tony doing? _____
He's drinking coffee. _____
Tony isn't typing a letter. _____
What's Tony wearing? _____
He's wearing shorts, sandals, a T-shirt and glasses. _____
What are you wearing? _____
I'm wearing trousers, a shirt and a tie. _____
What's she wearing? _____
She's wearing a blue dress, shoes, a brooch and earrings. _____
What's she doing? _____
She's talking to the teacher. _____
Who's wearing a white T-shirt? _____
What's the teacher doing? _____

UNIT 4

Would you like to live in this house?

LJ Patterson & Partners, Estate Agent, 14 Main Street, Lancaster
Tel: 01374 99476 / Fax: 01374 98345

Opening Times
Mon - Fri 9am - 5pm
Sat & Sun 10am - 4pm

For Sale
Price £95,000

17 Fairview Crescent
Lancaster

This attractive semi-detached house is pleasantly situated 2 minutes from the town centre. The house offers 2-storey accommodation including 3 bedrooms, a modernised kitchen, central heating and a patio.

Viewing by appointment only.

---

1 a Ask your neighbour.

1 What is the name of the estate agent?
2 What is the address of the house for sale?
3 What is the estate agent's telephone number?
4 What is the fax number?
5 What time do they close on Fridays?
6 Are they open on Sundays?
7 How much is the house?
8 Do I have to make an appointment to see the house?
9 Is the house in the country?
10 Does the house have central heating?

Check with your teacher.

2 a Listen to the cassette and write down the names of the rooms on the house plan below.

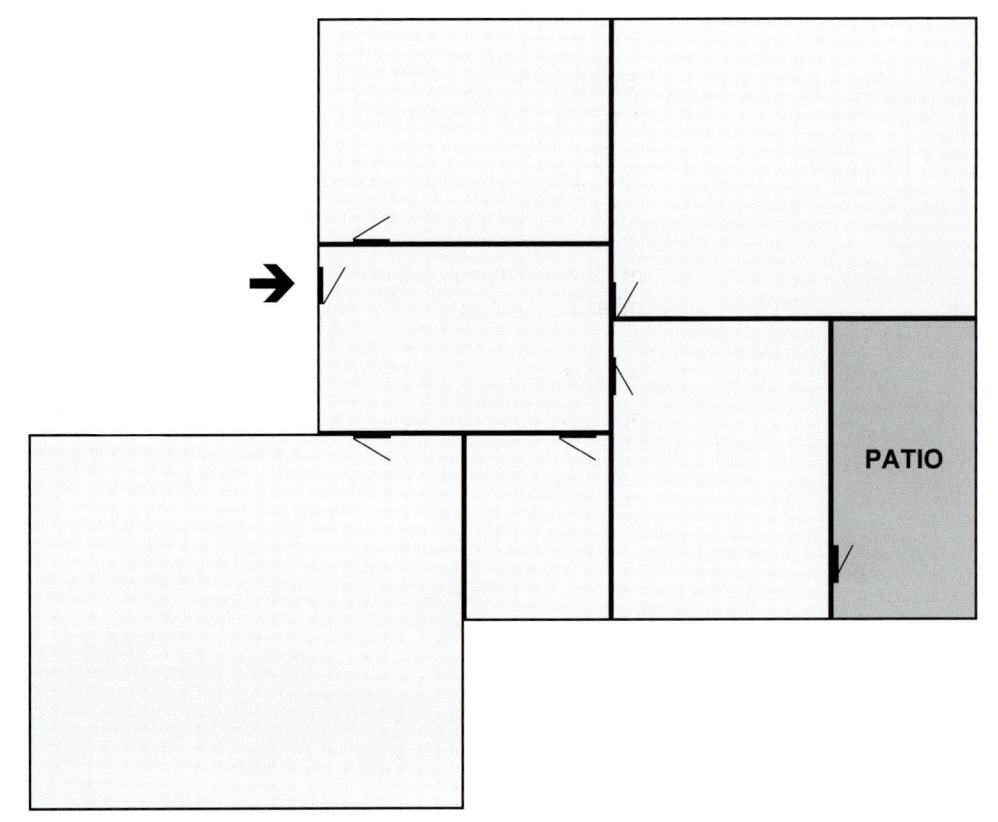

Check with your neighbour.

b Draw a plan of your own house.

c Tell your neighbour what the rooms are.

eg *This is the front door and this is the entrance hall. The first room on the left is a bedroom.*

3 **a** Alison lives in a block of flats in Sheffield but dreams of moving to a detached house in the country one day. Read the description of Alison's ideal home.

"My ideal home would be a detached house. It would have 9 rooms; a bathroom, a kitchen, a living room, a big dining room, a study, 3 bedrooms and an entrance hall. It would be made of stone and would be painted white. It would have views over mountains and a lake. It wouldn't have a balcony, air conditioning, a patio or satellite TV, but it would have central heating, a coal fire, a garage, a big garden, a wine cellar and a telephone. The nearest shop would be about 3 miles away, the nearest restaurant would be about 10 miles away and the nearest post office would be about 5 miles away. I would live there with my pet dog, Max."

b **Ask your neighbour.**

eg *Would you like to live in this house? Yes I would. No I wouldn't.*

c **Answer these questions about your ideal home in note form** ....

		you	your neighbour
1	What kind of house would it be?		
2	How many rooms would it have?		
3	Would it be in the town or country?		
4	What would it be made of?		
5	What colour would it be?		
6	What views would it have?		
7	Would it have a balcony?		
8	Would it have a patio?		
9	Would it have central heating?		
10	Would it have a coal fire?		
11	Would it have a garage?		
12	Would it have a garden?		
13	Would it have satellite TV?		
14	Would it have a wine cellar?		
15	Would it have a telephone?		
16	Would it have air conditioning?		
17	How far would the nearest shop be?		
18	How far would the nearest restaurant be?		
19	How far would the nearest post office be?		
20	Would you live there alone?		

d **Ask your neighbour about his/her ideal home.** ....

eg *What kind of house would your ideal home be? It would be a detached house.*

e **Tell your teacher about your ideal home.**

eg *My ideal home would be a detached house.*

4 a Translate the following.

Vocabulary

estate agent _____	next to _____
opening times _____	shower _____
for sale _____	outside _____
price _____	south facing _____
attractive _____	wonderful views _____
pleasantly situated _____	master bedroom _____
offer _____	garage _____
2-storey _____	mountains _____
accommodation _____	lake _____
modernised _____	balcony _____
central heating _____	air conditioning _____
patio _____	satellite TV _____
appointment _____	coal fire _____
front door _____	garden _____
entrance hall _____	wine cellar _____
approximately _____	telephone _____
on the left _____	10 minutes away _____
opposite _____	

Structures

It would be a detached house. _____

It would be made of stone. _____

It would be painted white. _____

It would have central heating. _____

It wouldn't have air conditioning. _____

I would live there alone. _____

This is the front door. _____

This is the entrance hall. _____

The first room on the left is a bedroom. _____

Would you like to live in this house? _____

Yes I would. _____

No I wouldn't. _____

What kind of house would it be? _____

It would be a detached house. _____

Would it have a balcony? _____

My ideal home would be a detached house. _____

UNIT 5

Do you have a computer?

1 a Match the sentences and the pictures.

1 The TV remote control has buttons. | b |
2 The cassette recorder has buttons. | |
3 The oven has dials. | |
4 The iron has a dial. | |
5 The hairdryer has a switch. | |
6 The computer keyboard has keys. | |

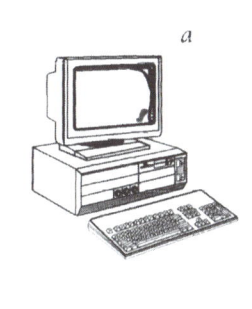

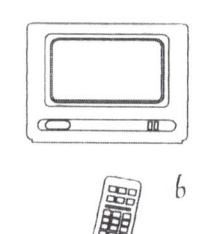

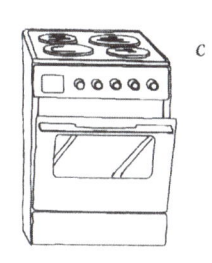

b Now complete the sentences below using the words in the box.

| press - turn |

eg   To operate the computer, you press the keys.

1 To operate the TV, you _____.
2 To operate the cassette recorder, you _____.
3 To operate the iron, you _____.
4 To operate the hairdryer, you _____.
5 To operate the oven, you _____.

Check with your teacher.

c Ask your neighbour.

eg   Do you have a computer? Yes I do. How do you operate it? I press the keys.

d Fill in the following about your class.

1 How many people in your class have a computer? _____
2 How many people in your class have a TV with remote control? _____
3 How many people in your class have an oven? _____
4 How many people in your class have an iron? _____
5 How many people in your class have a hairdryer? _____

2 a Here is a picture of an electric kettle. See if you can match the numbers and the words.

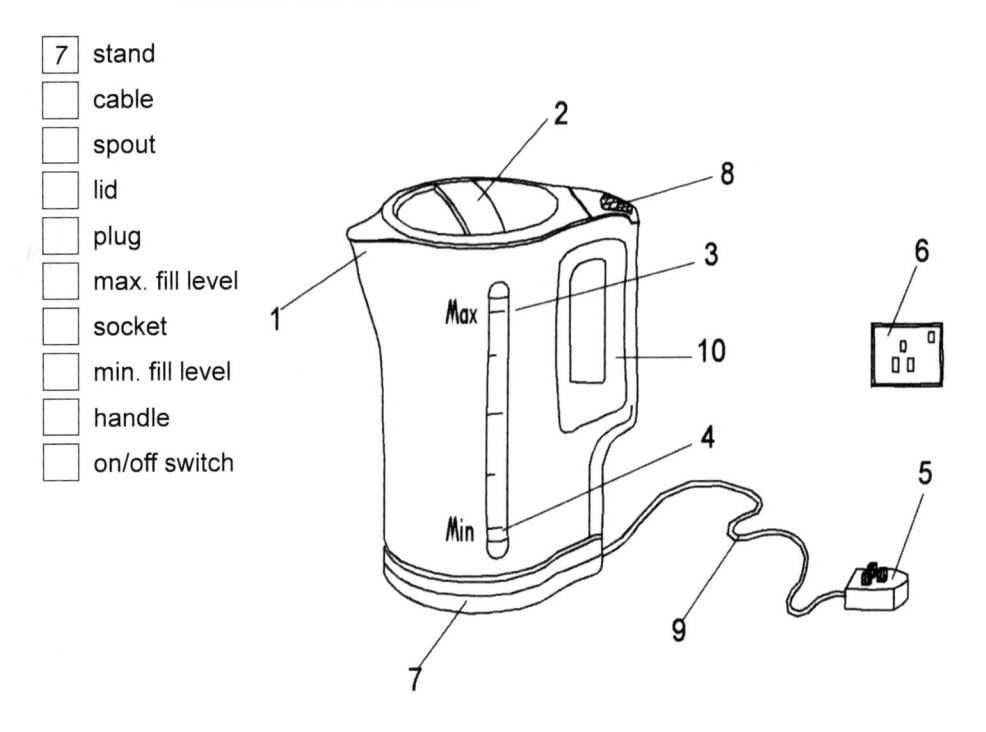

- [7] stand
- [ ] cable
- [ ] spout
- [ ] lid
- [ ] plug
- [ ] max. fill level
- [ ] socket
- [ ] min. fill level
- [ ] handle
- [ ] on/off switch

b Ask your neighbour these questions.

1 Have you ever used a kettle?
2 When was the last time you used it?
3 What did you use it for?

c Read the instructions.

Kettle Instructions

1 Take the kettle off the stand.
2 Remove the lid.
3 Check how much water is in it.
4 Fill the kettle to the required level.
5 Put the kettle back on the stand.
6 Put the plug in the socket and switch it on.
7 Put the on/off switch to the 'on' position.
8 Leave for a few minutes.
9 The kettle will automatically switch off when the water boils.
10 Take the kettle off the stand before pouring the water.

Guaranteed for 5 years.

d Ask your neighbour.

1 What do you have to do first?
2 What do you have to check?
3 What do you have to do with the plug?
4 Do you have to switch the kettle off?
5 What do you have to do before pouring the water?

3 a Match the pictures and the words.

- [i] kettle
- [ ] coffee machine
- [ ] toaster
- [ ] sewing machine
- [ ] mixer
- [ ] electric shaver
- [ ] telephone
- [ ] CD player
- [ ] vacuum cleaner

a) b) c) d) e) f) g) h) i)

b Ask your neighbour.

eg   How do you operate a telephone? You press the buttons.

c Fill in the following chart about yourself ....

(✓ = yes / x = no)

	you	your neighbour
Have you got a telephone?		
Have you got a sewing machine?		
Have you got a mixer?		
Have you got an electric shaver?		
Have you got a vacuum cleaner?		

d Ask your neighbour and fill in this column ....

e Fill in the following.

eg   What do you use an iron for? You use it for ironing clothes.

1   What do you use a _____ for? You use it for making and mending clothes.

2   What do you use a _____ for? You use it for making toast.

3   _____ ? You use it for cleaning your room.

4   What do you use a CD player for? _____ .

5   What do you use a mixer for? _____ .

f Ask your neighbour about the other objects in 3a.

g How to make toast. Put these instructions in the correct order.

_1_ Take a slice of bread.   ___ Take out the toast.
___ Put the bread in the toaster.   ___ Switch the toaster on.
___ Eat the toast.   ___ Put the plug in the socket.
___ Wait for the toaster to switch off automatically.   ___ Put some butter on the toast.

h Ask your neighbour.

1   How do you make a cup of coffee?
2   How do you make a cake?
3   How do you make a telephone call?

4 a Translate the following.

Vocabulary

computer	Computer
keyboard	Tastatur
iron	Eisen / Bügeleisen
oven	Ofen
hairdryer	Haartrockner / Föhn
remote control	Fernbedienung
key	Schlüssel
dial	Wählscheibe
button	Knopf
switch	Schalter
press	drücken
turn	drehen
operate	
electric kettle	
stand	stehen
cable	Kabel
spout	
lid	
plug	stecken

max. fill level	
socket	
min. fill level	
handle	
on/off switch	Ein / Aus Schalter
coffee machine	Kaffeemaschine
toaster	
vacuum cleaner	
CD player	
electric shaver	elektrischer Rasierer
sewing machine	
mixer	
mend	
toast	
clean	
slice of bread	
switch on/off	
butter	

Structures

The TV remote control has buttons. _____

To operate the computer you press the keys. _____

Do you have a computer? _____

Yes I do. _____

How do you operate it? _____

I press the keys. _____

Have you ever used a kettle? _____

Yes I have. _____

When was the last time you used it? _____

This morning. _____

What did you use it for? _____

To make a cup of tea. _____

What do you have to do first? _____

You have to take it off the stand first. _____

How do you operate a telephone? _____

You press the buttons. _____

What do you use an iron for? _____

You use it for ironing clothes. _____

UNIT 6

Life in the country is too quiet for me.

1 **a** **Ask your neighbour and point at the pictures.**

eg *Can you see a litter bin? Yes it's here.*

gate
birds
fence
queue
hedges
litter bin
bus stop
fruit trees
traffic lights
pedestrian crossing
parking meter
pavement
mini bus
hay bale
car park
stream
tractor
sheep
shops
forest

b **Fill in the following about yourself.**

		you	your neighbour
1	Do you live in a city?		
2	Do you live in a town?		
3	Do you live in a village?		
4	How many people live there?		
5	How far is the nearest shop?		
6	How far is the nearest bus stop?		
7	How far is the nearest restaurant?		
8	How long have you lived there?		
9	Would you like to move house?		
10	Can you see a bus stop from your living room?		

c **Ask your neighbour the questions.**

2 a Ask your neighbour questions using the words in the box.

eg   *Do you think life is quieter in the town or the country?*

| quiet | noisy | busy | hectic | exciting | boring | smelly |

b Read the following and mark in the box if you agree (✓), or disagree (x).

1   Life in the country is too quiet for me.   ☒
2   Life in the town is too busy for me.   ☑
3   Life in the country is too boring for me.   ☒
4   Life in the town is too hectic for me.   ☑
5   Life in the country is too noisy for me.   ☒
6   Life in the town is too noisy for me.   ☒
7   Life in the country is too smelly for me.   ☒
8   Life in the town is too smelly for me.   ☑
9   Life in the country is too exciting for me.   ☒
10 Life in the town is too quiet for me.   ☑

c Tell your neighbour what you think.

eg   *I agree with sentence 1. I think that life in the country is too quiet.*
     I disagree with sentence 2. I don't think that life in the town is too busy.

d Write down 3 advantages and 3 disadvantages of living in a town.

eg   *near to shops.*

Advantages

1 _____
2 _____
3 _____

Disadvantages

1 _____
2 _____
3 _____

e Tell your neighbour.

eg   *One advantage is that you are near to shops.*

f Write down 3 advantages and 3 disadvantages of living in the country.

Advantages

1 _____
2 _____
3 _____

Disadvantages

1 _____
2 _____
3 _____

g Ask your neighbour.

eg   *What are the advantages of living in the country?*

h Do you think there are more advantages of living in a town or in the country?

3 **a** **Look at photograph sequence 1 'A Walk in the Country' on the next pages and see if you can find the following items.**

trees   clouds   cows   a castle   a bridge   a gate

b **Ask your neighbour the following questions.**

eg *What can you see in photograph 1?*
I can see some houses, a car, some trees, a woman and a dog. The woman and her dog are walking along the pavement.

1. What can you see in photograph 2?
2. What can you see in photograph 3?
3. What can you see in photograph 4?
4. What can you see in photograph 5?
5. What can you see in photograph 6?

c **Now ask your neighbour these questions about the woman.**

eg *What's she doing in photograph 1?*
She's walking towards the houses.

1. What's she doing in photograph 2?
2. What's she doing in photograph 3?
3. What's she doing in photograph 4?
4. What's she doing in photograph 5?
5. What's she doing in photograph 6?

d **Read these sentences and then match them with the correct photographs.**

Yesterday morning Mrs Taylor took her dog, Brit, for a walk.

The sun was shining and it was a lovely day.

_3_ She stopped at a gate and enjoyed the view of the castle.
_1_ She walked through the village towards the terraced houses.
_4_ She crossed a bridge over a little stream.
_2_ She walked through some fields.
_5_ She walked down a narrow lane.

Her house was at the end of the lane. When she arrived home she made a cup of tea and gave Brit some water.

Check with your teacher.

e **Tell your neighbour the story using:**

'first', 'then', 'next', 'after that', 'finally'.

f **Now ask your neighbour these questions.**

1. What time of year do you think it is in the photographs? Why?
2. What time of day do you think it is in the photographs? Why?
3. What is the lady wearing?
4. When was the last time you went for a walk in the country? Where? Why?
5. Do you have any pets? Why (not)?

A Walk in the Country (Photograph Sequence 1)

25

4 a Translate the following.

Vocabulary

litter bin	
gate	Brücke Tor
hedges	
pedestrian crossing	
birds	Vogel
traffic lights	Ampel
fence	
queue	
bus stop	Bushaltestelle
fruit trees	
hay bale	
tractor	Trecker
sheep	Schaf
stream	Strom / kleiner Fluss
shops	Geschäfte
parking meter	Parkuhr
forest	Wald
mini bus	Kleinbus
pavement	
car park	Parkplatz

town	Stadt
country	Land
quiet	
noisy	leise
hectic	hektisch
boring	
busy	
smelly	stinkend
exciting	
castle	Schloss / Burg
village	
bridge	Brücke
narrow	
lane	Straße / Weg
field	Feld
first	zuerst
then	dann
next	als nächstes
after that	danach
finally	zum Schluss

Structures

Can you see a litter bin? Yes it's here. _____

Do you think life is quieter in the town or in the country? _____

Life in the country is too quiet for me. _____

I agree with sentence 1. _____

I think that life in the country is too quiet. _____

I disagree with sentence 2. _____

I don't think that life in the town is too busy. _____

One advantage is that you are near the shops. _____

What are the advantages of living in the country? _____

What can you see in photograph 1? _____

I can see some houses, a car, some trees, a woman and a dog. _____

The woman and her dog are walking along the pavement. _____

What's she doing in photograph 1? _____

She's walking towards the houses. _____

UNIT 7

What's the weather like?

1 a Here are some pictures of the weather. Match the descriptions and the pictures.

- [5] It's windy.
- [4] It's snowing.
- [5] It's cold and foggy.
- [2] It's hot and dry.
- [6] It's cold and dry.
- [3] It's raining.

b Ask your neighbour.

1 What's the weather like now?
2 What was the weather like yesterday?

c Complete the questions below and then answer what you like doing.

eg *What do you like doing in hot, dry weather? I like lying on the beach.*

1 _____ in cold, dry weather?
   I like walking my dog.

2 _____ in foggy weather?
   I like lying on my sofa.

3 _____ when it's raining?
   I like playing with my computer games.

4 _____ when it's snowing?
   I like lying on my sofa.

5 _____ in cold, wet weather?
   I like walking my dog.

d Ask your neighbour.

2 a Put the phrases in the correct place. It is now Wednesday morning!

1 tomorrow morning	6 this afternoon
2 last night	7 tomorrow night
3 yesterday afternoon	8 yesterday morning
4 the day after tomorrow	9 the day before yesterday
5 tonight	10 tomorrow afternoon

Monday	Tuesday	Wednesday	Thursday	Friday
9	2	this morning	1	4
	3	5	7	
	8	6	10	

b Ask your neighbour.

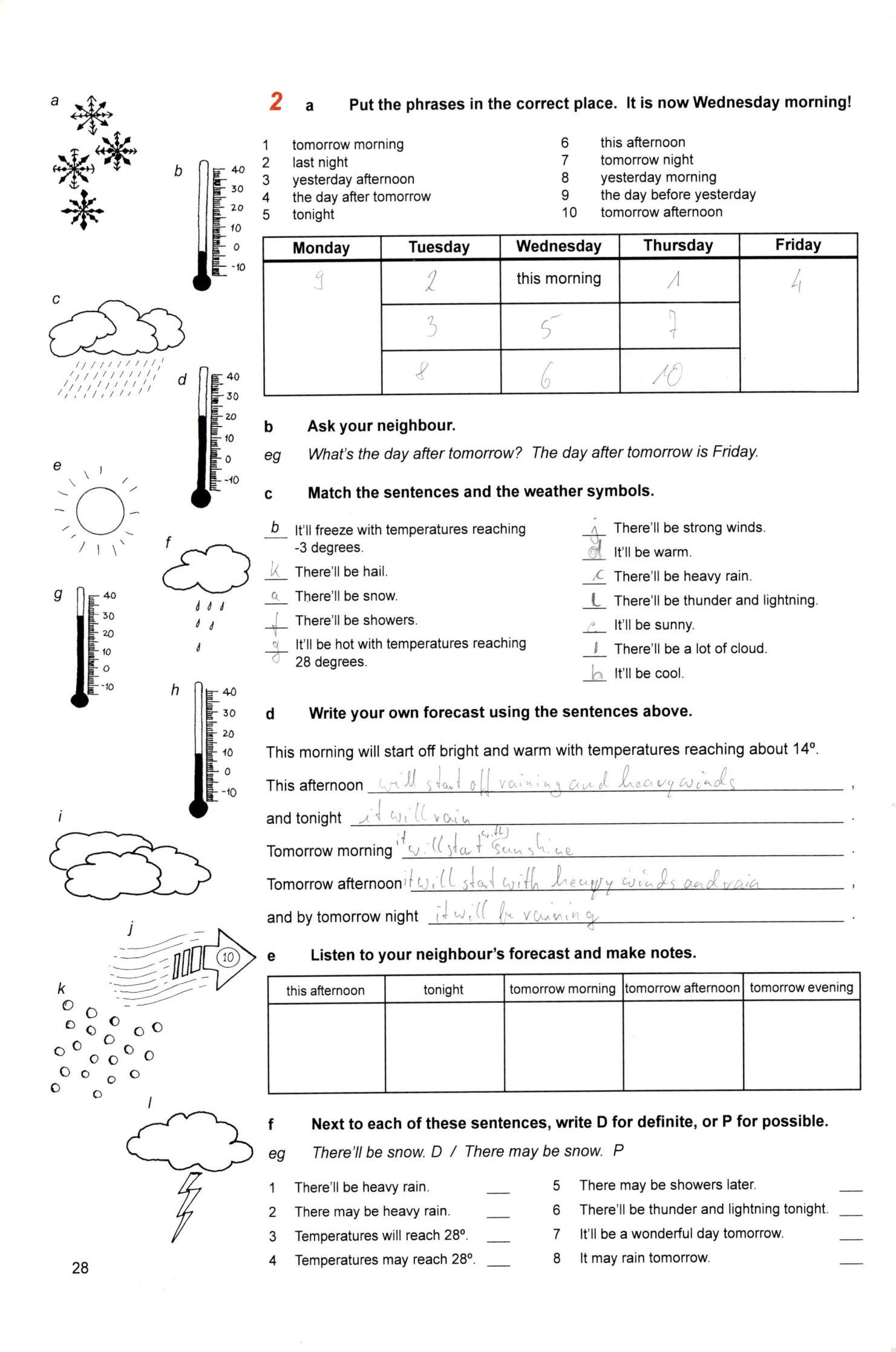

eg *What's the day after tomorrow? The day after tomorrow is Friday.*

c Match the sentences and the weather symbols.

_b_ It'll freeze with temperatures reaching -3 degrees.
_k_ There'll be hail.
_a_ There'll be snow.
_f_ There'll be showers.
_g_ It'll be hot with temperatures reaching 28 degrees.

_j_ There'll be strong winds.
_d_ It'll be warm.
_c_ There'll be heavy rain.
_l_ There'll be thunder and lightning.
_e_ It'll be sunny.
_i_ There'll be a lot of cloud.
_h_ It'll be cool.

d Write your own forecast using the sentences above.

This morning will start off bright and warm with temperatures reaching about 14°.
This afternoon _will start off raining and heavy winds_,
and tonight _it will rain_.
Tomorrow morning _it will start (with) sunshine_
Tomorrow afternoon _it will start with heavy winds and rain_,
and by tomorrow night _it will be raining_

e Listen to your neighbour's forecast and make notes.

this afternoon	tonight	tomorrow morning	tomorrow afternoon	tomorrow evening

f Next to each of these sentences, write D for definite, or P for possible.

eg *There'll be snow.* D / *There may be snow.* P

1 There'll be heavy rain. ___
2 There may be heavy rain. ___
3 Temperatures will reach 28°. ___
4 Temperatures may reach 28°. ___
5 There may be showers later. ___
6 There'll be thunder and lightning tonight. ___
7 It'll be a wonderful day tomorrow. ___
8 It may rain tomorrow. ___

3 a Listen to the cassette and fill in the missing information.

And now for the weather. In Scotland there will be ___strong winds___ coming in from the west this morning, but by lunchtime it will be calm and ___warm___ with temperatures rising to 16 degrees. In the north there will be ___rain___ and ___cloud___ which will clear by lunchtime, but it will remain ___cool___. Temperatures may reach ___10___ degrees. The Midlands will have a ___lovely day___ with ___sunshine___ and ___clear sky's___. In the south, however, there will be ___showers___ all day with temperatures averaging ___14___ degrees. Wales will have ___strong wind___ and ___hail___ in the morning, and may have some ___thunder___ and ___lightning___ later on. In the south west there may be some ___hail___ but this will have cleared up by lunchtime and in the afternoon there'll be ___sunshine___ and temperatures reaching ___20°___ degrees. In Northern Ireland there'll be ___cloud___ and ___rain___ in the morning but this will ___clear up___ by lunchtime.

Listen again and check.

b Now complete the weather map for <u>this</u> <u>morning</u>. Use the weather symbols from 2c.

29

4 a Translate the following.

Vocabulary

windy	windig
snowing	es schneit
cold	kalt
foggy	neblig
hot	heiß
dry	trocken
raining	es regnet
tomorrow morning	morgen früh
last night	letzte Nacht
yesterday afternoon	gestern Abend
the day after tomorrow	übermorgen
tonight	heute Nacht
this afternoon	heute Abend
tomorrow night	morgen Nacht
yesterday morning	gestern Morgen
the day before yesterday	vorgestern
tomorrow afternoon	morgen Abend
this morning	heute Morgen
freeze	frieren
temperatures	Temperatur
degrees	
hail	
snow	Schnee
showers	Regenschauer
strong winds	starken Wind
warm	warm
rain	Regen
thunder	Donnern
lightning	Blitz
sunny	sonnig
cloud	feucht kalt
cool	kalt

Structures

It's windy. _____

It's snowing. _____

What do you like doing in hot weather? _____

I like lying on the beach. _____

What's the day after tomorrow? _____

The day after tomorrow is Friday. _____

It'll freeze. _____

There'll be hail. _____

It'll be hot. _____

There'll be snow. _____

There'll be heavy rain. _____

There may be heavy rain. _____

There may be snow. _____

It may be cold. _____

UNIT 8

How do you get from the library to the golf club?

1 a Ask your neighbour.

eg   *What's number 1? It's a hospital.*

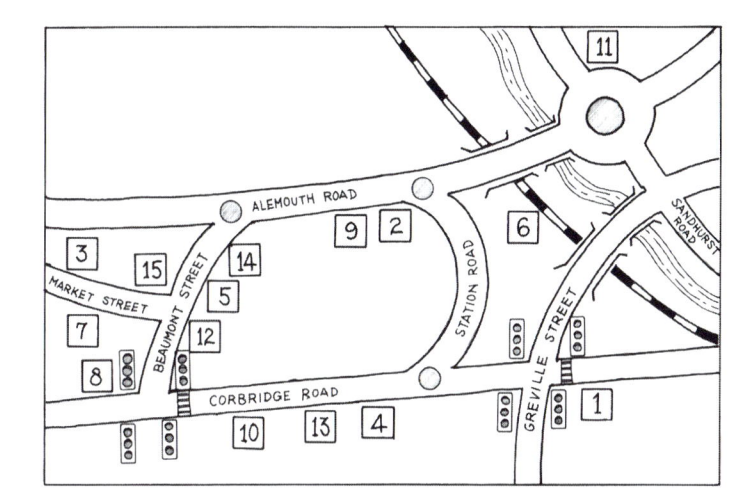

1 hospital
2 leisure centre
3 swimming pool
4 hotel
5 tourist information centre
6 railway station
7 bowling green
8 tennis court
9 car park
10 post office
11 golf club
12 library
13 bus station
14 museum
15 cinema

b Ask your neighbour questions like these.

eg   *Where's the hotel? It's in Corbridge Road next to the bus station.*

c Ask your neighbour these questions.

1 How many roundabouts can you see on the street plan?
2 How many bridges can you see on the street plan?
3 How many crossroads can you see on the street plan?
4 How many pedestrian crossings can you see on the street plan?
5 How many traffic lights can you see on the street plan?

d Where are you? Read the directions and write down where you are.

1 Go along Market Street and turn right into Beaumont Street. Turn left into Corbridge Road at the traffic lights. It's the first building on your right just after the pedestrian crossing.

   Where are you? _____

2 Go along Beaumont Street. Go past the library, the tourist information centre and the museum. Turn right into Alemouth Road at the roundabout and it's on your right next to the car park.

   Where are you? _____

3 Go along Station Road and turn right into Corbridge Road at the roundabout. Go past the hotel and it's on your left just before the post office.

   Where are you? _____

e Fill in the following.

eg   *To get from the hospital (1) to the swimming pool (3), you go along Corbridge Road. You go past the hotel, the bus station and the post office. Then you turn right at the traffic lights into Beaumont Street. Take the first left, go straight on for about 100 metres and the swimming pool is on your right just after the cinema.*

1 To get from the swimming pool (3) to the railway station (6), you go along __*Market*__ Street. Turn left into __*Beaumont*__ Street and then right at the roundabout. You go along __*Alemouth Road*__ Road and at the next roundabout you turn right into __*Station*__ Road. Go straight on for 50 metres and the railway station is on your left.

Unit 8   31

2   To get from the railway station (6) to the post office (10), you _go along_ Station Road. You _turn right_ into Corbridge Road. You _past_ the hotel and the bus station, and the post office is _on the left_.

f   Now ask your neighbour for directions.

eg   *How do you get from the library (12) to the golf club (11)?*

2   a   Fill in the following about your home town .....

	you	your neighbour
1 How many hospitals are there in your town?		
2 How many leisure centres are there in your town?		
3 How many hotels are there in your town?		
4 How many car parks are there in your town?		
5 How many cinemas are there in your town?		
6 How many libraries are there in your town?		
7 How many swimming pools are there in your town?		
8 How many railway stations are there in your town?		
9 How many golf clubs are there in your town?		
10 How many post offices are there in your town?		

b   Ask your neighbour the questions ....

c   Tell your teacher about your town.

d   Here is some information about the library, swimming pool and leisure centre. Listen to the cassette and fill in the missing information.

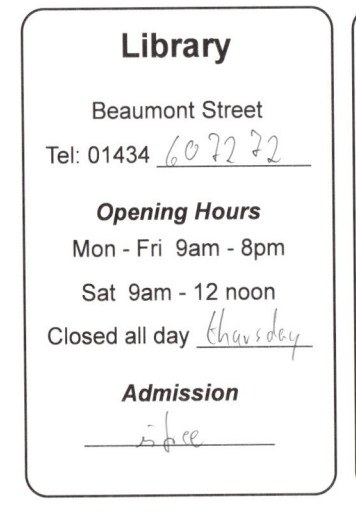

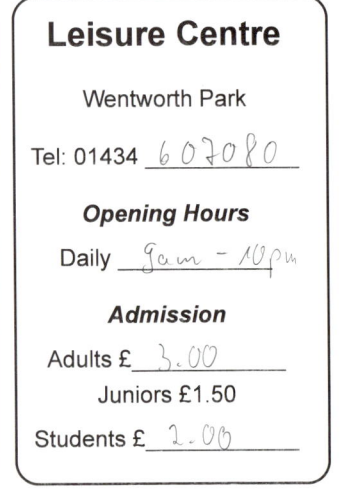

Library
Beaumont Street
Tel: 01434 _607272_
Opening Hours
Mon - Fri 9am - 8pm
Sat 9am - 12 noon
Closed all day _thursday_
Admission
free

Swimming Pool
Market Street
Tel: 01434 604903
Opening Hours
Weekdays:
12 noon - _9pm_
Weekends:
_9am_ - 8pm
Admission
Adults £1.80
Juniors £ _1.00_

Leisure Centre
Wentworth Park
Tel: 01434 _607080_
Opening Hours
Daily _9am - 10pm_
Admission
Adults £ _3.00_
Juniors £1.50
Students £ _2.00_

Listen again and check.

e   Ask your neighbour.

1   Where is the library located?
2   What is the telephone number of the swimming pool?
3   How much is admission to the swimming pool for an adult?
4   How much is admission to the leisure centre for a junior?
5   Is the leisure centre open every day?

f   Ask your neighbour 5 more questions.

3

a Match the pictures and the words.

| 5 | crossroads | 6 | no entry | 2 | give way *yield* | 1 | roundabout | 3 | traffic lights |
| 4 | stop | 10 | dead end | 8 | roadworks | 9 | junction | 7 | one-way street |

b Ask your neighbour.

1. How many roundabouts are there between your house and your school?
2. How many crossroads are there between your house and your school?
3. How many one-way streets are there between your house and your school?
4. How many sets of traffic lights are there between your house and your school?
5. How many roadworks are there between your house and your school?

c In Britain people drive on the left. Which side of the road do people drive on in your country?

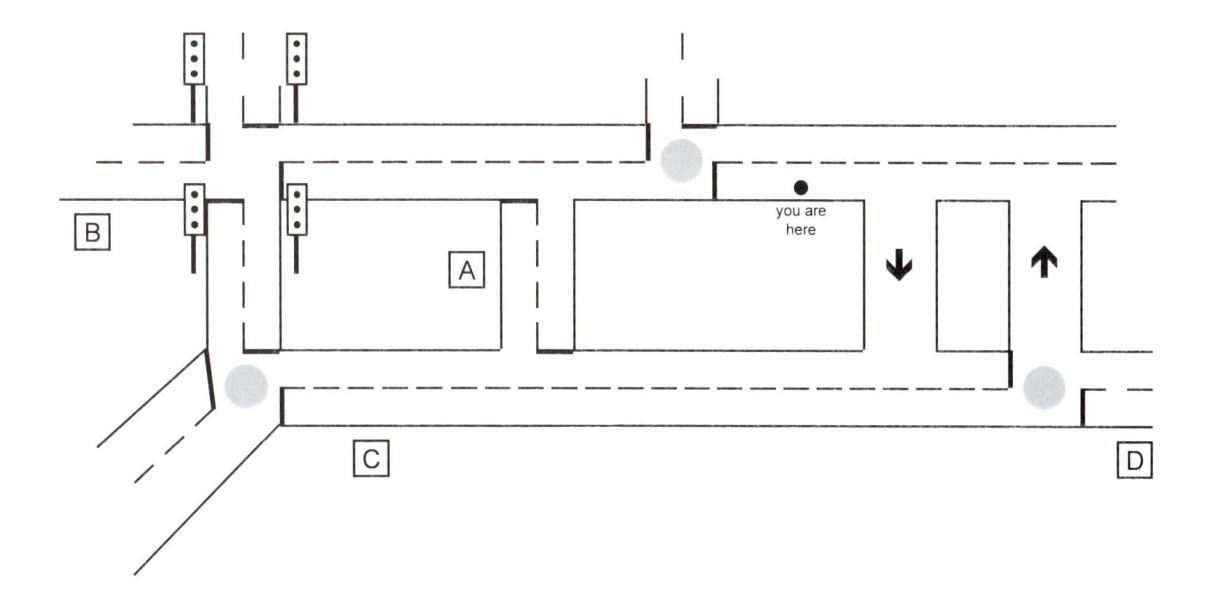

d This diagram shows the traffic system in Britain. Show your neighbour how you would drive to A, B, C and D. Make sure you are on the correct side of the road.

e Ask your neighbour these questions.

1. Do you think it would be difficult to drive on the left? Why (not)?
2. Do you think it would be easy to drive on the left? Why (not)?

4 a Translate the following.

Vocabulary

hospital _____
leisure centre _____
swimming pool _____
hotel _____
tourist information centre _____
railway station _____
bowling green _____
tennis court _____
post office _____
golf club _____
library _____
bus station _____
museum _____
cinema _____
roundabout _____
crossroads _____

opening hours _____
closed _____
admission _____
adults _____
juniors _____
daily _____
weekdays _____
weekends _____
students _____
no entry _____
give way _____
stop _____
one-way street _____
roadworks _____
junction _____
dead end _____

Structures

Where's the hotel? _____
It's on Corbridge Road next to the bus station. _____
How do you get to the golf club? _____
You go along Market Street. _____
You go past the post office. _____
You turn right into Beaumont Street. _____
You turn left into Beaumont Street. _____
Turn left at the traffic lights. _____
Turn right at the crossroads. _____
It's just before the post office. _____
It's just after the pedestrian crossing. _____
Take the first left. _____
Take the second left. _____
Take the first right. _____
Take the second right. _____
Go straight on. _____
Go straight on for about 100 metres. _____
The station is on your left. _____
The station is on your right. _____

UNIT 9

Have you ever been sailing?

1 a   Match the pictures and the activity.

_1_ sailing
___ pony trekking
___ camping
___ skiing
___ walking
___ shooting
___ mountain biking
___ motorcycling
___ fishing
___ climbing

Check with your neighbour.

b   Ask your neighbour these questions.

eg   *Which activity do you need a rope for? You need a rope for climbing.*

1   Which activity/activities do you need boots for?
2   Which activity/activities do you need a gun for?
3   Which activity/activities do you need a rod and bait for?
4   Which activity/activities do you need a lifejacket for?
5   Which activity/activities do you need a helmet for?

Check with your teacher.

c   Answer these questions about yourself in note form.

eg   *Have you ever been sailing?   Yes.   When?   Last summer.   Where?   Mediterranean.*

1   Have you ever been sailing? _____ When? _____ Where? _____
2   Have you ever been climbing? _____ When? _____ Where? _____
3   Have you ever been pony trekking? _____ When? _____ Where? _____
4   Have you ever been skiing? _____ When? _____ Where? _____
5   Have you ever been shooting? _____ When? _____ Where? _____
6   Have you ever been fishing? _____ When? _____ Where? _____
7   Have you ever been mountain biking? _____ When? _____ Where? _____
8   Have you ever been walking? _____ When? _____ Where? _____
9   Have you ever been motorcycling? _____ When? _____ Where? _____
10   Have you ever been camping? _____ When? _____ Where? _____

d   Ask your neighbour questions like these.

eg   *Have you ever been sailing? Yes I have. When was the last time you went sailing? It was last summer. Where did you go sailing? In the Mediterranean.*

e   Tell your teacher about yourself.

eg   *I've never been sailing. I've been climbing 4 times. Once in 1989 in the Dolomites, once in 1990 in the Alps and twice in Scotland. I can't remember when. I've been pony trekking once in Scotland. Never again!*

Glenhead Arms Hotel

Bed & Breakfast

Single Room £52
Twin/Double Room £92

Rates per room, per night.

Glenisla
Blairgowrie
Scotland
Tel   01575 582273
Fax 01575 582274

Summer Breaks

(2 nights or more)
Dinner, bed and breakfast
April - October £45
Rates per person, per day.
All rates inclusive of VAT at 17.5%.

Fishing Breaks

7-day stay £700 (Sat - Sat)
Includes dinner, B&B (bed and breakfast), picnic lunch, single room with private facilities and 6 days fishing.

Horse Riding Breaks

7-day stay £600 (Sat - Sat)
Includes dinner, B&B, picnic lunch, sharing twin/double room with private facilities and 6 days horse riding. Please bring own hat.

Golf Breaks

7-day stay £800 (Sat - Sat)
Includes dinner, B&B, lunch in clubhouse every day, sharing twin/double room with private facilities. Green fees extra.

All prices inclusive of VAT (Value Added Tax) at 17.5%.

---

2 **a** **Here is an advertising leaflet from the Glenhead Arms Hotel in Scotland. Look at the information and answer these questions.**

1   What is VAT? _____
2   How much is VAT? _____
3   How much is a single room for one night? _____
4   How much is a double room for one night? _____
5   What is B&B? _____

Check with your neighbour.

b **Answer the following.**

1   If I want a fishing break, is the picnic lunch included in the price? _____
2   If I want a golf break, is everything included in the price? _____
3   If I want to book a room, what number should I call? _____
4   If I want a summer break, is it £45 per person, or per room? _____
5   If I have a riding break, do I have to bring anything extra with me? _____

Check with your neighbour.

c **Ask your neighbour.**

1   Can I have a summer break in November?
2   Can I arrive for a golf break on a Tuesday?
3   How much does it cost for 3 nights in a single room in January?
4   How much does it cost for 3 nights in a single room in May?
5   How much does it cost for 2 nights in a double room in December?

3 a You have decided to take a short holiday. Choose one of the breaks available and fill in the booking form below.

Booking Form

Name ....

Address ....

....

Telephone ....

Fax ....

Please reserve the following accommodation:

single room ☐

twin room ☐

double room ☐

Date of Arrival ....

Date of Departure ....

fishing break ☐   golf break ☐

horse riding break ☐   summer break ☐

I/we enclose £ .... as full payment.

cheque ☐   amex ☐   visa ☐   mastercard ☐

Please enter card number:

☐ ☐ ☐ ☐   ☐ ☐ ☐ ☐
☐ ☐ ☐ ☐   ☐ ☐ ☐ ☐

Expiry Date ....

I understand and accept the conditions of booking.

Signed ....

Dated ....

---

b You are the receptionist at the Glenhead Arms Hotel. Your neighbour is going to telephone you and make a reservation. Fill in the booking form below during the telephone call.

Booking Form

Name ....

Address ....

....

Telephone ....

Fax ....

Please reserve the following accommodation:

single room ☐

twin room ☐

double room ☐

Date of Arrival ....

Date of Departure ....

fishing break ☐   golf break ☐

horse riding break ☐   summer break ☐

I/we enclose £ .... as full payment.

cheque ☐   amex ☐   visa ☐   mastercard ☐

Please enter card number:

☐ ☐ ☐ ☐   ☐ ☐ ☐ ☐
☐ ☐ ☐ ☐   ☐ ☐ ☐ ☐

Expiry Date ....

Booking made by:

Signed ....

Dated ....

4 a Translate the following.

Vocabulary

sailing _____	double _____
climbing _____	break _____
pony trekking _____	VAT (Value Added Tax) _____
camping _____	picnic lunch _____
skiing _____	private facilities _____
walking _____	golf _____
shooting _____	clubhouse _____
mountain biking _____	green fees _____
motorcycling _____	date of arrival _____
fishing _____	date of departure _____
rope _____	enclose _____
gun _____	full payment _____
rod _____	cheque _____
bait _____	amex _____
lifejacket _____	visa _____
helmet _____	mastercard _____
Mediterranean _____	expiry date _____
B&B (Bed & Breakfast) _____	signed _____
single _____	dated _____
twin _____	reservation _____

Structures

Which activity do you need a rope for? _____

You need a rope for climbing. _____

Have you ever been sailing? _____

Yes I have. _____

When was the last time you went sailing? _____

It was last summer. _____

Where did you go sailing? _____

In the Mediterranean. _____

I've never been sailing. _____

I've been climbing 4 times. _____

Once in 1989 in the Dolomites. _____

Once in 1989, once in 1990 and twice in Scotland. _____

I can't remember when. _____

I've been pony trekking once in Scotland. _____

Never again! _____

UNIT 10

Revision

1 a Ask your neighbour the following questions.

1. What's your name?
2. How do you spell it?
3. Where do you live?
4. What kind of house do you live in?
5. How many rooms does your house/flat have?
6. Which room do you eat in?
7. Which room do you work in?
8. Do you have a coat stand in your house/flat? Where?
9. Do you have a set of scales in your house/flat? Where? Why?
10. Can you name 3 objects in every room of your house/flat?

2 a Look at the information below and tell your neighbour about Roger and Edward.

eg   *Roger has a regular lifestyle. Edward doesn't have a regular lifestyle.*

	Roger	Edward
have a regular lifestyle	✓	✗
start work at the same time every day	✓	✗
have a company car	✗	✓
travel a lot in his job	✗	✓
go home every night	✓	✗
go to bed at different times every night	✗	✓

b Complete the sentences below about yourself using:

always, normally, often, sometimes, rarely, never.

1. I _____ have breakfast at the same time.
2. I _____ start work at the same time.
3. I _____ work in the same place.
4. I _____ have lunch at the same time.
5. I _____ go to bed at the same time.

c Ask your neighbour the following questions.

1. How many days a week do you work?
2. Do you sometimes work at weekends?
3. How long does it take to get to work?
4. How long do you have for lunch?
5. What time do you have breakfast?
6. What time do you have lunch?
7. What do you do in the evenings?
8. Do you have a company car?
9. Do you travel a lot in your job?
10. What time do you go to bed?

3 a Describe the people in the picture to your neighbour. They have to guess who you are describing. You may describe their clothes, their appearance, and what they are doing.

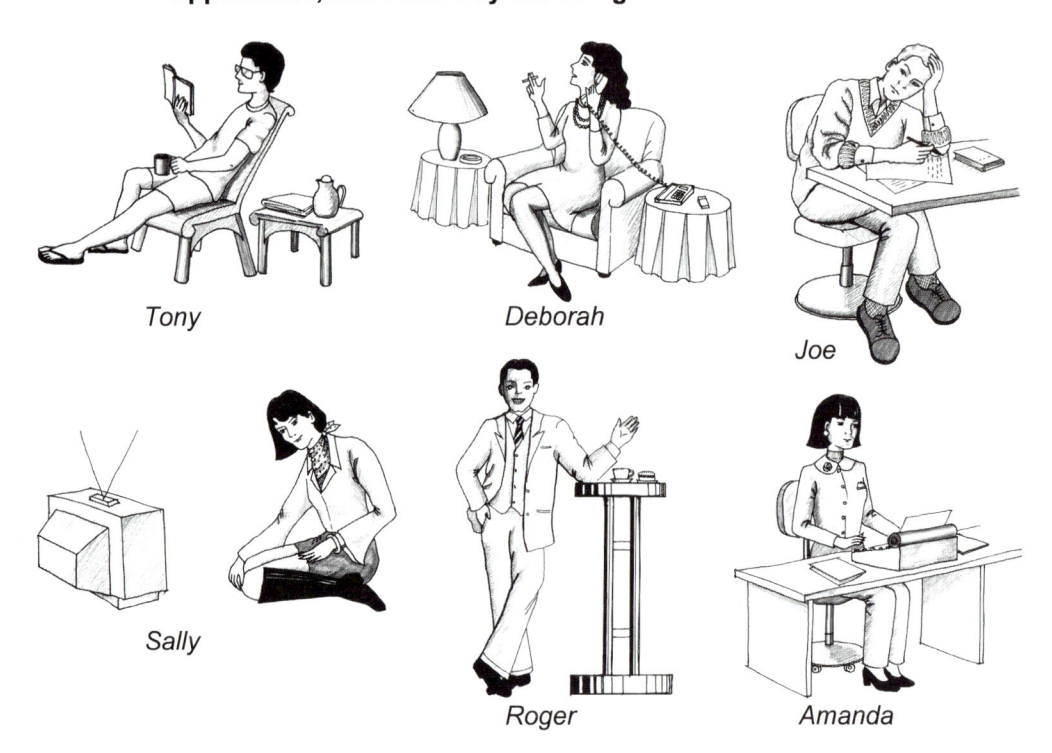

Tony *Deborah* *Joe*

Sally *Roger* *Amanda*

b Look at the other people in your class and ask your neighbour these questions.

1 Can you see anyone who is wearing a skirt?   Who is it?
2 Can you see anyone who is wearing a tie?   Who is it?
3 Can you see anyone who is wearing a brooch? Who is it?
4 Can you see anyone who is wearing a suit?   Who is it?
5 Can you see anyone who is wearing a scarf?   Who is it?

4 a Ask your neighbour these questions about their ideal home.

1 How many rooms would it have?   6   What would it be made of?
2 Which rooms would it have?   7   What colour would it be?
3 What views would it have?   8   How far would the nearest shop be?
4 Would it have central heating?   9   What kind of house would it be?
5 Would it have air conditioning?   10 Would you live there alone?

5 a How many objects can you name in your house which have:

a) keys b) dials c) buttons d) switches?

b What is it? See if you can guess and then compare with your neighbour.

1 You use it for making clothes.   4 You use it for making cakes.
2 You use it for cleaning your room.   5 You use it for making toast.
3 You use it for listening to music.

c How do you make a slice of toast? What do you do first? What do you do after that? Tell your neighbour.

6 **a** Look at the words and then put a 'C' next to it if you would find it in the country, and a 'T' next to it if you would find it in the town. You may put a 'C' and a 'T' if you would find them in both.

1 queues ___
2 traffic lights ___
3 sheep ___
4 hedges ___
5 fences ___

6 shops ___
7 bus stops ___
8 litter bins ___
9 pedestrian crossings ___
10 forests ___

b **Now try and explain the words to your neighbour.**

eg *You often find queues outside shops when people are waiting to buy something.*

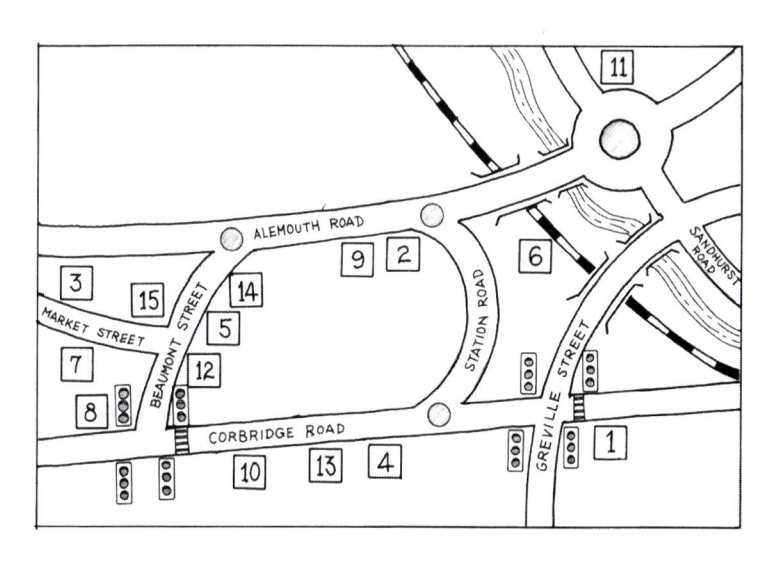

c **Ask your neighbour these questions.**

1 Do you live in a town, a city, or a village?
2 How far is the nearest bus stop from your house/flat?
3 How long have you lived there?
4 What can you see from your bedroom window?
5 Would you like to move house/flat? Why (not)?

d **Discuss with your neighbour the advantages and disadvantages of living in the country, or living in the town.**

7 **a** **Today is Wednesday 10 January. Answer these question and then check with your neighbour.**

1 What was the day before yesterday? _____
2 What is the day after tomorrow? _____
3 When was Tuesday 9 January? _____
4 When is Friday 12 January? _____
5 What is tomorrow? _____

8

8 **a** **Ask your neighbour these questions using the street plan.**

1 How do you get from the hospital (1), to the railway station (6)?
2 How do you get from the swimming pool (3), to the post office (10)?
3 How do you get from the railway station (6), to the library (12)?
4 How do you get from the golf club (11), to the swimming pool (3)?
5 How do you get from the library (12), to the hospital (1)?

b **Now ask your neighbour about their own home town.**

1 How many hospitals are there in your town?
2 How many leisure centres are there in your town?
3 How many libraries are there in your town?
4 How many car parks are there in your town?
5 How many post offices are there in your town?

c **Ask your neighbour these questions.**

1 Why would you go to a library?
2 Why would you go to a railway station?
3 Why would you go to a swimming pool?
4 Why would you go to a hotel?
5 Why would you go to a tourist information centre?

9 **a** **Which activity is it? Look at the equipment and then write next to it which activity/activities it is. When you have finished, check with your neighbour.**

eg   a rod and bait - fishing.

1 a rope   _____
2 a lifejacket   _____
3 a helmet   _____
4 a pair of boots   _____
5 a tent   _____

b **Ask your neighbours these questions.**

1 Have you ever been sailing?   When? Where?
2 Have you ever been climbing?   When? Where?
3 Have you ever been fishing?   When? Where?
4 Have you ever been mountain biking?   When? Where?
5 Have you ever been camping?   When? Where?

10 **a** **You are now going to tell your neighbour about yourself. Try and keep talking for at least 3 minutes. Here are some things you can talk about.**

- your name, age, address
- your daily routine
- your house/flat
- the town where you live
- your ideal home
- disadvantages and advantages of living where you do.

UNIT 11

Have you ever travelled on the London Underground?

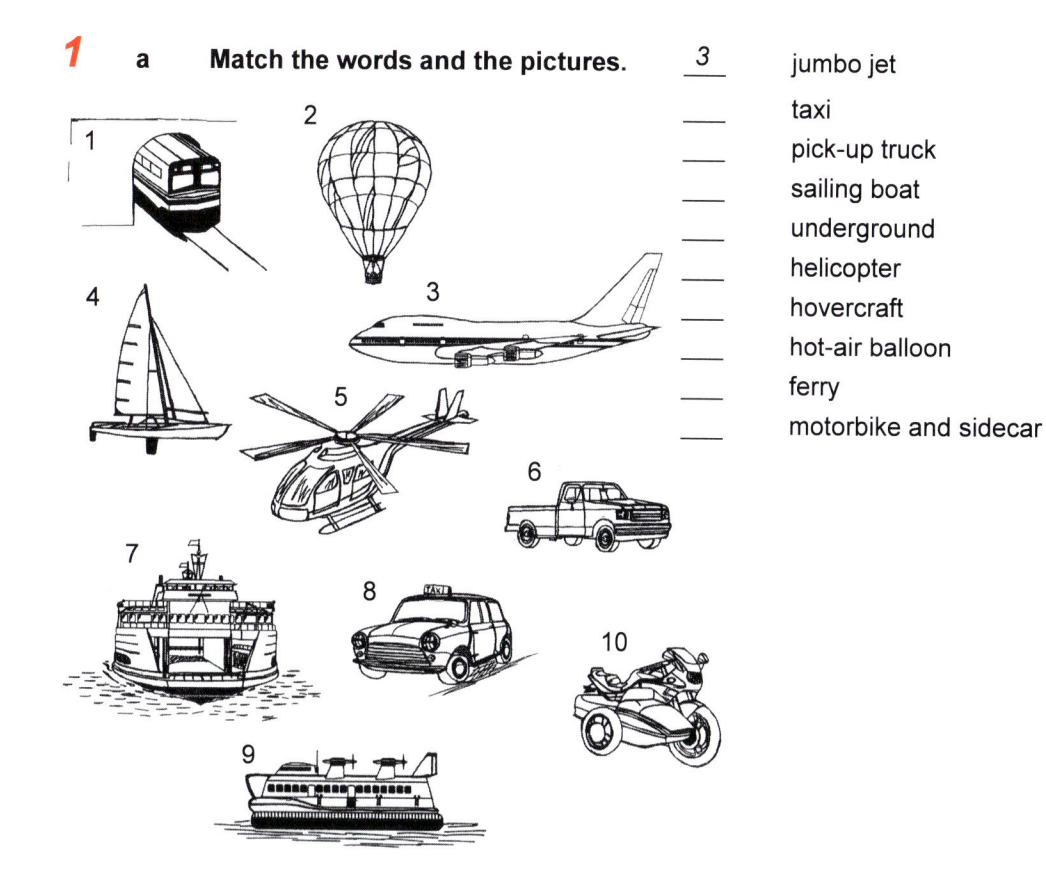

1 a Match the words and the pictures.

- _3_ jumbo jet
- ___ taxi
- ___ pick-up truck
- ___ sailing boat
- ___ underground
- ___ helicopter
- ___ hovercraft
- ___ hot-air balloon
- ___ ferry
- ___ motorbike and sidecar

b Now point at the pictures and ask your neighbour.

eg What's this? It's a jumbo jet.

c Ask your neighbour questions like these.

eg Have you ever travelled by jumbo jet?
Yes, when I went to America. I went by jumbo jet because it's the fastest way to get there.

d Now ask your neighbour these questions.

eg How would you go to America? I would go by jumbo jet because it's the fastest.

1. How would you go to work or college every day?   Why?
2. How would you visit friends in another town?   Why?
3. How would you go on holiday to Britain?   Why?
4. How would you go shopping?   Why?
5. How would you go to your English lesson?   Why?

e Tell your teacher about your neighbour.

f Ask your neighbour about different means of transport.

eg Do you like travelling by bus? No I don't like travelling by bus because it's always full. I have to walk to the bus stop and wait for a bus to come. I prefer travelling by car.

1. Do you like travelling by train? Why (not)?
2. Do you like travelling by motorbike? Why (not)?
3. Do you like travelling by plane? Why (not)?
4. Do you like travelling by bicycle? Why (not)?
5. Do you like travelling by ship? Why (not)?

2

Key to Lines

- Bakerloo
- Central
- Circle
- District
- Hammersmith & City
- Jubilee
- Metropolitan
- Northern
- Piccadilly
- Victoria

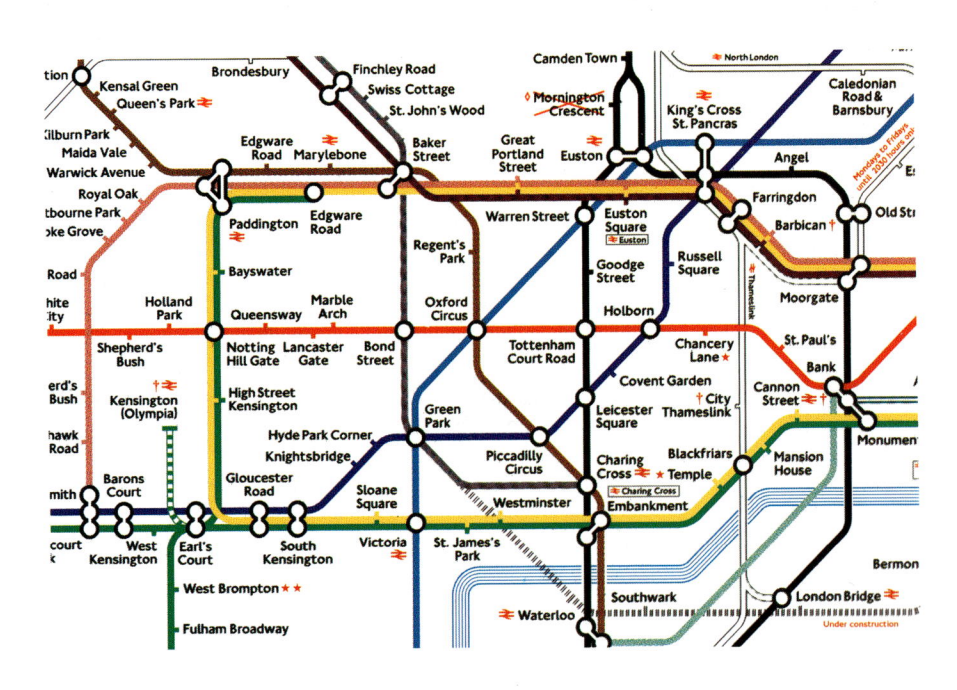

a **Ask your neighbour the following questions.**

eg *Which line is Bond Street on? It's on the Jubilee line and the Central line.*

1 Which line is Goodge Street on?
2 Which line is Marble Arch on?
3 Which line is Regent's Park on?
4 Which line is St Paul's on?
5 Which line is Knightsbridge on?

b **Look at the example.**

eg *How do you get from Victoria to Covent Garden?*
The best way is to take the Victoria line to Green Park. You can change there to the Piccadilly line and the third stop is Covent Garden.

Now you try. How do you get from Paddington to Marble Arch? _____

_____

Check with your neighbour.

c **Ask your neighbour 3 more questions.**

eg *How do you get from Baker Street to the Embankment?*
The best way is to take the Bakerloo line. It's only 5 stops and you don't have to change.

d You are going to hear some information about opening and closing times for the stations below. Listen to the cassette and make notes.

	Monday - Friday	Saturday	Sunday
Aldwych Station			
Barbican Station			
City Thameslink Station			
Mornington Crescent			
Further Information			

Instructions for Use
1. Select type of ticket.
2. Select destination, eg Paddington.
3. Read display to find out price of ticket.
4. Insert required money into slot.
5. Take ticket from ticket slot.
6. Take change (if any).

Bayswater Road

TICKETS

Display

Money 10p, 50p, £1

£5, £10, £20
change given

- adult single
- adult return
- junior single
- junior return
- 1-day travel card
- 3-day travel card

- Edgware Road A
- Marylebone A
- Baker Street A
- Great Portland Street A

- Warren Street A
- Euston Square A
- Kings Cross St Pancras B
- Farringdon B
- Barbican B
- Moorgate B
- Liverpool Street B
- Aldgate B
- Tower Hill B
- Monument C
- Mansion House C
- Blackfriars C
- Temple C

- Embankment C
- Westminster C
- St James' Park C
- Victoria D
- Sloane Square D
- South Kensington D
- Gloucester Road D
- High Street Kensington D
- Notting Hill Gate D
- Paddington A

TICKET

Standard Prices	Adult Single	Adult Return	Junior Single	Junior Return
Zone A	£1.00	£2.00	£0.50	£1.00
Zone B	£1.50	£3.00	£0.75	£1.50
Zone C	£1.80	£3.60	£0.90	£1.80
Zone D	£2.20	£4.40	£1.10	£2.20

1-day Travel Card £5.00 / 3-day Travel Card £15.00

3

a Fill in the following.

eg How much is an adult single to Baker Street? £1.

1 How much is an adult return to Paddington? _____.
2 How much is a junior single to Gloucester Road? _____.
3 How much is a junior return to the Embankment? _____.
4 How much is an adult single to Tower Hill? _____.
5 How much is a 3-day travel card? _____.

b Ask your neighbour 5 more questions.

eg How much is an adult single to Blackfriars? £1.80.

c Now answer these questions.

eg Which button do I press first? You press the type of ticket you want first.

1 Which button do I press next? _____.
2 How do I know how much the ticket costs? _____.
3 Does the machine accept 5p pieces? _____.
4 Does the machine give change? _____.
5 Where do I get my ticket from? _____.

d Ask your neighbour.

1 How do I buy a return ticket to Notting Hill Gate?
2 How does my 8 year old daughter buy a single ticket to Marylebone?
3 If I want to buy a ticket for several journeys on one day, what kind of ticket should I buy?
4 Have you ever travelled on the London Underground? When? Why?
5 Where else would you find a machine like this?

4 a Translate the following.

Vocabulary

jumbo jet _____	rebuilding _____
taxi _____	pay your fare _____
pick-up truck _____	fine _____
sailing boat _____	adult single _____
underground _____	adult return _____
helicopter _____	junior single _____
hovercraft _____	junior return _____
hot-air balloon _____	1-day travel card _____
ferry _____	3-day travel card _____
motorbike and sidecar _____	select _____
to prefer _____	destination _____
peak hours _____	display _____
open _____	insert _____
repair work _____	slot _____

Structures

Have you ever travelled on the London Underground? _____

Have you ever travelled by jumbo jet? _____

I went to America by jumbo jet. _____

It was the fastest way to get there. _____

How would you go to America? _____

I would go by jumbo jet because it's the fastest. _____

Do you like travelling by bus? _____

I don't like travelling by bus. _____

It's always full. _____

I have to walk to the bus stop. _____

I have to wait for a bus to come. _____

I prefer travelling by car. _____

Which line is Bond Street on? _____

It's on the Jubilee and Central line. _____

How do you get from Victoria to Covent Garden? _____

The best way is to take the Victoria line to Green Park. _____

You can change there to the Piccadily line. _____

The third stop is Covent Garden. _____

It's only 5 stops and you don't have to change. _____

How much is an adult single to Baker Street? _____

Which button do I press first? _____

You press the type of ticket you want first. _____

UNIT 12

What's the best holiday you've ever had?

1 a Put the words in the column you think is correct before reading the stories.

Los Angeles   Yosemite Park   Scone Palace   greyhound bus   Boston   California   golf   wet
air-conditioning   drive-ins   foggy   whisky distillery   motels   New York   Grand Canyon   salmon
Death Valley   convertible car   Glencoe   waterproof trousers   hamburgers   mosquito repellant

UNITED STATES OF AMERICA	SCOTLAND

b Read the paragraphs below and mark in the box if they are Story A (Clive's holiday to the USA) or Story B (Nick's holiday to Scotland).

1 He returned the hired car to Las Vegas and took a plane back to New York where he caught his connecting flight back to London. A friend picked him up in London and gave him a lift back to Manchester and that was the end of the holiday.   story **A**

2 Last summer Clive went on holiday to the USA for 3 weeks. He started off from Manchester where a friend gave him a lift to the motorway junction. From there he hitched down to London and took the tube and then a taxi to Gatwick Airport.   story ☐

3 There were roadworks on the M1 motorway so it took longer than usual but at about 11.30pm he arrived at the hotel in Glencoe.   story **B**

4 In the last few days he went fishing in the River Tay, one of the best salmon fishing rivers in Scotland. On the last day he visited Scone Palace, then he got back in the car and drove south, and that was the end of his holiday.   story ☐

5 He visited Dalwhinnie Distillery where they produce malt whisky. He saw how they made the whisky and at the end of the tour he was invited to taste the whisky. It tasted very good. The weather was still foggy and wet when he came out.   story ☐

6 It was his first time to the USA and he decided the best way to see it would be to travel to California by train, which he did. The train took 72 hours to get there. Unfortunately the journey wasn't as interesting as he had hoped, but he definitely saw a lot of the USA .   story ☐

7 He travelled across the Atlantic in a jumbo jet and after 8 hours he arrived in New York. He had friends, Peggy and Phil, in Boston so he took a greyhound bus up there. He rang Phil from Boston bus station which was very busy and dirty. Phil came and collected him on his motorbike.   story ☐

8 The weather in Boston was lovely and warm and he spent the next few days walking around Boston. After he had seen all the sights, he decided to head west.   story ☐

9 Last summer Nick went on holiday to Scotland for 3 weeks. He lives in Brighton but loves the mountains and countryside. He packed his rucksack with waterproof trousers and jackets and took some mosquito repellent and one Friday morning he got in his car and drove north.   story ☐

10 The weather cleared up the next day so he played a round of golf in the morning at Dalmunzie, the highest 9-hole course in Britain. The wind was very strong so he did not play very well, but he thoroughly enjoyed the game.   story ☐

11 He went to the Grand Canyon and took a helicopter ride over it. He also visited Yosemite Park and Death Valley, and soon the 3 weeks were gone.   story ☐

12 The first few days he climbed mountains near the hotel. He was lucky with the weather and it didn't rain at all. He met a lot of people and in the evenings he ate and drank in the hotel before going to bed.   story ☐

13 Then the weather turned bad; it was foggy and wet so he decided to leave Glencoe and visit some other places.   story ☐

14 He arrived in Los Angeles at 3pm and hired a convertible car. However, the next day he changed it for a car with air conditioning as the weather was too hot. He travelled around and saw a lot. He ate hamburgers which he bought from drive-ins and stayed in motels.   story ☐

c Put the paragraphs in the correct order.

Story A (Clive / USA) _____

Story B (Nick / Scotland) _____

Check with your teacher.

2 a Answer the following questions about the best holiday you have ever had in note form using one or two words. Do not write full sentences.

eg   Where did you go? Ireland.

1   Where did you go? _____
2   How long were you there? _____
3   Did you stay in one place or travel around? _____
4   What was the accommodation like? _____
5   Who did you go with? _____
6   What did you see? _____
7   How did you get there? _____
8   What was the weather like? _____
9   Why was it the best holiday ever? _____
10 Would you go back again? _____

b   Ask your neighbour about their best holiday.

eg   Where did you go? I went to Ireland.

c   Now tell your class about yourself.

eg   The best holiday I've ever had was in 1993 when I went to Ireland.

d   Ask your neighbour.

1   What is this an advertisement for?
2   What is the address of the company?
3   What number do I dial to fax a reservation?
4   How much is it for 2 people on a motoring holiday?
5   What is another name for Finland, Sweden and Denmark?

Check with your neighbour.

Finland, Sweden and Denmark

Finest lake and seaside Chalets

Hotel Touring City Breaks

Our specialist programme of motoring holidays
£210 per person.

Scandinavia awaits your visit!

Skandika Holidays, 8 Rhos Way, Wrexham
Tel 01978 843241 / Fax 01978 9120719

LONDON

Best rates in London!

single from £20
double from £15 per person
families 3/4/5 from £13 p.p.

Windsor Cottage Hotel
12 Persevny Road
London   W1 2LT
Tel 0171 374 9087
Fax 0171 385 2147

5 minutes from
Piccadilly tube station.

Call, fax or write now!
Welcome to London

---

e   Ask your neighbour.

1   What is this an advertisement for?
2   What is the name of the hotel?
3   What is the address of the hotel?
4   How much is a double room for 2 people?
5   How much is a room for a family of 3?
6   What is the post code of the hotel?
7   What is the fax number?
8   Which is the nearest underground station?
9   How can I reserve a room?
10 Is this hotel cheaper than other hotels in London?

f   Ask your neighbour.

Would you prefer to go to London or Scandinavia? Why?

3 a Look at photograph sequence 2 'Going on Holiday' on the next pages. John and his wife, Lucy, are going on holiday. His mother, Freda, is going to look after their house while they're away. Describe the people to your neighbour.

b Match the sentences below and the photographs.

1 She's putting the cat out. `3`
2 She's packing a suitcase. ☐
3 He's saying goodbye to his mother. ☐
4 He's putting the suitcases in the car. ☐
5 She's putting the milk bottles out. ☐

c Now ask your neighbour these questions.

1 What's she doing in photograph 1?
2 What's she doing in photograph 2?
3 What's she doing in photograph 3?
4 What's he doing in photograph 4?
5 What's he doing in photograph 5?

d Look at the photographs and complete these sentences using 'before' or 'after'.

eg She put the milk bottles out before she put the cat out.

1 She packed the case _____ she put the milk bottles out.
2 She put the cat out _____ she put the milk bottles out.
3 She gave the suitcase to her husband _____ she put the cat out.
4 He put the suitcases in the car _____ they drove away.
5 They said goodbye to his mother _____ they packed the car.

e Read this text and then answer the questions below.

Last Saturday Lucy and John got up early. John went to the bathroom and washed himself. He got dressed, went to the kitchen and made breakfast. Lucy washed and dressed herself and then they had breakfast together. After breakfast Lucy went back to the bedroom and opened her wardrobe. She took out her suitcase and started to pack. She packed a pair of sandals, a dress, 2 skirts, 3 blouses, a pair of shorts, a pair of earrings, a bracelet, a necklace, a jacket and a scarf. Then she took the suitcase downstairs and gave it to John. She went back to the bedroom and found John's suitcase under the bed. She opened it and packed 3 pairs of socks, 2 pairs of trousers, 2 shirts, a T-shirt, a tie, a jacket and 2 pairs of shoes. She took the suitcase downstairs and gave it to John. Then she went into the kitchen, washed the milk bottles and put them out. She went inside to look for the cat but she couldn't find it. After half an hour she found the cat asleep on her bed. She picked it up, carried it downstairs and put it out. John put the cases in the car and Lucy gave the house keys to his mother. They got into the car, said goodbye to his mother and drove away.

1 Who made breakfast? _____
2 How many skirts did Lucy pack? _____
3 Where was John's suitcase? _____
4 Where did Lucy find the cat? _____
5 Who did they give the house keys to? _____

f Work with your neighbour. You are going to continue the story. Use these questions to help you.

1 Where did they go on holiday?
2 How long did they stay?
3 Where did they stay?
4 What did they do in the mornings, afternoons and evenings?
5 What was the weather like?

g Now tell your class about John and Lucy's holiday.

Going on Holiday (Photograph Sequence 2)

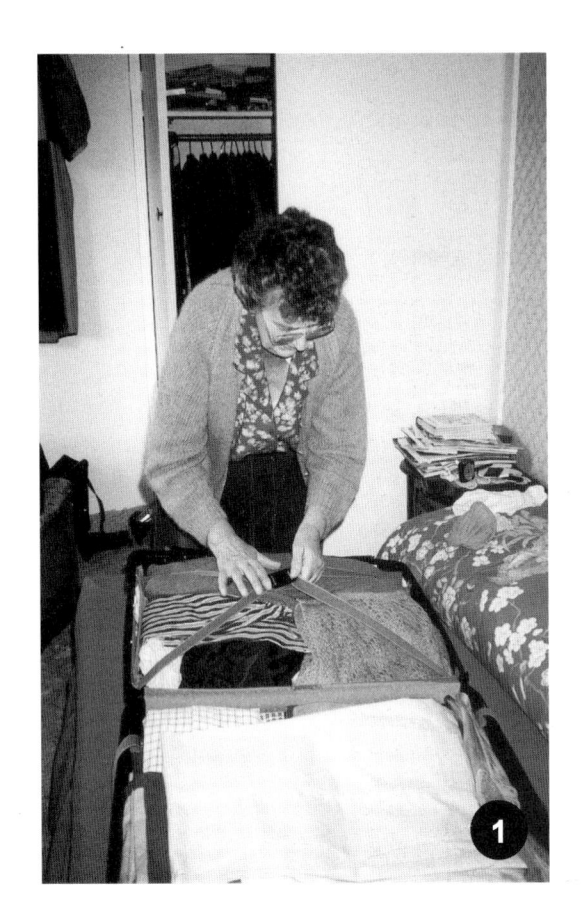

50

51

4 a Translate the following.

Vocabulary

salmon _____
waterproof trousers _____
motels _____
mosquito repellent _____
drive-ins _____
lucky _____
to pack _____
the weather turned bad _____
produce _____
to invite _____
to taste _____
thoroughly _____
to collect _____
to see the sights _____
to head west _____
unfortunately _____
advertisement _____
seaside _____
chalets _____
motoring holiday _____
per person _____
wife _____
mother _____
husband _____
to put out _____
suitcase _____
cat _____
milk bottles _____
before _____
after _____
to drive away _____
to look after _____
to wash _____
to find _____
asleep _____
to carry _____
house keys _____

Structures

What's the best holiday you've ever had? _____
Where did you go? _____
I went to Ireland. _____
The best holiday I've ever had was in 1993. _____
She's putting the cat out. _____
She put the milk bottles out before she put the cat out. _____

UNIT 13

Has flight JG971 from Tokyo arrived yet?

1 a Listen to the cassette and fill in the missing information.

DEPARTURES			
Flight Number	Destination	Gate	Comments
BA 739	Copenhagen	7	Boarding
UL 504	Brussels	23	Final Call
BM 805	Glasgow	19	Boarding
KL 433	Amsterdam	3	Proceed to Gate 3
SA 191	Madrid	11	check in desk
LA 731	Berlin	14	Delayed
Passenger Information			
Passenger _Kevin Allen_ to go to the airport information desk.			

Listen again and check.

Compare with your neighbour.

b Ask your neighbour.

1. Have you ever travelled by plane?
2. How often do you travel by plane?
3. Do you like flying? Why (not)?
4. What was your best flight? Why?
5. What was your worst flight? Why?

c What is most important for you when you're flying?

✓✓ = very important   ✓ = important   x = not important

☐ good, calm weather		☐ punctual departure and arrival	
☐ smooth landing		☐ duty free goods	
☐ good food		☐ safety	
☐ free drinks		☐ travelling with somebody	
☐ friendly cabin crew		☐ getting your luggage back	

d Ask your neighbour.

eg Is good, calm weather important for you when you're flying? Yes it is.

e Tell your teacher about yourself.

eg For me the most important thing is good, calm weather.
I hate flying in bad weather.

Unit 13

2 a Look at the information below and ask your neighbour.

eg Has the plane from Tokyo arrived yet? No it hasn't.

1 Has the plane from Berlin arrived yet?
2 Has the plane from Bucharest arrived yet?
3 Has the plane from Beijing arrived yet?
4 Has the plane from Dubai arrived yet?
5 Has the plane from Paris arrived yet?

		ARRIVALS			Time Now 11:20
Flight Number	Scheduled Arrival Time	Estimated Arrival Time	Landed Time	Arriving From	Flight Information
JG 971	11:00	11:44		TOKYO	Delayed
EA 391	11:05		11:07	BERLIN	Baggage in Hall
HX 472	11:10		11:10	BUCHAREST	Landed
WV 714	11:15			BEIJING	Cancelled
YI 362	11:20	11:30		DUBAI	Delayed
QZ 580	11:25			PARIS	On Time

b Match up the flight numbers, where they are from and the flight information.

1 JG 971   Tokyo
2 QZ 580   Paris
3 WV 714   BEIJING

4 EA 391   Berlin
5 HX 472   Bucharest
6 YI 362   Dubai

It's on time.   [2]
It's been delayed.   [6]
It's already landed.   [5]

It's been delayed.   [1]
The baggage is in the hall. [4]
It's been cancelled.   [3]

Check with your teacher.

c Ask your neighbour 5 questions.

eg Has flight JG 971 from Tokyo arrived yet? No it hasn't. It's been delayed.

d Ask your neighbour.

1 Has flight YI 362 been delayed?
2 Has flight HX 472 been cancelled?
3 Has flight JG 971 arrived?

e Write 5 more questions.

eg Has flight YI 362 been delayed?

1 _____ ?
2 _____ ?
3 _____ ?
4 _____ ?
5 _____ ?

Check with your teacher.

f Ask your neighbour your questions.

LONDON - MUNICH

Depart: Heathrow Airport
BA flights   Terminal 1 (min check in time at gate - 20 mins)
Other flights Terminal 2 (min check in time at gate - 30 mins)

Arrive: Munich Airport

Frequency	Aircraft			
1234567	Dep	Arr	Via	Flight
12345..	0700	0830	non-stop	LH 971
1234567	0820	1145	Düsseldorf	BA 709
12345..	1005	1135	non-stop	LH 391
1.3.5..	1200	1330	non-stop	BA 743
1.34.6.	1445	1800	Frankfurt	LH 242
1234567	1745	2105	Hanover	LH 372
.2.4.6.	1905	2035	non-stop	BA 552
12.456.	2025	2205	non-stop	LH 721

(1 = Monday / 7 = Sunday)

Flight Enquiries

Flight Reservations   0171-322-9476
Flight Information   0171-391-4672
Cargo Sales Office   0171-242-9733

24-hour service

3 a Look at the information and ask your neighbour.

eg *Does the 0820 plane fly on Sundays? Yes it does.*

1 Does the 1445 plane fly on Tuesdays?
2 Does the 2025 plane fly on Saturdays?
3 Does the 1200 plane fly on Tuesdays?
4 Which days does the 1905 plane fly on?
5 Which days doesn't the 1200 plane fly on?

b Answer the following questions.

eg *What time does the 0820 arrive? It arrives at 1145.*

1 What time does the 1745 arrive? _____ .
2 What time does flight BA 709 depart? _____ .
3 Is flight BA 552 non-stop? _____ .
4 Which flight goes via Düsseldorf? _____ .
5 Which terminal does flight BA 709 leave from? _____ .

Check with your neighbour.

c Ask your neighbour 5 more questions.

eg *Which flight goes via Hanover? Flight LH 372.*

d Ask your neighbour the following questions.

1 Which number do I ring if I want to find out departure times?
2 What is the latest check in time for flight LH 391?
3 Can I reserve a ticket at 3am?
4 If I have to be in Munich for 1430, which flight should I take?
5 If I have to be in Munich at 1300, which flight should I take?

Check with your teacher.

4 a Translate the following.

Vocabulary

departures	landed time
flight number	flight information
comments	yet
boarding	on time
final call	delayed
check in	already
smooth	landed
cabin crew	baggage in hall
punctual	cancelled
arrival	frequency
duty free goods	aircraft
safety	via
luggage	enquiries
arrivals	reservations
scheduled arrival time	cargo sales
estimated arrival time	24 hour service

Structures

Has flight JG 971 from Tokyo arrived yet?
Is good calm weather important for you when you're flying?
For me the most important thing is good, calm weather.
I hate flying in bad weather.
Has the plane from Tokyo arrived yet?
No it hasn't.
Yes it has.
It's been delayed.
It's already landed.
Has flight YI 362 been delayed?
Does the 0820 plane fly on Sundays?
Yes it does.
What time does the 0820 arrive?
It arrives at 1145.
Which flight goes via Hanover?
Flight LH 372.

UNIT 14

When's the next train to Corbridge?

1 a Match the pictures and the words.

3 handbag
6 sports bag
9 holdall
4 suitcase
8 briefcase
1 rucksack
5 box
10 garment bag
7 vanity case
2 hat box

Check with your neighbour.

b Ask your neighbour.

eg What's number 1? It's a rucksack.

c Look at the instructions for the left luggage locker below and then answer these questions.

eg When should I key in the number? When I want to retrieve my luggage.

1 What colour is the light when I take my ticket? _It's green_ .
2 What number do I key in to retrieve my luggage? _The number of your ticket_ .
3 Does the machine give change? _____ .
4 When do I insert the money? _When the green light is on_ .
5 How do I know how much it costs? _It's shown on the Display_ .

d You want to leave a suitcase in the left luggage locker. Discuss with your neighbour what you have to do.

e Tell your teacher how to use the left luggage locker.

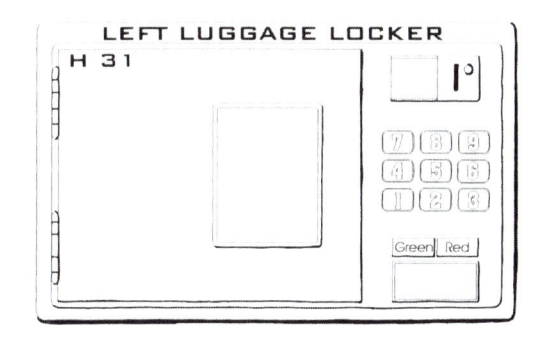

Instructions for Use
1 Place luggage in locker.
2 Close locker and wait for green light.
3 Insert required amount as shown on display (no change is given).
4 Wait for red light.
5 Take ticket.

To Retrieve Luggage
1 Key in the number on your ticket.
2 Wait for door to open.
3 Take your luggage.

2 **a** Listen to the cassette and fill in the missing information.

TRAIN TIMETABLE				
Platform	Departure Time	Destination	Via	Comments
7	12:06	York	Durham Darlington	on time
5	12:15	Birmingham	Manchester Preston	on time
4	12:17	Glasgow		delayed
2	12:24	London	Darlington York	on time
3	12:25	Cardiff		cancelled
6	12:30	New Castle		on time

Listen again and check then compare with your neighbour.

b Look at the following information and answer the questions below.

eg   When is New Year's Day? Monday January 1.

Bank and Public Holidays

New Year's Day	Mon	Jan 1
Good Friday	Fri	Apr 5
Easter Monday	Mon	Apr 8
May Day Holiday	Mon	May 6
Spring Bank Holiday	Mon	May 27
Summer Bank Holiday	Mon	Aug 26
Christmas Day	Wed	Dec 25
Boxing Day	Thur	Dec 26

1 When is Spring Bank Holiday? _Mon May 27_ .
2 When is Summer Bank Holiday? _____ .
3 When is May Day Holiday? _____ .
4 When is Boxing Day? _____ .
5 When is Easter Monday? _____ .

c Ask your neighbour 5 questions.

eg   What is August 26?   It's Summer Bank Holiday.

d How many bank and public holidays do you have in your country?

3 a It's Thursday and you're in Newcastle. Look at the train timetable below.

1   It's 0715. When's the next train to Corbridge? _____ .
2   It's 0935. When's the next train to Corbridge? _____ .
3   It's 1700. When's the next train to Corbridge? _____ .

Train Timetable Newcastle - Hexham											
	x	+	o	+	*	o	*	+	*	*	+
Newcastle	0700	0725	0800	0815	..07	1610	1645	1705	1845	1905	2300
Dunstable	0705	0730	0805		..12	1615	1650		1850	1910	2305
Metro Centre	0710	0735	0810		..17	1620	1655		1855	1915	2310
Blaydon	0715	0740	0815		..22	1625	1700		1900	1920	2315
Wylam	0720	0745	0820		..27	1630	1705		1905	1925	2320
Prudhoe	0725	0750	0825		..32	1635	1710		1910	1930	2325
Stocksfield	0730	0755	0830		..37	1640	1715		1915	1935	2330
Corbridge	0735	0800	0835		..42	1645	1720		1920	1940	2335
Hexham	0740	0805	0840	0835	..47	1650	1725	1725	1925	1945	2340

<u>Bank and Public Holidays</u>

x every day, except Sunday   + only weekdays   o every day, including bank holidays   * every day, except bank holidays

b Now ask your neighbour these questions.

eg   *What time does the 0800 train arrive in Prudhoe? It arrives at twenty five past eight.*

1   What time does the 0800 train arrive in Stocksfield?
2   What time does the 0725 train arrive in Hexham?
3   What time does the 1407 train arrive in Wylam?
4   What time does the 1645 train arrive in the Metro Centre?
5   What time does the 2300 train arrive in Blaydon?

c Ask your neighbour 5 more questions.

eg   *What time does the 1705 train arrive in Hexham? It arrives at twenty five past five.*

d Answer the following questions.

eg   *I have to be in Stocksfield for 0845. Which train should I take? You should take the 0800.*

1   I have to be in Prudhoe for 1150. Which train should I take? _____ .
2   I have to be in Corbridge for 0900. Which train should I take? _____ .
3   I have to be in the Metro Centre for 0945. Which train should I take? _____ .
4   I have to be in Hexham for 1200. Which train should I take? _____ .
5   I have to be in Stocksfield for 1430. Which train should I take? _____ .

e Ask your neighbour 5 more questions.

eg   *I have to be in Hexham for 1730. Which train should I take? You should take the 1705 express.*

f Answer the following questions

eg   *Does the 1705 run on Sundays? No, it only runs on weekdays.*

1   Does the 0800 run on Good Friday? _____ .
2   Does the 1307 run on Sundays? _____ .
3   Does the 0725 run on Wednesdays? _____ .
4   Does the 1845 run on Boxing Day? _____ .
5   What is the last train to run on Saturday night? _____ .

4 a Translate the following.

Vocabulary

handbag _____
sports bag _____
holdall _____
briefcase _____
rucksack _____
box _____
garment bag _____
vanity case _____
hat box _____
left luggage locker _____
place _____
to retrieve _____
to key in _____
no change is given _____

delay _____
apology _____
due to _____
derailment _____
New Year's Day _____
Good Friday _____
Easter Monday _____
May Day Holiday _____
Spring Bank Holiday _____
Summer Bank Holiday _____
Christmas Day _____
Boxing Day _____
express _____

Structures

When's the next train to Corbridge? _____
When should I key in the number? _____
When I want to retrieve my luggage. _____
When is New Year's Day? _____
Monday January 1. _____
What is August 26? _____
It's Summer Bank Holiday. _____
What time does the 0800 train arrive in Prudhoe? _____
It arrives at twenty five past eight. _____
What time does the 1705 arrive in Hexham? _____
It arrives at twenty five past five. _____
I have to be in Stocksfield for 0845. _____
Which train should I take? _____
You should take the 8 o'clock. _____
Does the 1705 run on Sundays? _____
No, it only runs on weekdays. _____

UNIT 15

I think that cars are the safest way to travel.

1 a Fill in the following using a tick (✓) for yes or a cross (x) for no and a question mark (?) for don't know.

	comfortable	safe	expensive	slow	crowded	enjoyable	healthy	convenient	environmentally friendly
cars	✓	✓	✓	x	?	x	✗	✓	x
buses	x	✓	x	✓	✓	x	✗	x	✓
trains	✓	✓	x	x	x	✓	x	✓	✓
motorbikes	✓	x	✓	x	x	✓	x	x	x
bicycles	x	x	x	✓	x	✓	✓	x	✓

b Fill in the following.

I think that ___cars___ are the most comfortable way to travel.

I think that ___trains___ are the safest way to travel.

I think that ___motorbikes___ are the most enjoyable way to travel.

I think that ___buses___ are the most convenient way to travel.

I think that ___bicycles___ are the most environmentally friendly way to travel.

c Ask your neighbour what he/she thinks.

eg *I think that cars are the most comfortable way to travel. What do you think? I think they're very comfortable but the disadvantages are that they're expensive and not very environmentally friendly.*

d Fill in the following in note form.

eg *What are the advantages of cars? Comfortable, safe and convenient. Take you door to door. You can leave when you want.*

1 What are the disadvantages of buses? ___expensive, enjoyable, not comfatable, crowded___

2 What are the advantages of trains? ___They are safe, convenient, environmentally friendly, read a Book___

3 What are the disadvantages of cars? ___expensive, somtimes slow, not environmentally___

4 What are the advantages of buses? ___safe, environmentally,___

5 What are the disadvantages of trains? _____

e Ask your neighbour the questions above.

2 a Read the following information.

"...and now for the traffic news. The M1 motorway northbound is blocked between junctions 3 and 4 due to an overturned lorry. Tailbacks are already 2 miles long. Drivers are requested to leave the motorway at junction 3 and follow police diversion signs. Meanwhile, roadworks due to worn-out surface on the M25 are causing congestion between junctions 24 and 25. Drivers are advised to avoid this section."

15 injured in motorway pile-up

A pile-up on the M4 last night was caused by careless driving according to the police.

11 cars were involved in the pile-up which happened at about 6.30pm last night and 15 people were taken to hospital.

A police spokesman said "Motorists were driving at speeds over 70mph despite the thick fog and visibility of around 100 yards. We were lucky that no one was seriously injured."

One of the drivers who was in hospital last night suffering from whiplash said "I was driving at around 40mph because of the bad conditions. Suddenly I saw brake lights ahead. I braked hard but could not avoid the cars in front."

Sheila Jameson who was travelling in the inside lane said "They were all travelling like maniacs - far too fast and far too close. I'm surprised nobody was killed. People who drive like that shouldn't be allowed on the roads."

Police have reminded motorists to drive with extra care when conditions are bad.

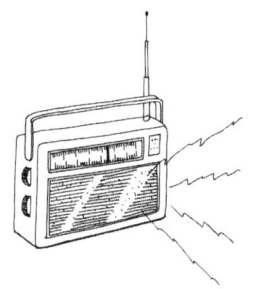

"Yesterday afternoon traffic congestion caused smog levels in central London to rise to a dangerous level. Motorists were requested to turn off their engines at traffic lights and when standing in traffic jams. People living in the area were advised to close all windows and keep children inside. It is feared that levels will rise again today."

b Ask your neighbour. What do you think these words mean?

1 tailback   3 seriously injured   5 whiplash   7 brake lights   9 motorist
2 pile-up   4 traffic jam   6 bad conditions   8 smog   10 overturned

Check with your teacher.

c Fill in the following in note form. Use the information from the text, as well as your own examples.

Problem	Cause
accidents	eg driving too fast/drivers falling asleep
roadworks	
diversions	
congestion	
smog	

d Discuss these in your group.

eg   What causes accidents? I think that people drive too fast or they drive when they are tired. They're both very dangerous.

3 a Read the following statements and decide if you agree, disagree, or if you don't know. Put a tick (✓) in the box.

		agree	disagree	don't know
1	Motorways should have more lanes.	☐	☐	☐
2	Public transport is not efficient.	☐	☐	☐
3	The driving test is too easy.	☐	☐	☐
4	I can't remember the last time I went by train.	☐	☐	☐
5	I don't know how much it costs to come to my English lesson by bus.	☐	☐	☐
6	Cars should be made which don't go faster than 120km.	☐	☐	☐
7	I want to open my windows when I want, not when it's safe.	☐	☐	☐
8	Motorways should be privatised.	☐	☐	☐
9	I take public transport more than once a week.	☐	☐	☐
10	Bad drivers should be banned.	☐	☐	☐

b Discuss your answers with 2 neighbours.

eg *I think that motorways should have more lanes. What do you think? I agree - there are too many cars on the road and if there were more lanes there wouldn't be as many accidents.*

c Read the following text.

Whether you listen to the radio, watch TV, or read newspapers, you will always hear some traffic news. Occasionally you will hear some good news (eg repairs to the road are now finished) but normally you will hear bad news - traffic jams, road repairs, accidents. Of course, when this happens people do not decide to put their car in the garage and take public transport. No they stay in their cars and find other roads, side roads and B-roads in order to continue their journey. Statistics show that more and more new cars are being sold. By 2010 the number of cars will have doubled. This is not just Britain, this is true of most cities in the world and many towns in more developed countries. The problems created are not just traffic problems. More traffic means more pollution, more exhaust fumes going into the air which are breathed in by pedestrians and children as well as motorists. More traffic means more accidents. But whose responsibility is it to take action? Who should be doing something about it now? Some people say it is the government's responsibility - they should build better roads which need fewer repairs, wider roads with more lanes, and more roads. Others say it is the individual's responsibility. We should all use public transport wherever possible and when we have to travel by car, try to find somebody else going to the same place and travel together in one car. If you look at cars on any road today, 90% only have one person in them. So it's clear that some solution has to be found. The question is, what is the best solution?

d Read the sentences and based on the text write T for true, or F for false.

eg *Traffic news is normally bad news. T*

1 Fewer cars are being sold. _____
2 This problem is world-wide. _____
3 There will be twice as many cars in 2010. _____
4 More traffic means fewer accidents. _____
5 10% of cars on the road have more than 1 person in them. _____

Check with your teacher.

4 a Translate the following.

Vocabulary

comfortable _____	to brake hard _____
safe _____	inside lane _____
expensive _____	maniacs _____
slow _____	far too close _____
crowded _____	killed _____
enjoyable _____	to remind _____
healthy _____	extra care _____
convenient _____	whether _____
environmentally friendly _____	occasionally _____
disadvantage _____	good news _____
advantage _____	repairs _____
traffic news _____	bad news _____
northbound _____	traffic jams _____
blocked _____	road repairs _____
overturned _____	accidents _____
tailbacks _____	side roads _____
drivers _____	B-roads _____
to leave _____	to continue _____
diversion signs _____	journey _____
meanwhile _____	true _____
congestion _____	developed countries _____
to avoid _____	pollution _____
injured _____	exhaust fumes _____
pile-up _____	to breathe in _____
spokeswoman _____	pedestrians _____
speed _____	responsibility _____
despite _____	to build _____
visibility _____	fewer _____
seriously injured _____	wider _____
to suffer from _____	individual _____
whiplash _____	public transport _____
bad conditions _____	solution _____
suddenly _____	privatised _____
brake lights _____	banned _____

Structures

I think that cars are the most comfortable way to travel. _____
I think that buses are the safest way to travel. _____
What do you think? _____
I think they're very comfortable. _____
The disadvantages are that they're expensive. _____
What causes accidents? _____
I think people drive too fast or they drive when they are tired. _____
I think that motorways should have more lanes. _____
I agree. _____

UNIT 16

Going Shopping

1

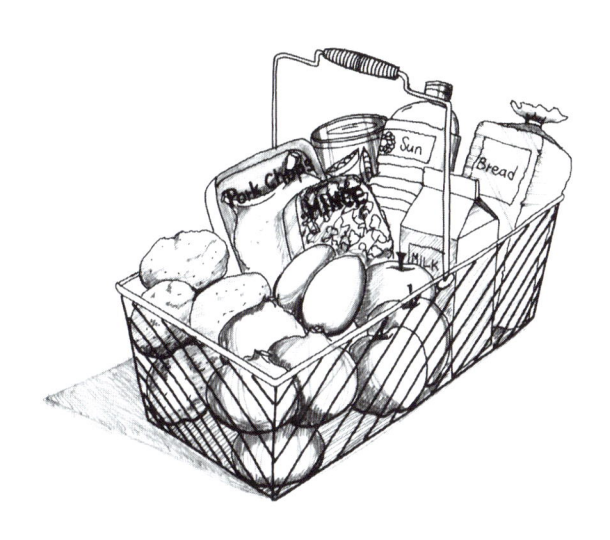

a   See if you can find these items in the shopping basket.

Bread, milk, eggs, potatoes, onions, tinned peas, cooking oil, apples, mince and pork chops.

b   Write down 8 items which you normally buy when you go shopping.

1. _bread_ ✓
2. _potatoes_
3. _cigarettes_
4. _milk_ ✓
5. _yoghurt_
6. _butter_
7. _chewing gum_
8. _meat_

c   Ask 3 neighbours what they buy and then tell your teacher which items all of you buy.

d   Answer the following questions using 'always', 'usually', 'sometimes', 'seldom', 'never'

	you	your neighbour
1 How often do you eat at home?	usually	always
2 How often do you go shopping?	always	seldom
3 How often do you cook for yourself?	always	sometimes
4 How often do you cook for other people?	sometimes	seldom
5 How often does someone else cook for you?	seldom	usually
6 How often do you wash up?	always/never	seldom
7 How often do you eat the same thing?	seldom	seldom
8 How often do you eat frozen food?	seldom	seldom
9 How often do you eat from tins or packets?	seldom	seldom
10 How often do you eat too much?	never	seldom

e   Ask your neighbour and note down the answers

f   Tell your teacher about your neighbour.

eg   My neighbour normally eats at home. He seldom cooks for himself and never cooks for other people. His wife usually cooks for him...

2 a Look at the words and put them in one of the columns below.

deodorant	cat food	soap	grapes	milk	leeks	barbecue sauce
curry sauce	cheese	dog food	carrots		cherries	mayonnaise
oranges	bananas	toothpaste	potatoes		salad dressing	shampoo
cabbage	butter	apples	shower gel	onions	tomato sauce	yoghurt

I know what it is	I think I know what it is	I don't know what it is
	grapes = Weintrauben cherries = Kirschen	leeks = Lauch toothpaste = Zahnpasta cabbage = Kohl

b Compare with 2 neighbours.

Ask your teacher the words you don't know.

c Where would you find these in a supermarket? Work with your neighbour and put the above words in one of the categories.

Dairy Products (Milch-)
- milk
- cheese
- butter
- yoghurt

Fruit
- grapes
- cherries
- oranges
- bananas
- apples

Toiletries
- deodorant
- soap
- toothpaste
- shampoo
- shower gel

Pet Food (Haustier)
- cat food
- dog food

Sauces
- barbecue-
- curry-
- mayonnaise
- salad dressing
- tomato-

Vegetables
- leeks
- carrots
- potatoes
- cabbage
- onions

Check with your teacher.

3 a Here is a plan of a supermarket. The following items are missing: sauces, ordinary fruit, tinned fruit, biscuits, tea and coffee, mixers, spirits, rice, sugar and fresh meat.

Listen to the cassette and put the items in the correct place. You may listen to it twice.

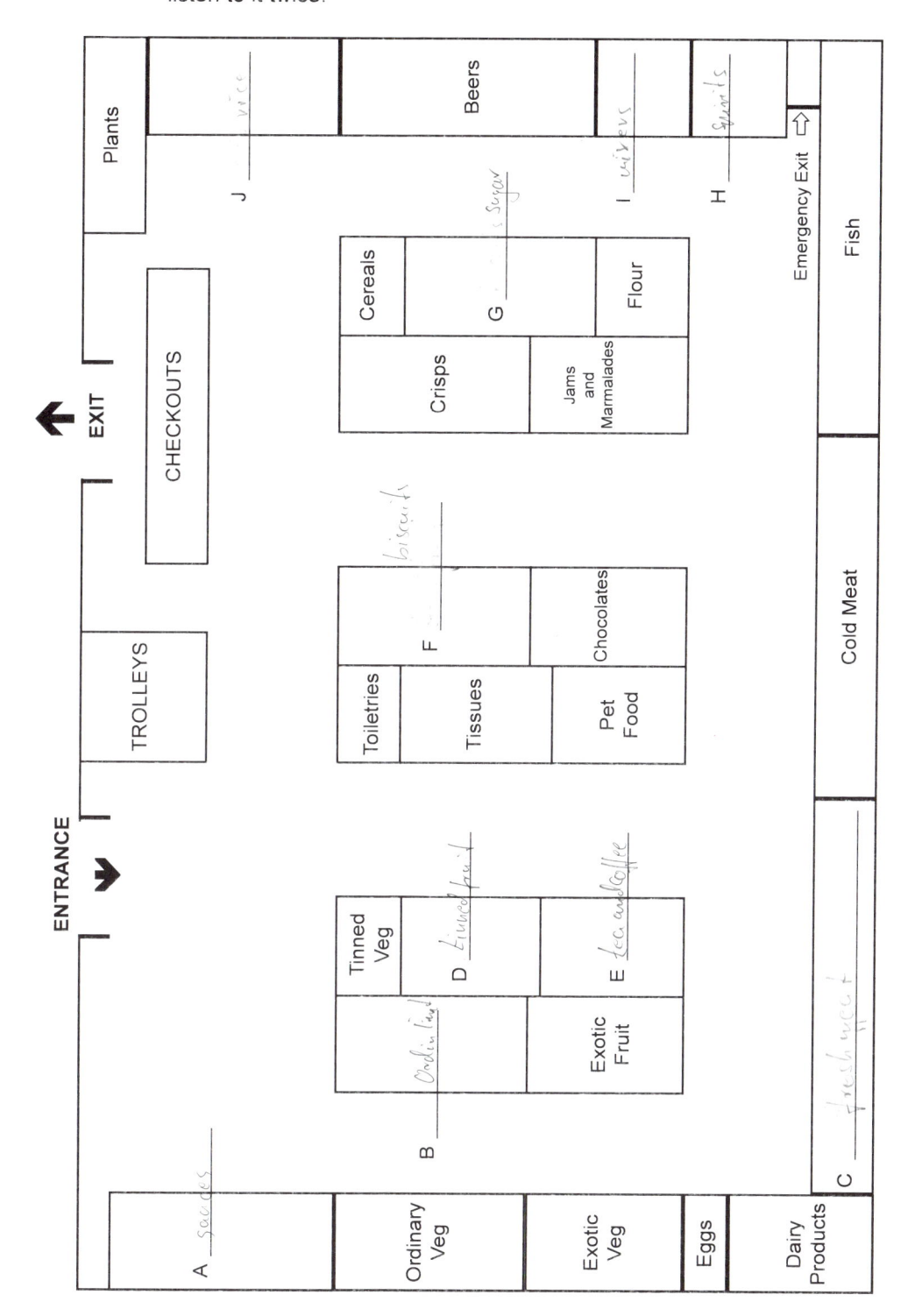

[Plan of supermarket with handwritten annotations:
- A: sauces
- B: ordinary fruit
- C: fresh meat
- D: tinned fruit
- E: tea and coffee
- F: biscuits
- G: sugar
- H: spirits
- I: mixers
- J: rice

Labelled sections: Plants, Beers, Emergency Exit, Fish, Cereals, Flour, Crisps, Jams and Marmalades, Checkouts, Exit, Toiletries, Tissues, Chocolates, Pet Food, Cold Meat, Trolleys, Entrance, Tinned Veg, Exotic Fruit, Ordinary Veg, Exotic Veg, Eggs, Dairy Products]

b **Ask your neighbour.**

eg *Where are the crisps? They're next to the jams and marmalades.*

1 Where are the trolleys?   4 Where are the tissues?
2 Where is the cold meat?   5 Where is the pet food?
3 Where is the emergency exit?   6 Where are the cereals?

c **Ask your neighbour 5 more questions.**

eg *Where are the tinned vegetables? They're opposite the toiletries.*

4 a Translate the following.

Vocabulary

shopping basket _____
to contain _____
tinned peas _____
mince _____
pork chops _____
deodorant _____
curry sauce _____
bananas _____
cabbage _____
cat food _____
dog food _____
grapes _____
salad dressing _____
shower gel _____
cherries _____
leeks _____
tomato sauce _____
barbecue sauce _____
mayonnaise _____
yoghurt _____
dairy products _____
toiletries _____

pet food _____
sauces _____
trolleys _____
checkouts _____
entrance _____
exit _____
ordinary _____
exotic _____
tinned vegetables _____
tinned fruit _____
fresh meat _____
cold meat _____
jams _____
marmalades _____
crisps _____
cereals _____
flour _____
emergency exit _____
biscuits _____
rice _____
spirits _____
mixers _____

Structures

My neighbour normally eats at home. _____
He seldom cooks for himself. _____
He never cooks for other people. _____
His wife usually cooks for him. _____
Do you know what deodorant is? _____
I know what it is. _____
I think I know what it is. _____
I don't know what it is. _____
Where are the crisps? _____
They're next to the jams and marmalades. _____
The tissues are between the toiletries and the pet food. _____
The trolleys are on the left when you walk in. _____
Where are the tinned vegetables? _____
They're opposite the toiletries. _____

UNIT 17

Eating Out

1 a Look at the information and answer the questions below.

eg What kind of food does the Jasmin Garden serve?

It serves Chinese food.

Jasmin Garden Chinese Restaurant

66 Victoria Road, Wrexham
Tel 01978 443322

Mandarin Chinese Specialities

Party Bookings Welcome

Licensed Bar

Opening Hours:
Mon - Thu 10am - 11.15pm
Fri & Sat 10am - 11.45pm
Sun 1pm - 11.15pm

Fortini's Restaurant

78-80 King George Street
Blackpool
Tel 01253 462613

Real Italian Cuisine

Licensed Bar

Open 7 days a week
11am - 2.30pm
6pm - 11pm

Shalimar Indian Restaurant

19 Trent Street, Derby
Tel 01332 242464

Specialist Tandoori Dishes

Opening Hours
Daily 11am - 2.30pm / 6pm - 12am

Licensed Bar

Royal Country Restaurant

24 Markington Place
Stratford-upon-Avon
Tel 01789 516437

Traditional English Dishes

Sunday Lunches
Roast Beef and Yorkshire Pudding £5.25

Opening Times
Mon - Sat 12pm - 2pm / 6.30pm - 10pm
Sun 12pm - 2pm / 7pm - 9pm

---

1 When is the Royal Country Restaurant open on Sunday? _____
2 Which restaurant is in Blackpool? _____
3 What is the telephone number of the Indian restaurant? _____
4 01978 is the area code for which town? _____
5 Which restaurant closes daily at midnight? _____

b Ask your neighbour the following questions.

eg What is the address of the Indian restaurant? It's 19 Trent Street, Derby.

1 Can I drink wine in the Italian restaurant?
2 What is the telephone number of the Italian restaurant?
3 In which restaurant can I order a Sunday lunch?
4 Which restaurant opens at 7pm on Sunday evenings?
5 What time does the Chinese restaurant close on Saturdays?

c Match the menu below and the restaurant from 1a.

1 *Royal Country Restaurant*   2 *Fortini's Restaurant*   3 *Jasmin Garden Chinese*   4 *Shalimar Indian Restaurant*

chicken soup	garlic bread	bird's nest soup	poppadoms
roast lamb and mint sauce	spaghetti carbonara	sweet 'n' sour pork	basmati rice, naan bread
potatoes, carrots and peas	ice cream	boiled rice	tandoori chicken
apple pie		lychees	assam tea

Check with your teacher.

d Ask your neighbour the following questions.

1 When was the last time you were in a restaurant?
2 Who were you with?
3 What kind of food did it serve?
4 What did you eat?
5 Would you recommend the restaurant?

e Tell your teacher about your neighbour.

2 a Look at the information and ask your neighbour the following questions.

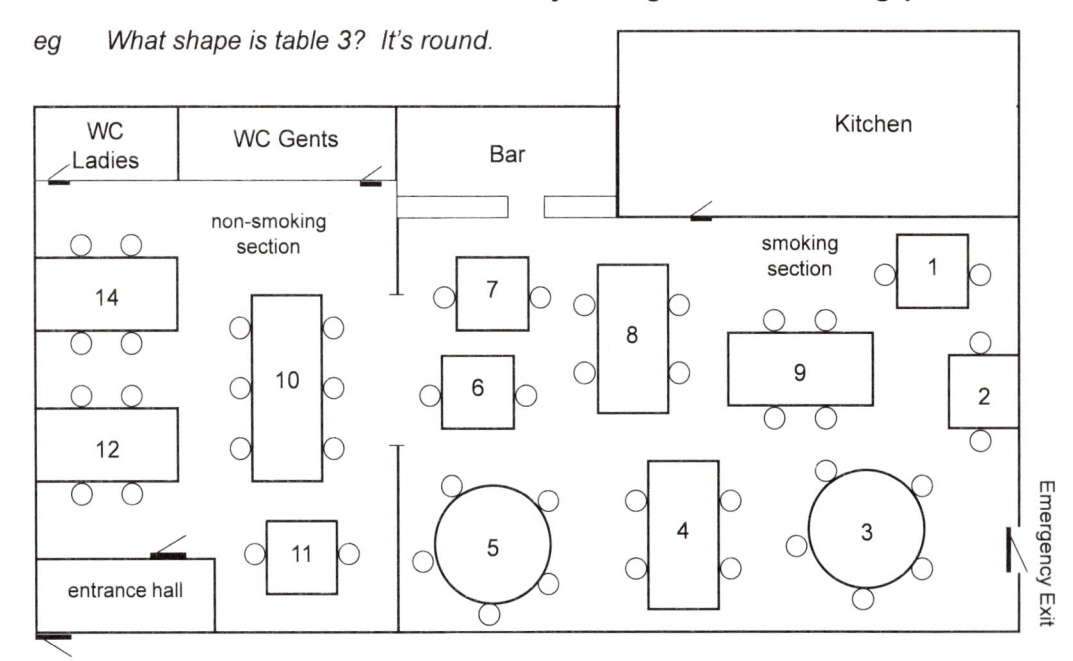

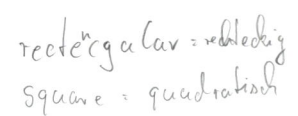

eg *What shape is table 3? It's round.*

rectangular = rechteckig
square = quadratisch

[Restaurant floor plan showing: WC Ladies, WC Gents, Bar, Kitchen. Non-smoking section with tables 14, 12, 10, 11. Smoking section with tables 1, 2, 9, 8, 7, 6, 5, 4, 3. Entrance hall at bottom left, Emergency Exit on right.]

1 What shape is table 8?
2 How many tables are there altogether?
3 Which table number is missing? Do you know why?
4 How many square tables are there?
5 Which tables are non smoking tables?

b Here is the reservations diary for the Royal Country Restaurant. Listen to the cassette and fill in the missing information. You will hear the cassette twice.

Royal Country Restaurant - Reservations - Saturday November 5							
6.00	Mr Nixon	(4 people)	Table 14	8.30		(people)	Table
6.30	Walkers	(4 people)	Table 8	9.00		(people)	Table
6.30	Johnsons	(2 people)	Table 1	9.30	Benfords	(2 people)	Table
7.00	Taylors	(4 people)	Table 4	10.00		(people)	Table
7.30	Mr Armstrong	(5 people)	Table 5				
7.30	Mrs Brown	(6 people)	Table 10				
8.00	Bell	(2 people)	Table 2/11				

c Ask your neighbour the following questions.

eg *Who will have table 14? Mr Nixon.*

1 Who will have table 5?
2 Will the Johnsons have table 1?
3 Is table 3 a smoking table?
4 How many people are in Miss Brown's party?
5 What time are the Benfords coming?

d Answer the following questions (you may listen to the cassette again).

eg *What time is the first reservation? It's at 6.00pm*

1 Are the Taylors regular visitors?
2 How old is Mr Armstrong's daughter?
3 What is Miss Brown celebrating?
4 Do the Benfords smoke?
5 Is Saturday night normally busy?

Check with your teacher.

Menu

Soup of the Day £2.15
Prawn Cocktail £2.30
Paté with Toast £2.20
Roast Beef and Yorkshire Pudding £6.75
Roast Lamb and Mint Sauce £6.75
Roast Pork and Apple Sauce £7.35
Roast Turkey and Cranberry Jelly £6.95
All served with boiled potatoes and vegetables.
Ice Cream (strawberry, vanilla) £1.90
Apple Crumble £2.50
Cheese and Biscuits £2.20
Coffee and Mints £1.30

Wine List

White	Glass	Bottle
German		
Liebfraumilch	80p	£5.95
Piesporter	85p	£6.15
Italian		
Lambrusco	75p	£5.25
Frascati	85p	£6.25
Australian		
Jacobs Creek	85p	£6.10
Red		
Italian		
D'Abruzzo Montepulcciano	90p	£7.95
Californian		
Paul Masson	85p	£7.10
French		
St Emilion	£1.10	£8.95

3   a   Fill in the following.

eg   soup - paté
The soup is cheaper than the paté.
The paté is more expensive than the soup.

beef - lamb
The beef is the same price as the lamb.

1   prawn cocktail - paté _____

2   ice cream - apple crumble _____

3   lamb - beef _____

4   lamb - turkey _____

5   Liebfraumilch - Lambrusco _____

Check with your teacher.

b   Look at the menus again. Decide what you would like to eat and fill in the following.

1   What would you like as a starter? _____
2   What would you like as a main course? _____
3   What would you like for dessert? _____
4   Would you like coffee and mints? _____
5   What would you like to drink with your meal? _____

c   Roleplay in a restaurant. A customer (C) is ordering a meal from the waiter/waitress (W). Read the dialogue through then practise ordering a meal for yourself.

W   Good evening. Can I help you?
C   Yes please, I'd like a table for two.
W   Come this way please. Here's the menu.
W   Are you ready to order?
C   Yes please. What's the soup of the day?
W   It's cream of tomato.
C   Okay, we'll have 2 soups and then one roast beef and one roast pork.
W   One beef, one pork, fine. Would you like anything to drink with the meal?

C   Yes please, a bottle of D'Abbruzo Montepulcciano
W   Okay, fine.
    (later)
W   Was everything all right?
C   Yes thanks. Can we have the bill please?
W   Yes of course. Here's your bill.
C   Okay here you are, keep the change.
W   Thank you.

4 a Translate the following.

Vocabulary

Indian _____
Chinese _____
specialities _____
specialist _____
party bookings _____
licensed bar _____
cuisine _____
traditional _____
roast beef _____
yorkshire pudding _____
to serve _____
to recommend _____
round _____
square _____
rectangular _____
soup of the day _____
paté _____

prawn cocktail _____
roast lamb with mint sauce _____
roast pork with apple sauce _____
roast turkey with cranberry jelly _____
boiled potatoes _____
ice cream _____
strawberry _____
vanilla _____
apple crumble _____
cheese and biscuits _____
mints _____
wine list _____
French _____
German _____
Australian _____
Californian _____

Structures

What kind of food does the Jasmin Garden serve? _____
It serves Chinese food. _____
What is the address of the Indian restaurant? _____
It's 19 Trent Street, Derby. _____
What shape is table 3? _____
It's round. _____
Who will have table 14? _____
Mr Nixon. _____
What time is the first reservation? _____
It's at 6.00 pm. _____
The soup is cheaper than the paté. _____
The paté is more expensive than the soup. _____
The beef is the same price as the lamb. _____
Come this way please. _____
Are you ready to order? _____
Was everything all right? _____
Keep the change. _____

UNIT 18

Eating In

1   **a**   Match the words and the pictures.

_3_ casserole dish
_5_ frying pan
_1_ kettle
_6_ pot
_4_ saucepan
_2_ roasting tray

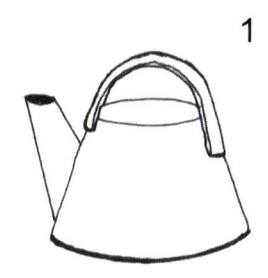

Check with your teacher.

b   Answer the following questions using the words from 1a.

eg   Which would you use to roast a chicken? A roasting tray.

1   Which would you use to fry potatoes? _____ .
2   Which would you use to boil water? _____ .
3   Which would you use to make a cheese sauce? _____ .
4   Which would you use to boil potatoes? _____ .
5   Which would you use to make a chicken casserole? _____ .

Check with your neighbour.

c   Ask your neighbour these questions.

1   Have you ever visited people in another country?
2   Did they prepare a typical meal for you?
3   How many courses did it have?
4   What did they make?
5   Did you enjoy it?

d   Discuss with your neighbour.

1   What is a typical meal for your country?
2   How many courses does a typical meal have?
3   How would you make it?
4   What do you normally drink with it?
5   Which pots/pans would you use?

2 a Match the abbreviations and the words.

lb   g   tblsp   tsp   ml   fl oz   ½   ⅓

1 tablespoon _tblsp_   2 pound _lb_   3 millilitre _ml_   4 fluid ounces _fl oz_

5 teaspoon _tsp_   6 gram _g_   7 a half _½_   8 a third _⅓_

b Look at the recipe for tomato and basil soup.

- Tomato and Basil Soup -

Ingredients

1½ lb (700g) tomatoes
(chopped in quarters)
1 medium onion (chopped small)
1 medium potato (chopped small)
1½ tblsp olive oil
10 fl oz (275ml) stock
1 clove garlic (crushed)
1 tsp dried basil
salt and pepper

Instructions

1 Heat the oil in a saucepan.

2 Add the onion and potato and soften them slowly. This takes 10 - 15 minutes.

3 Add the tomatoes, stir well and let them cook for one minute. Pour in the stock and stir. Add the basil, salt and pepper and crushed garlic. Cover and leave to simmer for 25 minutes. Taste to check before serving.

---

c Answer the following questions.

eg How much basil do you need? 1 teaspoon.

1 What do you have to do first? _____.
2 How much oil do you need? _____.
3 Do the tomatoes have to be crushed? _____.
4 Do you add the tomatoes before the stock? _____.
5 How many millilitres is 10 fluid ounces? _____.

d Look at the instructions below and answer these questions.

eg What is this? It's an instant soup.

1 What do you do first? _____
2 Do you need a pan? _____
3 How much water do you add? _____
4 Do you need a spoon? _____
5 What flavour is it? _____

e Ask your neighbour

eg Do you prefer home-made soup or instant soup? Why?

f Tell your teacher about yourself.

eg I prefer home-made soup because it tastes better.

Cream of Tomato Soup
Instant Cup Soup
Instructions for Use
1 Empty packet into cup or mug.
2 Pour on ⅓ pint (190ml) of boiling water.
3 Stir well.

3 **a** Look at the information and ask your teacher about food you don't know.

Good Luck Food Palace
12 Marine Parade, Leeds, LS1 7JH
(0113) 2573157
Takeaway
We are open during Chinese New Year
Home Deliveries available
Telephone orders welcome

Duck Dishes	
Roast Duck with Mushrooms	£4.25
Roast Duck with Pineapple	£4.25
Chicken Dishes	
Fried Chicken with Pineapple	£3.25
Fried Chicken with Lemon Sauce	£3.65
Beef Dishes	
Fried Beef with Onion	£3.25
Fried Beef with Mushrooms	£3.25
Pork Dishes	
Fried Pork with Pineapple	£3.25
Fried Pork Chinese Style	£3.45
Set Meal for 2 Persons	£16.00

Joe's Fish 'n' Chip Shop
17 Ashford Road, Kendal
Tel 01539 243941
Open
Mon - Sat 11.30am - 1.30pm
Mon - Sat 4.30pm - 9.30pm
Closed on Sundays
Telephone your orders and they'll be ready for collection.

Cod & Chips	£2.25
Scampi & Chips	£2.25
Fishcake & Chips	£2.10
Steak 'n' Kidney Pie	£1.60
Chicken 'n' Mushroom Pie	£1.50
Sausage	£1.20
Portion of Chips	60p
Extra Portions	
Curry Sauce	50p
Mushy Peas	50p

Francesca's Italian Takeaway
Open 7 days a week
143 South Street, Perth
Tel 01738 667829
Delivery Service Available
no extra charge

Pizzas	10"	12"	**Pastas**	
Margherita Cheese & Tomato	£2.80	£4.00	Spaghetti Marinara Tomato Sauce & Seafood	£4.30
Romana Cheese, Tomato & Ham	£3.20	£4.70	Lasagne Freshly Made	£3.30
Funghi Cheese, Tomato & Mushroom	£3.00	£4.70	Tagliatelle al Tonno Tomato Sauce & Tuna	£4.20

Diwan-E-Kash
4/5 County Mills, Edinburgh
Tel 0131 606575
Takeaway Menu
15% Discount
Open daily
12 noon to 1.45pm / 6pm to 11.15pm
Sunday 6.30pm to 10.30pm

Poppadom	35p
Bhuna Beef Served with a special blend of spices - medium hot	£4.90
Balti Gosth Tender diced lamb - very spicy	£5.70
Chicken Vindaloo Very hot	£4.30
Lamb Korma Cooked with fresh cream and coconut - very mild	£4.90

b Answer the following questions.

eg How much is curry sauce? It's 50p.

1 How much is cod & chips? _____.

2 Is roast duck with mushrooms cheaper than fried beef with mushrooms? _____.

3 What is the area code for Leeds? _____.

4 How much is steak 'n' kidney pie and a portion of chips? _____.

5 What is on a pizza funghi? _____.

c Ask your neighbour 5 more questions.

eg What's the name of the Chinese restaurant? The Good Luck Food Palace.

d Practise ordering a takeaway meal with your neighbour.

eg Hello, I'd like to order a pizza Romana, 12 inch please.
Will you collect it or would you like it delivered?
I'll collect it in half an hour.
Okay, what's the name?
Simon Rogers.
Fine, see you soon.
Bye.

4 a Translate the following.

Vocabulary

casserole dish _____   salt _____
frying pan _____   pepper _____
pot _____   chopped _____
saucepan _____   crushed _____
roasting tray _____   dried _____
tablespoon _____   to heat _____
pound _____   to add _____
millilitre _____   to soften _____
fluid ounce _____   slowly _____
teaspoon _____   to stir _____
gram _____   to simmer _____
to roast _____   delivery service _____
to fry _____   takeaway _____
courses _____   available _____
recipe _____   no extra charge _____
tomatoes _____   closed on Sundays _____
onion _____   discount _____
potato _____   spice _____
olive oil _____   mild _____
stock _____   medium _____
garlic _____   cream _____
basil _____   coconut _____

Structures

Which would you use to roast a chicken? _____
A roasting tray. _____
How much basil do you need? _____
1 teaspoon. _____
What is this? _____
It's an instant soup. _____
Do you prefer home-made soup or packet soup? _____
I prefer home-made soup because it tastes better. _____
How much is curry sauce? It's 50p. _____
What's the name of the Chinese restaurant? _____
I'd like to order a pizza. _____
I'll collect it in half an hour. _____
What's the name? _____

UNIT 19

A pint of beer please.

1 a Read the following text.

In England and Wales pubs can only open between 11am (opening time) and 11pm (closing time). If you go to a pub you will hear the owner (landlord) shouting "last orders please" at 10.50pm. When you hear this you have 10 minutes to order your last drink of the evening. At 11pm the landlord will shout "time please". When you hear this you may not order any more drinks, however, you do have 20 minutes to enjoy your last drink. This time is called "drinking up time". The pubs in England and Wales are normally empty by 11.30pm. In Scotland pubs can open for 12 hours maximum, but there is no legal closing, or opening time. Most pubs all over Britain serve food as well (bar snacks) and normally offer hot meals as well as sandwiches. In fact many pubs in Britain serve excellent food.

b Ask your neighbour.

eg   What is "opening time"? It's when pubs open.

1. Who is the landlord?
2. How long is "drinking up time"?
3. What are the differences between pubs in England and Scotland?
4. When does the landlord shout "time please"?
5. Do most pubs serve food as well?

c Ask your neighbour.

*eg   What would you like to drink?
I'd like a gin and tonic please.
Ice and lemon?
Yes please.
Anything else?
A glass of coke please.
Ice and lemon?
No thanks. How much is that?
That's £2.60.
Here you are.
Thanks and here's your change.*

d Practise the dialogue with your neighbour.

The Globe Inn
24 Stamford Road, Oakleigh

Price List

Lager	pint	£1.60	Vodka	£1.30
	half	£0.80	Gin	£1.30
Bitter	pint	£1.60	Whisky	£1.20
	half	£0.80	Coke half	£0.80
Cider	pint	£1.50	Fruit Juice	£0.85
	half	£0.75	Glass of Wine	£0.90
Peanuts		£0.40	Mixers	£0.50
Crisps		£0.40	*(tonic, lemonade, etc)*	

All prices include VAT @ 17.5%

2 a Match the definition and the phrases and then check with your teacher.

eg   *What is happy hour?*
     Happy hour is an hour (or more) when drinks are cheaper than normal.

Happy hour is... 4
Quiz night is... 3
Karaoke is... 1
Darts is... 2
A double is... 5

1 An idea from Japan. People can sing their favourite songs to background music. The best singers can win prizes.
2 A game where people throw darts at a board on the wall.
3 An evening when groups of people answer questions on different topics. There are often prizes.
4 An hour (or more) when drinks are cheaper than normal.
5 Two normal measures of spirits (eg whisky, gin, vodka).

eg = for example

b Look at the notices and answer the questions below.

eg   *When is karaoke night? It's on Saturday 14.*

Darts Competition
Tuesday 17
Entry Free

Karaoke night
Saturday 14
8pm onwards
All welcome
Prizes to be Won

Quiz Night
every Friday night
8pm
£3 per team entry
Prizes up to £10

Bar Snacks
Open Daily
Lunchtime 12pm - 2.30pm
Evenings 5pm - 8.30pm
Kiddies Menu available

Happy Hour
5.30pm - 6.30pm
Thursday - Sunday
All Pints 95p
Doubles for the price of singles

1 What time does happy hour start? _____
2 What time do they stop serving bar snacks in the evening? _____
3 How much can a team win on quiz night? _____
4 Can I get a bar snack at Sunday lunchtime? _____
5 How much is a pint during happy hour? _____

Check with your teacher.

c Ask your neighbour.

eg   *What's happening on Tuesday 17? It's darts night.*

1 How often is the quiz night?
2 What time does the karaoke night start?
3 Is a double the same price as a single during happy hour?
4 Are there any prizes on the karaoke evening?
5 Do I have to pay to enter the darts competition?

Check with your teacher.

d Ask your neighbour.

1 Do you have happy hour in your country?
2 Have you every played darts?
3 What pub games do people play in your country?

e Tell your teacher.

3 a **You are going to take part in a pub quiz. Work in groups of 3. Make up a name for your team.**

Listen to the questions on the cassette and write down the answers. You may discuss these in your group and you may listen to the question 3 times. Your teacher will check your answers at the end of each section (answers must be in English).

QUIZ CARD

Name of Team_____

House and Home
1. keys
2. Town
3. Bedroom
4. ___
5. ___

Total Correct 3

Transport and Travel
1. Airplane ✓
2. Gates
3. Car ✓
4. leaving ✓
5. Ship ✓

Total Correct 4

Food and Drink
1. ___
2. Italian Rd
3. Yes
4. carrots
5. Banana

Total Correct 4

Environment and Weather
1. dog
2. Bookshop ✓
3. ice
4. Winter
5. no

Total Correct 4

Languages
1. italian
2. 26
3. Sisters ✓
4. France
5. Spanish

Total Correct 4

Sport and Hobbies
1. trekking
2. swimming ball ✓
3. shipping ✓
4. ___
5. ___

Total Correct 1

Now add up your score to find your final total.

Final Total _____

Which group has the most correct answers?

b **Work in groups of 3. Each group makes up 5 questions. When you are ready ask the other groups your questions.**

4 a Translate the following.

Vocabulary

opening time	Öffnungszeit
closing time	Geschäftsschluss
landlord	
owner	Besitzer
last orders	letzte Bestellung
time please	
drinking up time	
empty	leer
legal	rechtens
bar snacks	kleine Imbiss
happy hour	verbilligte Stunde
quiz night	nächtliches Fragespiel
karaoke	Playback singen
darts	Pfeil werfen
competition	Turnier

Structures

What is "opening time"? ____
It's when pubs open. ____
What would you like to drink? ____
I'd like a gin and tonic please. ____
Ice and lemon? ____
Yes please. ____
Anything else? ____
A glass of coke please. ____
How much is that? ____
That's £2.60. ____
What is happy hour? ____
Happy hour is an hour (or more) when drinks are cheaper than normal. ____
When is karaoke night? ____
It's on Saturday 14. ____
What's happening on Tuesday 17? ____
It's darts night. ____

UNIT 20

Revision

to move house = Umziehen

1 **a** **Ask your neighbour these questions.**

1. What means of transport would you use to go on holiday to Britain? Why?
2. What means of transport would you use to go shopping? Why?
3. What means of transport would you use to go on holiday to America? Why?
4. What means of transport would you use to move house? Why?
5. What means of transport do you use to go to your English lesson? Why?
6. Do you like travelling by train? Why (not)?
7. Do you like travelling by motorbike? Why (not)?
8. Do you like travelling by plane? Why (not)?
9. Do you like travelling by bicycle? Why (not)?
10. Do you like travelling by ship? Why (not)?

2 **a** **Now tell your neighbour about the best holiday you've ever had. Use the following questions as a guide.**

accommodation = Unterkunft / Hotel

1. Where did you go?
2. How long were you there?
3. Did you stay in one place or travel around?
4. What was the accommodation like?
5. Who did you go with?
6. What did you see?
7. How did you get there?
8. What was the weather like?
9. Why was it the best holiday you've ever had?
10. Would you go back again?

3 **a** **Ask your neighbour these questions.**

1. Have you ever travelled by air?
2. How often do you travel by air?
3. Do you like flying?
4. What was your best flight?
5. What was your worst flight?

b **Look at the information and ask your neighbour about the flights.**

eg Has the plane from Athens arrived yet? Yes it has.

ARRIVALS					Time Now 08:10
Flight Number	Scheduled Arrival Time	Estimated Arrival Time	Landed Time	Arriving From	Flight Information
GA 247	08:00	07:55	07:55	ATHENS	Baggage in Hall
SA 495	08:05	08:05	08:05	MADRID	Landed
IA 297	08:10	08:45	_____	DUBLIN	Delayed
DA 373	08:15	08:15	_____	FRANKFURT	On Time
IT 444	08:20	08:30	_____	ROME	Delayed

c **Now ask your neighbour questions like this.**

eg Has flight number DA373 been delayed? No it hasn't. It's on time.

d **Tell your neighbour the status of each flight.**

eg Flight GA247 has already landed and the baggage is in the baggage hall.

Unit 20

4 a Ask your neighbour 10 questions about the bank and public holidays below.

eg *When is Spring Bank Holiday?*
    What is August 26?

Bank and Public Holidays		
New Year's Day	Mon	Jan 1
Good Friday	Fri	Apr 5
Easter Monday	Mon	Apr 8
May Day Holiday	Mon	May 6
Spring Bank Holiday	Mon	May 27
Summer Bank Holiday	Mon	Aug 26
Christmas Day	Wed	Dec 25
Boxing Day	Thu	Dec 26

b Look at the timetable below and ask your neighbour 5 questions.

eg *What time does the 0800 train arrive in Corbridge?*
    Does the 0907 train run on bank holidays?

Newcastle - Hexham

	x	+	o	+	*	o	*	+	*	*	+
Newcastle	0700	0725	0800	0815	..07	1610	1645	1705	1845	1905	2300
Dunstable	0705	0730	0805		..12	1615	1650		1850	1910	2305
Metro Centre	0710	0735	0810		..17	1620	1655		1855	1915	2310
Blaydon	0715	0740	0815		..22	1625	1700		1900	1920	2315
Wylam	0720	0745	0820		..27	1630	1705		1905	1925	2320
Prudhoe	0725	0750	0825		..32	1635	1710		1910	1930	2325
Stocksfield	0730	0755	0830		..37	1640	1715		1915	1935	2330
Corbridge	0735	0800	0835		..42	1645	1720		1920	1940	2335
Hexham	0740	0805	0840	0835	..47	1650	1725	1725	1925	1945	2340

Bank and Public Holidays

x every day, except Sunday   + only weekdays   o every day, including bank holidays   * every day, except bank holidays

5 a Ask your neighbour these questions.

1 Which means of transport do you think is the most comfortable? Why?
2 Which means of transport do you think is the safest? Why?
3 Which means of transport do you think is the most convenient? Why?
4 Which means of transport do you think is the most enjoyable? Why?
5 Which means of transport do you think is the most environmentally friendly? Why?

b Note down one advantage and one disadvantage of each of these means of transport and then compare with your neighbour. See if you agree or disagree.

	advantages	disadvantages
cars		
buses		
trains		
motorbikes		
ships		

5   **c**   **Read these statements and discuss with your neighbour whether you agree or disagree.**

1. The driving test in my country is too easy.
2. Public transport is too expensive.
3. There are too many cars on the road.
4. People would not use cars if petrol was more expensive.
5. I always take public transport if I can.

6   **a**   **Read these questions and say how often you do these things using always, usually, sometimes, seldom, never.**

1. How often do you do eat at home?   _____
2. How often do you go shopping?   _____
3. How often do you cook for yourself?   _____
4. How often do you eat frozen food?   _____
5. How often do you eat from tins or packets?   _____
6. How often do you eat the same thing?   _____

Tell your neighbour about yourself.

b   **Here are 5 items which you can buy in a supermarket. Tell your neighbour why you would buy them and what you would do with them.**

eg   *I would buy milk to make a sauce or to put on my cornflakes or to drink.*

1 butter   2 apples   3 toothpaste   4 tomatoes   5 shampoo

7   **a**   **Here is an advertisement for the Royal Country Restaurant.**

Ask your neighbour 5 questions about it.

eg   *What is the area code?*

Royal Country Restaurant

24 Markington Place
Stratford-upon-Avon
Tel 01789 516437

Traditional English Dishes
Sunday Lunches
Roast Beef and Yorkshire Pudding £5.25

Opening Times:
Mon - Sat 12pm - 2pm / 6.30pm - 10pm
Sun 12pm - 2pm / 7pm - 9pm

---

b   **Now ask your neighbour these questions.**

1. When was the last time you were in a restaurant?
2. Who were you with?
3. Where did you go?
4. What did you eat?
5. Would you recommend the restaurant?

8 a Answer these questions and then compare with your neighbour.

1   What would you use a frying pan for? _____

2   What would you use a kettle for? _____

3   What would you use a saucepan for? _____

4   What would you use a roasting tray for? _____

5   What would you use a casserole dish for? _____

b Look at the advertisement below and ask your neighbour 5 questions about the information.

eg   *Is the restaurant open on Sunday?*

Francesca's Italian Takeaway

Open 7 days a week
11.30am - 11.00pm

143 South Street, Perth, PH1 8TW
Tel 01738 667829
Fax 01738 167888

Delivery Service Available
no extra charge

---

9 a Here are some words and phrases to do with pubs. Try and explain them to your neighbour.

1   opening times
2   landlord
3   closing time
4   last orders
5   bar snacks

10 a You are going to tell your neighbour about yourself now. Try and keep talking for at least 4 minutes. Here are some ideas to help you.

- the best holiday you have ever had
- advantages and disadvantages of public transport in your town
- what you normally buy in the supermarket and why
- what you normally eat
- the last time you were in a restaurant
- your best and worst flight

UNIT 21

Rubbish and Recycling

1 a   Match the objects and the words.

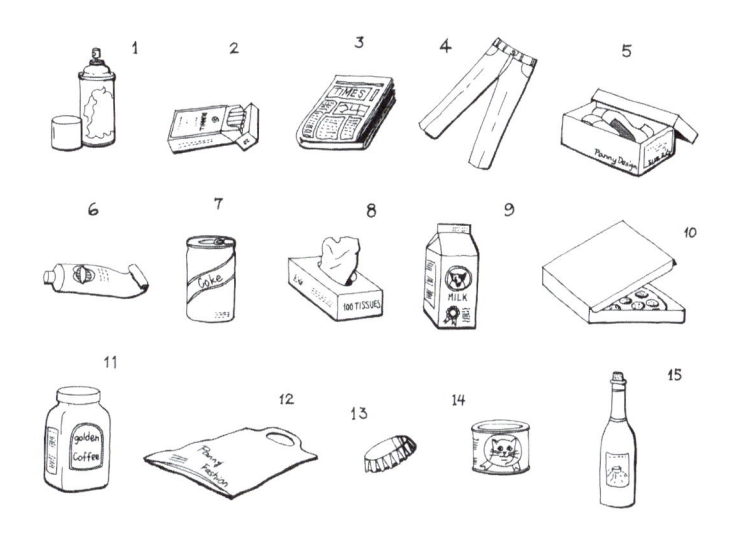

_2_ cigarette packet
_8_ tissues
_11_ jar
_4_ trousers
_15_ bottle
_7_ can
_13_ bottle top
_14_ tin
_1_ aerosol can
_5_ shoe box
_12_ plastic bag
_3_ newspaper
_9_ carton
_6_ tube of toothpaste
_10_ pizza box

Check with your neighbour.

b   Which of these can you recycle? Put the objects in the correct places.

BOTTLE BANK   SAVE A CAN BANK   TEXTILE BANK   PAPER BANK

Non-recyclable items: _____

c   What do you do with your empty cans? Put a tick (✓) in the correct box.

I throw them away ☐   I take them to a recycling bank ☐   I use them again ☐

d   Ask your neighbour.

1   What do you do with your empty bottles?
2   What do you do with your old newspapers?
3   What do you do with your old clothes?
4   What do you do with your empty tins?
5   What do you do with your plastic bags?

e   Fill in the following.

1   Is your household rubbish collected? _____
2   How often is it collected? _____
3   Who collects it? _____
4   Where is it collected from? _____
5   Where does it go to? _____

f   Ask your neighbour.

2 a Did you know...?

1 The average European family throws away 50 kilograms of paper per year.
2 The average European family throws away 60 kilograms of metal per year.
3 The average European family throws away 45 kilograms of plastic per year.

Do you think your family throws away more or less? _____

b What did you throw away last week? ....

Fill in the following about yourself.
   eg   *2 cans, 3 tins, 2 jars.*

	you	your neighbour
drink cans	0	0
food tins	0	0
jars	3	0
bottles	2	0
newspapers	6	7
cartons	8	5
tissues	many	4
cigarette packets	12	0
plastic bags	3 or 4	6
pizza boxes	0	0

c Ask your neighbour and fill in the information ....

d If you multiply these numbers by 52 you will find out how many of each object your neighbour throws away per year (approximately!).

1 How many cans does your neighbour throw away per year? _____0_____
2 How many tins does your neighbour throw away per year? _____0_____
3 How many jars does your neighbour throw away per year? _____0_____
4 How many bottles does your neighbour throw away per year? _____0_____
5 How many newspapers does your neighbour throw away per year? ___365___
6 How many cartons does your neighbour throw away per year? _____
7 How many tissues does your neighbour throw away per year? _____
8 How many cigarette packets does your neighbour throw away per year? _____
9 How many plastic bags does your neighbour throw away per year? _____
10 How many pizza boxes does your neighbour throw away per year? _____

Find out who throws the most away and who throws the least away.

3   a   Match the descriptions and the words.

1 I put rubbish in these.
2 I need this to tie parcels up.
3 I need this when I go to the toilet.
4 I use this to kill flies.
5 I take these when I have a headache.
6 I use this to keep my furniture clean.
7 I need these when I cut myself.
8 I need this to make my hair stay in the same place.
9 I use this to decorate my flat.
10 I use this to wash my clothes.

_5_ headache tablets ✓
_1_ bin bags
_7_ plasters ✓
_9_ wallpaper
_3_ toilet paper ✓
_6_ furniture polish ✓
_10_ washing powder ✓
_2_ string (Band/Senkel)
_8_ hairspray ✓
_4_ fly spray ✓

b   Ask your neighbour.

eg   *What do you need headache tablets for? You need them when you have a headache.*

c   Put the words in 3a in the correct category. What do you buy them in?

Packet *eg headache tablets*
plasters
washing powder
string (sometimes)

Roll fly spray
hairspray
furniture polish
toilet paper
bin bag

Can plaster

d   You are in a shop. Look at the price list and ask your neighbour.

eg   *Can I have a packet of washing powder please?*
Yes of course. Here you are. Anything else?
No thank you.
That's £1.92 please.

Price List

tablets   £1.30
bin bags   £1.99
plasters   72p
washing powder   £1.92
hairspray   99p
wallpaper   £2.85
toilet paper   32p
furniture polish 99p
string   £1.08
fly spray   £1.29

e   You buy chocolates in a box, orange juice in a carton and shampoo in a bottle. What else do you buy in boxes, cartons and bottles?

List 2 things.

boxes   _____   _____
cartons _____   _____
bottles _____   _____

f   Read through the questionnaire. Make sure you understand the questions, then fill in your answers.

Questionnaire		yes	it depends	no
1	When you go shopping, do you take a bag with you?	X		
2	Do you think supermarkets should give plastic bags free of charge?			X
3	Do you buy products in refillable containers?	X		
4	Do you buy brand products?		X	
5	Do you think packaging is a waste of money?		X	

g   Ask your neighbour the questions, then ask why or why not.

eg   *When you go shopping do you take a bag with you?*
Yes, because it's easier to carry my shopping home.

4 a Translate the following.

Vocabulary

cigarette packet _____	parcels _____
tissues _____	flies _____
jar _____	to decorate _____
bottle _____	headache tablets _____
can _____	bin bags _____
bottle top _____	plasters _____
tin _____	wallpaper _____
aerosol can _____	toilet paper _____
shoe box _____	furniture polish _____
plastic bag _____	washing powder _____
carton _____	string _____
tube _____	hairspray _____
to recycle _____	fly spray _____
bottle bank _____	packet _____
save-a-can bank _____	roll _____
textile bank _____	it depends _____
paper bank _____	free of charge _____
non-recyclable items _____	refillable _____
to throw away _____	containers _____
household rubbish _____	brand products _____
average _____	packaging _____
to tie up _____	waste of money _____

Structures

I throw my empty bottles away. _____

I take my empty bottles to a recycling bank. _____

I use my empty bottles again. _____

What do you need headache tablets for? _____

You need them when you have a headache. _____

Can I have a packet of washing powder please? _____

Yes of course. _____

Here you are. _____

Anything else? _____

No thank you. _____

That's £1.92 please. _____

Can I have a roll of bin bags please? _____

Can I have a can of hairspray please? _____

When you go shopping do you take a bag with you? _____

Yes, because it's easier to carry my shopping home. _____

UNIT 22

Where can you buy a safety pin?

1 a Match the objects and the words.

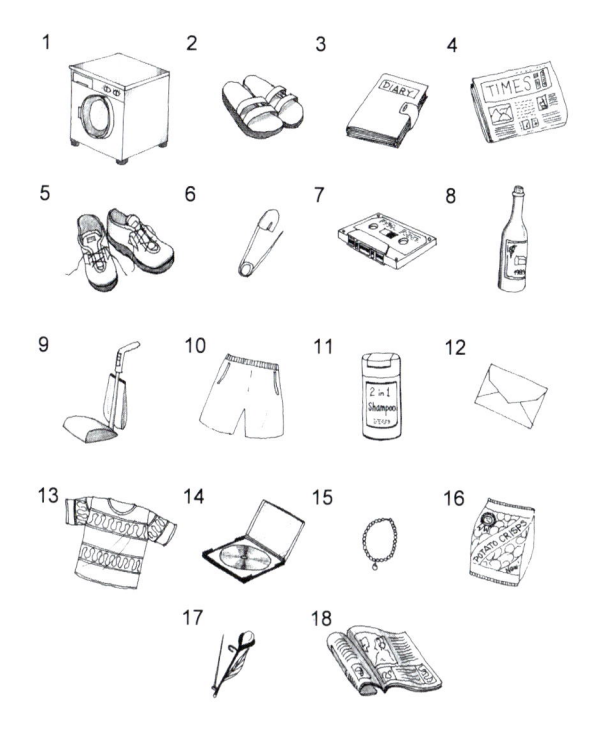

_6_	safety pin
_17_	brooch
_1_	washing machine
_13_	T-shirt
_7_	cassette
_12_	envelope
_14_	CD
_4_	newspaper
_8_	bottle of wine
_15_	necklace
_9_	vacuum cleaner
_18_	magazine
___	trainers
_10_	shorts
_2_	sandals
_11_	shampoo
_16_	crisps
_3_	diary

b Put the objects where you would buy them.

Electrical Shop	Jeweller's	Music Shop
eg washing machine	necklace	cassette
vacuum cleaner	brooch	CD

Chemist's	Shoe Shop	Stationer's
shampoo	sandals	magazine
	trainers	

Clothes Shop	Off-Licence	Newsagent's
safety pin	(Trinkhalle)	Diary
shorts	bottle of wine	newspaper
T-shirt	crisps	envelope

c Ask your neighbour.

eg *Where can you buy a safety pin? You can buy a safety pin at a chemist's.*

Think of one other item which you can buy in each of these shops.

d Ask your neighbour about these items.

eg *Where can you buy a pair of boots? In a shoe shop.*

2 a Put the words in one of these categories.

flowers
petrol
socks
jewellery
magazine
birthday card
sticky tape b
whisky
handbag
chocolate
shoes
coat
CD
hairdryer
newspaper
maps b
plants
diary
iron
perfume
belt
wrapping paper c
cassette
envelopes
beer
books

a I know what these words mean.

_____
_____
_____

b I think I know what these words mean.

_____
_____
_____
_____

c I don't know what these words mean.

_____
_____
_____

b Compare your list with your neighbour's and look up the words you don't know.

c Fill in the following. Tick (✓) the boxes to show what you can buy in each shop (you may tick more than 1 box).

	flowers	socks	jewellery	magazine	birthday card	sticky tape	whisky	handbag	shoes	coat	chocolate	hairdryer	CD	plants	maps	newspaper	iron	diary	perfume	belt	wrapping paper	cassette	envelopes	beer	books	petrol
newsagent's			X													X		X								
garage	X				X							X														X
off-licence					X																	X		X		
stationer's				X							X												X			
chemist's																			X							
book shop				X	X								X		X						X	X			X	
music shop											X							X								
electrical shop										X			X													
shoe shop		X						X	X																	
clothes shop		X						X	X																	
florist's	X			X							X									X						
jeweller's			X																							

d Ask your neighbour.

eg   *Where can you buy flowers? You can buy them in a garage or a florist's.*

e Tell your neighbour about the last time you bought any of these items.

eg   *I rarely buy flowers. The last time was for my Mother's birthday. I bought them from a garage because I had forgotten it was her birthday.*

3 a You've just arrived at your holiday apartment and the receptionist is telling you about local shopping facilities. Listen to the cassette and note down the names of shops A and F and the opening times. You will hear the cassette twice.

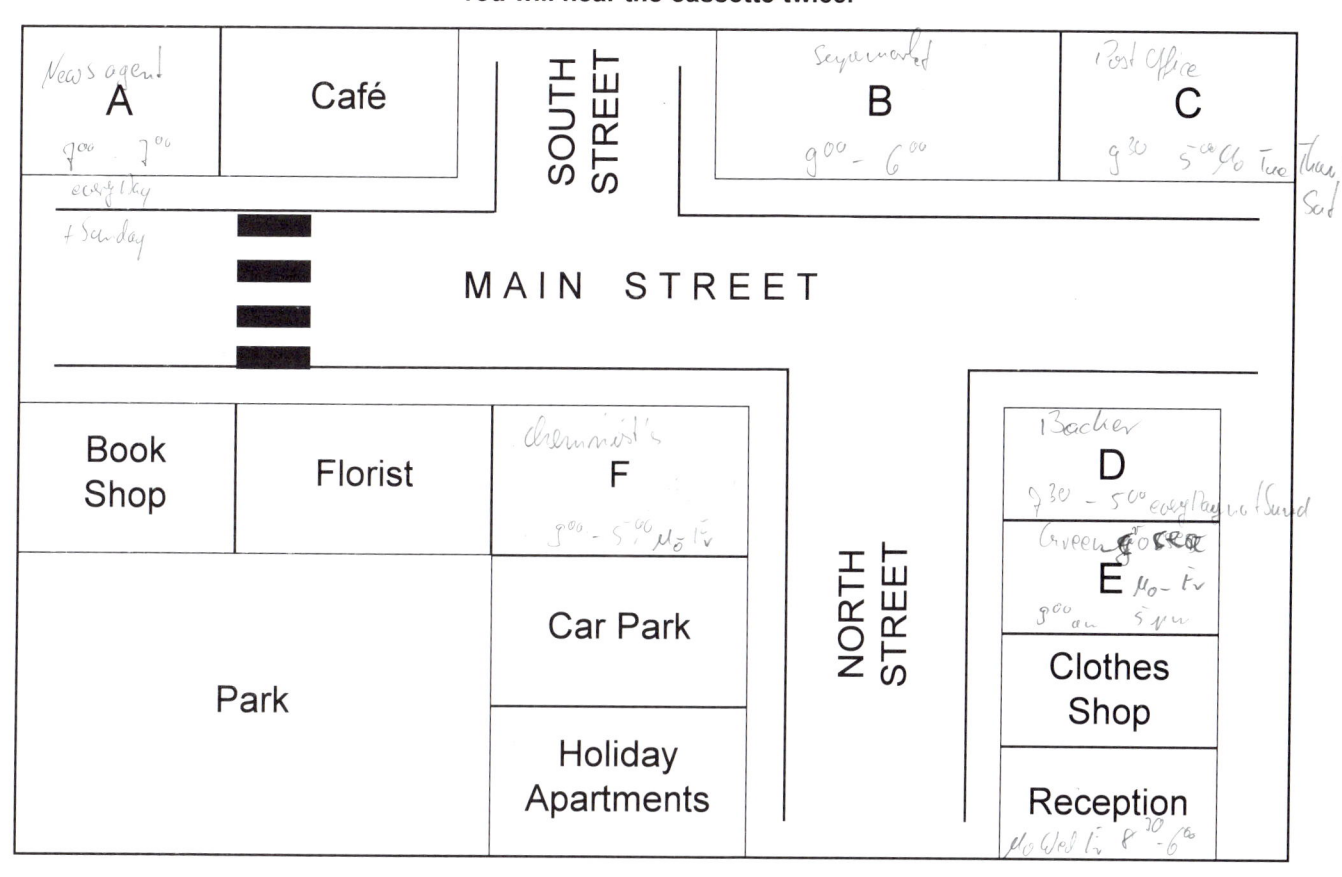

Map annotations:
- A: Newsagent, 9:00 – 7:00, every day + Sunday
- Café
- B: Supermarket, 9:00 – 6:00
- C: Post Office, 9:30 – 5:00 (Mo–Sat, Two than 1ᵒ Sat)
- F: Chemist's, 9:00 – 5:00 Mo–Fr
- D: Baker, 7:30 – 5:00 every day no Sund
- E: Green Grocer, Mo–Fr 9:00 am – 5 pm
- Reception: Mo Wed Fr 8:30 – 6:00
- Book Shop, Florist, Car Park, Holiday Apartments, Park, Clothes Shop
- Streets: SOUTH STREET, MAIN STREET, NORTH STREET

b Now ask your neighbour questions.

eg What time does the baker's close?

c Answer the following questions.

1. Which shop has got a red door? _____
2. Is the supermarket cheap? _____
3. Where can you buy postcards? _____
4. Which shop opens at 7.30am? _____
5. Which days does the receptionist work? _____

d Ask your neighbour the following questions.

1. How do I get to the chemist's?
2. Where is the newsagent's?
3. What time does the post office close on Wednesdays?
4. How do I get to the post office?
5. What time does the chemist's close?

e Ask your neighbour 5 more questions.

eg How do I get to the newsagent's?
You go down North Street. Turn left at the end. It's on the other side of the road, just after the pedestrian crossing.

f Make a list of 3 things you need from each of the shops. You are the customer and your neighbour is the shop assistant. Your neighbour starts the roleplay.

eg Hello. Can I help you?

4 a Translate the following.

Vocabulary

safety pin _____	birthday card _____
washing machine _____	sticky tape _____
cassette _____	maps _____
envelope _____	plants _____
CD _____	diary _____
wine _____	perfume _____
magazine _____	belt _____
trainers _____	wrapping paper _____
shampoo _____	beer _____
electrical shop _____	bookshop _____
jeweller's _____	florist's _____
music shop _____	supermarket _____
chemist's _____	baker's _____
shoe shop _____	holiday apartment _____
off-licence _____	receptionist _____
newsagent's _____	shopping facilities _____
stationer's _____	reception _____
clothes shop _____	greengrocer's _____
flowers _____	half-day closing _____
petrol _____	foreign newspapers _____
jewellery _____	

Structures

Where can you buy a safety pin? _____

You can buy a safety pin at a chemist's. _____

Where can you buy a pair of boots? _____

In a shoe shop. _____

Where can you buy flowers? _____

You can buy them in a garage or a florist. _____

I rarely buy flowers. _____

The last time was for my Mother's birthday. _____

I bought them from a garage because I had forgotten it was her birthday. _____
_____

How do I get to the newsagent's? _____

You go down North Street. _____

Turn left at the end. _____

It's on the other side of the road, just after the pedestrian crossing. _____
_____

UNIT 23

How many metres are there in a kilometre?

1 a   Look at the following information.

Measurements (approximations)

Area
1 square foot = 0.09 square metres (m²)
1 square yard = 0.84 square metres (m²)
1 acre = 4046 square metres (m²)

Weight
1 ounce (oz) = 28 grams
1 pound (lb) = 0.45 grams
1 stone = 6.4 kilograms

Fluids
1 pint = 0.57 litres
1 gallon = 4.5 litres

Length
1 inch = 2.5 centimetres (cm)
1 foot = 30 centimetres
1 yard = 90 centimetres
1 mile = 1.6 kilometres (km)

Temperature

°C	°F
-30	-22
-20	-4
-10	14
0	32
5	41
10	50
15	59
20	68
25	77
30	86
35	95
40	104
45	113
50	122

b   Ask your neighbour the following questions.

eg   *How many centimetres are there in an inch?   There are 2.5 centimetres in an inch.*

1   How many grams are there in an ounce?
2   How many litres are there in a gallon?
3   How many kilometres are there in a mile?
4   How many square metres are there in an acre?
5   How many kilograms are there in a stone?

c   Say whether the following are true (✓) or false (x).

eg   *20°F is colder than 20°C.*   ☑

1   A kilometre is shorter than a mile.   ☐
2   A square foot is smaller than a square metre.   ☐
3   A pound is heavier than a kilogram.   ☐
4   14°F is colder than 14°C.   ☐
5   A pint is more than a litre.   ☐

d   Fill in the following.

eg   *There are 28 grams in an ounce.*

1   There are _____ litres in a pint.
2   There are _____ grams in a pound.
3   There are _____ centimetres in an inch.
4   There are _____ centimetres in a foot.
5   There are _____ inches in a foot.

2 a Match the phrase and the definition.

1 bargain ☐ When all items are sold at discount but no new items are bought.
2 closing down sale ☐ When old items are sold at discount and new items are bought.
3 end of season sale ☐ An item which is cheaper than normal.

```
- Special Offer -
Heineken Lager
89p can (50ml cans)
2 cans for the price of 1
While Stocks Last
```

```
CLOSING DOWN SALE
Everything has to go
All Items
½ Price
```

```
Bargain Counter
Every item
99p
```

```
This Week Only
Tomatoes
Save 16p per lb
75p   59p
```

```
Buy one get one
FREE
Buy any CD from this stand and get
another from this stand FREE
```

```
End of Season
Sale
everything reduced
by 30%
```

b Answer the following questions.

eg How much is one item from the bargain counter? 99p.

1 If I buy 2 cans of Heineken lager, is it more expensive than if I buy 1 can? _____
2 If I buy 3 items from the bargain counter, how much will it cost? _____
3 If I buy 2lbs of tomatoes this week, how much will it cost? _____
4 If I buy 1 CD from this stand, can I get a second one from another stand free? _____
5 In the end of season sale, how much is everything reduced by? _____

c Ask your neighbour.

eg How much are 2 cans of Heineken lager? 89p.

1 How much do tomatoes usually cost per pound?
2 Is everything in the closing down sale reduced by 50%?
3 How much lager is in each can?
4 How much do I save per pound of tomatoes I buy?
5 How long does the special offer on Heineken lager last?

d Ask your neighbour.

1 When was the last time you bought an item in a sale or special offer?
2 What was it?
3 Why did you buy it?
4 Do you look for special offers? Why (not)?
5 Do you usually go to sales? Why (not)?

e Tell your teacher about your neighbour.

3 **a** You are with a tour group who are visiting a shopping centre. The tour guide is about to give you some information. Look at the following and put a question mark (?) against the information you think you will hear.

	?	✓		?	✓
where you are now	___	___	what time the shops close	___	___
the time now	___	___	how to get to the nearest railway station	___	___
where you will meet	___	___	where the bus is parked	___	___
what time you will meet	___	___	which restaurant is the cheapest	___	___
the names of all the shops	___	___	where you can get money from	___	___

b Listen to the cassette and tick (✓) the information you hear. Did you hear what you expected?

✎ Notes

c Look at the following diagram and listen to the cassette again. Make notes as you listen to the information and then compare with your neighbour.

KING'S HALL SHOPPING CENTRE - FIRST FLOOR LAYOUT PLAN

```
┌──────────┬───────────┬──────────┬───────────┬───┬──────────┐
│Electrical│Stationer's│ Florist's│Newsagent's│ B │  Indian  │
│  Shop    │           │          │           │   │Restaurant│
├──────┬───┤           │          │           │   │          │
│ WC   │   │           │          │           │   │          │
├──────┘   │  ┌────────┬──────┬───┴───────┐   │   ├──────────┤
│          │  │Seating │ Cafe │           │   │   │          │
│  A       │  │ Area   │      │           │   │   │  Post    │
│          │  ├────────┼──────┤           │   │   │  Office  │
│          │  │  Bank  │      │           │   │   │          │
│          │  │        │First │Information│   │   ├──────────┤
│          │  │        │ Aid  │  Bureau   │   │   │          │
│          │  │        │Centre│           │   │   │Chemist's │
├──────────┴──┴────────┼──────┴───────────┤   │   │          │
│  Department Store    │   Shoe Shop      │Boutique│        │
└──────────────────────┴──────────────────┴───────┴──────────┘
```

d Answer the following questions.

1 What closes at 3 o'clock? _____

2 What is closed for redecoration? _____

3 What will happen at 4.45pm on the dot? _____

4 When does the first aid centre close? _____

5 Where is the end of season sale? _____

e Ask your neighbour these questions.

1 Can I get money after 3 o'clock?
2 Where is the shoe shop?
3 What time is the local band playing?
4 How can I pay in shops?
5 Where is the bus parked?

4 a Translate the following.

Vocabulary

measurements _____
approximations _____
area _____
square metre _____
fluids _____
weight _____
length _____
temperature _____
bargain _____
closing down sale _____
end of season sale _____
special offer _____
item _____
to save _____
reduced _____
meeting point _____
on the dot _____
cash machine _____
redecoration _____
department store _____
first aid centre _____

Structures

How many metres are there in a kilometre? _____
How many centimetres are there in an inch? _____
There are 2.5 centimetres in an inch. _____
20º F is colder than 20º C. _____
There are 28 grams in an ounce. _____
How much is one item from the bargain counter? _____
How much are two cans of Heineken lager? _____

UNIT 24

At the Supermarket

1 **a** Look at photograph sequence 3 'At the Supermarket' on the next pages and put the photographs in the correct order.

1 *eg B*   3 _____   5 _____   7 _____
2 _____   4 _____   6 _____

b Tell your neighbour and explain why you chose that order.

eg I think that B is the first photograph because the trolley is empty.

c What has Mrs Mills just done? Read the sentences below and write which photograph each sentence refers to.

eg She has just picked up a bag of potatoes.   ☐ F

1 She has just put some bananas on the scales. ☐
2 She has just given the assistant some money. ☐
3 She has just picked up a carton of orange juice. ☐
4 She has just left the supermarket. ☐
5 She has just taken the celery out of the trolley. ☐
6 She has just taken a shopping trolley from the trolley park. ☐

d Ask your neighbour these questions.

eg What has she just done in photograph A? She's just taken the celery out of the trolley.

1 What has she just done in photograph B?
2 What has she just done in photograph C?
3 What has she just done in photograph D?
4 What has she just done in photograph E?
5 What has she just done in photograph F?
6 What has she just done in photograph G?

e Now ask your neighbour these questions about the photographs.

eg What do your think she's holding in her left hand in photograph G?
    I think she's holding a shopping list in her left hand.

1 What do you think she's saying to the assistant in photograph D?
2 What do you think she's holding in her left hand in photograph C?
3 What is she wearing?
4 How much are beef tomatoes?
5 What time of year do you think it is? Why?

f Ask your neighbour these questions.

1 When was the last time you went to a supermarket?
2 Where was the supermarket?
3 What did you buy?
4 Do you often go to that supermarket?
5 How do you get there?

At the Supermarket (Photograph Sequence 3)

EVERYDAY
LOW PRICE
Try our
brand
for quality
and value
SAFEWAY
D

These scales are for your guidance only.
SALTER
E

SPECIAL OFFER
Beef
Tomatoes
Class I
Loose Per lb
SAVE 16p Per lb
75p
59p
Green
Peppers
CANNED
SOUPS
F

Fruit Juice
G

2 a Listen to the cassette. Jamie and Gillian are writing a list of the shopping they need and deciding who is going to get what. You will hear the dialogue twice. Write down who is going to buy what.

Jamie's Shopping List	Gillian's Shopping List

b Listen again and answer the following in note form.

1 Where do they want to park the car? _____

2 Where do they want to buy the toilet rolls from? Why? _____

3 Where do they want to buy the eggs from? Why? _____

4 What does Jamie want to buy from the off-licence? _____

5 What does Jamie want to buy from the newsagent's? _____

c Ask your neighbour about 5 items on the shopping lists.

eg *Where do you buy washing up liquid? In the supermarket.*
 Why do you buy it there? Because it's cheap and convenient.

d You are going shopping with your neighbour. Make a list of 9 items which you and your neighbour want to buy.

1 _____	4 _____	7 _____
2 _____	5 _____	8 _____
3 _____	6 _____	9 _____

e Decide who will get what.

eg *I'll get the washing up liquid. Can you get the toilet rolls?*

f Tell your teacher what you've decided.

eg *I'm going to get the washing up liquid from the supermarket.*
 My neighbour's going to get the toilet rolls from the chemist's.

3 a Look at the advertisement below and answer the questions.

eg *What is this an advertisement for? It's an advertisement for a TV and video recorder.*

1 What is the name of the shop? _____
2 What is the telephone number? _____
3 When are they open? _____
4 What do they sell? _____
5 What is the address? _____

END OF SEASON SALE

- Everything Reduced -

Save money when you buy yourself and your family a new TV and/or video recorder from Walker's Electrical Shop.

Grundy C211343   21" colour TV

Save £30

Comes complete with trolley stand.
Normal Price £399.99
Sale Price £369.99

Walker's Electrical Shop
42-44 Sands Way
Oldham
OD21 5TU
Tel: (0161) 793211

Mon - Sat: 9am - 5.30pm

Grundy VTM 112 Video Recorder

Includes remote control
Normal Price £339.99
Save £40
Sale Price £299.99

---

b Ask your neighbour these questions about the advertisement.

eg *What type of video recorder is it? It's a Grundy VTM 112.*

1 How much does the video recorder normally cost?
2 How big is the TV?
3 How much does the TV cost in the sale?
4 If I buy the TV and the video recorder in the sale, how much will it cost?
5 How much do I save if I buy the TV in the sale?

c Now ask your neighbour these questions.

1 Would you buy this TV?   Why? Why not?
2 Do you prefer to pay for something monthly?
3 Do you prefer to pay in a lump sum? Why (not)?
4 If you have a TV, how did you pay for that?
5 What monthly instalments do you pay?

d You have seen this advertisement in the newspaper and have decided to buy the Grundy C211343 21" colour TV. Telephone the shop and ask if they still have one. Check the price and tell them how you are going to pay. Arrange when you will collect it. You are the customer and your neighbour is the assistant. Start the roleplay.

eg *Walker's Electrical Shop. Susan speaking. How can I help you?*

4 a Translate the following.

Vocabulary

trolley _____	frozen chicken _____
to pick up _____	butcher's _____
to put _____	sausages _____
to take _____	piece of beef _____
shopping list _____	tinned food _____
cooking oil _____	peas _____
washing up liquid _____	milk _____
toothpaste _____	eggs _____
soap _____	free-range _____
bread _____	silver foil _____
large white loaf _____	advert _____
small brown loaf _____	TV _____
vegetables _____	video recorder _____
fruit _____	normal price _____
peppers _____	sale price _____
mushrooms _____	to include _____
lettuce _____	to buy _____
cauliflower _____	to pay for _____
apples _____	lump sum _____
meat _____	monthly instalments _____

Structures

I think that B is the first photograph because the trolley is empty. _____
She has just picked up a bag of potatoes. _____
What has she just done in photograph A? _____
She's just taken the celery out of the trolley. _____
What do you think she's holding in her left hand in photograph G? _____
I think she's holding a shopping list in her left hand. _____
Where do you buy washing up liquid? _____
In the supermarket. _____
Why do you buy it there? _____
Because it's cheap and convenient. _____
I'll get the washing up liquid. _____
Can you get the toilet rolls? _____
I'm going to get the washing up liquid from the supermarket. _____
My neighbour's going to get the toilet rolls from the chemist's. _____
What's this an advertisement for? _____
It's an advertisement for a TV and video recorder. _____
What type of video recorder is it? _____
It's a Grundy VTM 112. _____
Susan speaking. _____
How can I help you? _____

UNIT 25

Which department is it in?

1 a Ask your neighbour the following questions.

1. Is there a department store in your town?
2. What is it called?
3. Where is it?
4. How often do you go there? Why?
5. Is it cheaper or more expensive than other shops?

b Match the objects and the words.

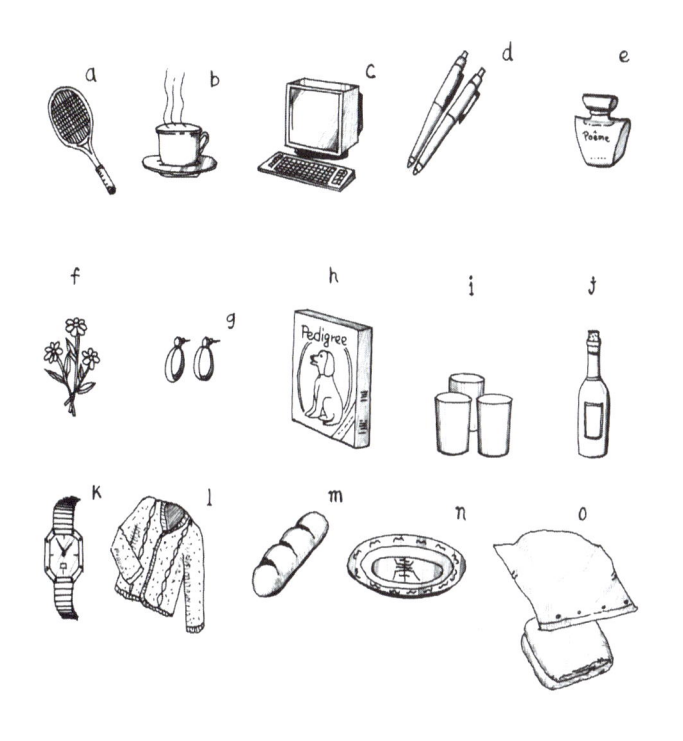

h	dog food
a	tennis racket
o	sheet and pillow case
d	pens
f	flowers
k	watch
i	glasses
e	perfume
m	loaf of bread
g	earrings
n	china plate
l	woollen cardigan
c	computer
b	cup of coffee
j	bottle of wine

c Point at the pictures and ask your neighbour.

eg What's this? It's a tennis racket. What are these? They're pens.

d Here are approximate prices for some items in England. Ask your neighbour and fill in the prices for his/her country.

eg In England a cup of coffee costs about £1.35. How much does it cost in your country?

a cup of coffee	£1.35	1,-	a set of glasses	£18.99	6,-
a packet of dog food	£1.22	57,-	a bottle of perfume	£24.99	20,-
a tennis racket	£32.49	300,-	a loaf of bread	72p	2,50
a sheet and pillow case	£12.79	60,-	a pair of earrings	£3.99	500,-
a set of pens	£14.99	100,-	a china plate	£6.25	30,-
a bunch of flowers	£3.99	20,-	a woollen cardigan	£23.49	100,-
a watch	£29.99	180,-	a computer	£999.99	1599,-

e Tell your teacher.

eg A cup of coffee is more expensive in England than it is in my country but a loaf of bread is cheaper in my country.

Department Store Guide

Basement
- coffee shop
- telephone
- shoe repairs
- glass and chinaware
- jewellery

First Floor
- ladies' accessories
- knitwear
- men's accessories
- tobacco
- magazines
- children's clothes and shoes

Third Floor
- boutique
- restaurant
- furs and leather
- lingerie
- WC/ladies
- ladies' fashions

Ground Floor
- bakery
- cosmetics
- florist
- watches
- health food shop
- information
- cash machine
- wine shop

Second Floor
- ladies' shoes
- men's fashions and shoes
- customer service department
- stationery
- suitcases
- WC/men
- hair salon
- sports wear and equipment

Fourth Floor
- bed linen
- electrical equipment
- fabrics
- furniture
- paints and wallpapers
- household equipment
- pet supplies
- accounts

2 a Which department would you go to? Look at the Department Store Guide and write the department next to the word.

dog food _Fourth Floor / pet supplies_   watch _jewelly watches_   china plate _____

tennis racket _____   glasses _glass and chinaware_   woollen cardigan _____

sheet and pillowcase _bed linen_   perfume _cosmetics_   computer _____

pens _stationery_   bread _bakery_   cup of coffee _coffee shop_

flowers _florist_   earrings _jewellery_   bottle of wine _wine shop_

Check with your neighbour.

b Fill in the following. Which floor would you go to?

eg If I wanted a cup of coffee, I would go to the coffee shop in the basement.
If I wanted to buy a diary, I would go to the stationery department on the second floor.

1 If I wanted to change my hairstyle, _____.
2 If I wanted to exchange a cardigan, _____.
3 If I wanted to go to the toilet, _____.
4 If I wanted to make a phone call, _____.
5 If I couldn't find what I wanted, _____.

c Ask your neighbour.

eg Can you name 3 things you would buy in the wine shop?
A bottle of red wine, a can of beer and a bottle of whisky.

1 Can you name 3 things you would buy in the furniture department?
2 Can you name 3 things you would buy in the stationery department?
3 Can you name 3 things you would buy in the men's fashion department?

d Ask your neighbour the following questions.

eg Which floor is the cash machine on? It's on the ground floor.
Why would you go there? I would go there to take out some money.

1 Which floor is the restaurant on? Why would you go there?
2 Which floor is the health food shop on? Why would you go there?
3 Which floor are the magazines on? Why would you go there?
4 Which floor is the telephone on? Why would you go there?
5 Which floor is the customer service department on? Why would you go there?

3 a You are going to listen to an announcement in a department store on the cassette. Put a question mark (?) next to the information you think you will hear.

? ✓   ? ✓

☐ ☐ the time now   ☐ ☐ what to do in case of fire

☑ ☑ information about special offers   ☑ ☑ information about departments which are closed today

☑ ☐ what each department sells   ☐ ☑ where to go if you have any questions

☑ ☐ where the exits are   ☐ ☐ where the nearest car park is

b Listen to the cassette and put a tick (✓) next to the information you hear. Did you hear what you expected?

c Here is the layout plan for 2 floors of the department store. Listen again and make notes below.

GROUND FLOOR LAYOUT PLAN

- Wine Shop | Florist
- Lift | stairs
- Cosmetics | Health Food Shop | Watches
- Bakery | Cosmetics
- Info. | escalator | Cash-point Machine | Cosmetics

SECOND FLOOR LAYOUT PLAN

- Customer Services | WC | Men's Shoes | Ladies' Shoes
- Lift | stairs
- Hair Salon | Men's Fashions | Stationery
- Suitcases | escalator | Sportswear & Equipment

Opening Times: Mon - Sat 9am - 6pm / Late Night Shopping: Thu 9am - 8.30pm

✎ **Notes**

bargl Flue = aiels
you welcome = gorn gschehen

d Ask your neighbour the following questions and then check with your neighbour.

1. What is £3 cheaper than normal today? *BO Whisky*
2. What time is the demonstration of fitness equipment? *8:30 pm for 0.5h*
3. How long is the WC closed? *3:00 - 3:30 pm*
4. Which special offer is available only while stocks last? *Day cream*
5. Which day of the week is it? Why? *Look at opening time / is thursday*

e Roleplays in the supermarket. Work with your neighbour.

1. You bought a dress for your daughter last week but it is too small. Go to the customer service department and see if you can exchange if for a larger one.
2. You have heard that there is a special offer in the hair salon. You decide to change your hairstyle. Go to the hair salon and arrange an appointment.
3. You are at the information desk on the ground floor. You want to buy a tennis racket. Find out which department you should go to and how to get there.

4 a Translate the following.

Vocabulary

a packet of dog food _____	men's accessories _____
a tennis racket _____	tobacco _____
a sheet _____	children's clothes _____
a pillow case _____	second floor _____
a set of pens _____	customer service point _____
a bunch of flowers _____	stationery _____
a set of glasses _____	WC men _____
a bottle of perfume _____	hair salon _____
a loaf of bread _____	sportswear and equipment _____
a pair of earrings _____	third floor _____
a china plate _____	boutique _____
a woollen cardigan _____	restaurant _____
guarantee _____	furs and leather _____
latest technology _____	lingerie _____
ready to go _____	WC ladies _____
department store guide _____	bed linen _____
basement _____	electrical equipment _____
coffee shop _____	fabrics _____
shoe repairs _____	furniture _____
glass and chinaware _____	paints and wallpapers _____
ground floor _____	household equipment _____
bakery _____	pet supplies _____
cosmetics _____	accounts _____
wine shop _____	to exchange _____
first floor _____	to return _____
knitwear _____	

Structures

What's this? It's a tennis racket. _____
What are these? They're pens. _____
In England a cup of coffee costs £1.35. _____
How much does a cup of coffee cost in your country? _____
A cup of coffee is more expensive in England than it is here. _____
A loaf of bread is cheaper in England than it is in my country. _____
If I wanted a cup of coffee, I would go to the coffee shop in the basement. _____
If I wanted to buy a diary, I would go to the stationery department on the second floor. _____
Can you name 3 things you would buy in the wine shop? _____
A bottle of red wine, a can of beer and a bottle of whisky. _____
Which floor is the cash machine on? _____
It's on the ground floor. _____
Why would you go there? _____
I would go there to take out some money. _____

UNIT 26

What's the code for Cork?

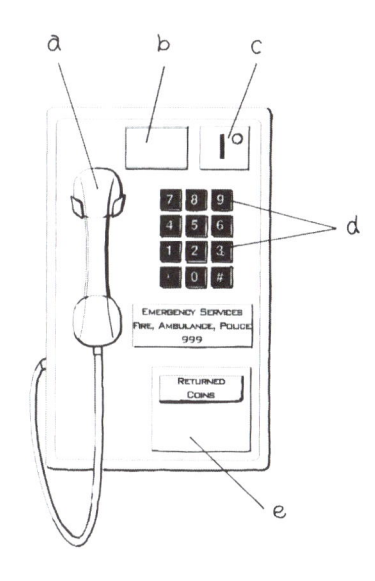

1 a Match the letters and the words.

_a_ receiver
___ coin slot
___ returned coins slot
___ display
___ keys

b Point at the pictures and ask your neighbour.

eg What's this? It's the receiver. What do you do with it? You speak into it.

c Read the instructions below and put them in the correct order.

___ listen for the dialling tone
_1_ pick up the receiver
___ dial the number
___ take the returned coins

___ replace the receiver
___ insert your money (minimum 10p)
___ speak
___ listen for the ringing tone

d Close your book and tell your neighbour how to make a phone call.

eg First you lift up the receiver. Then...

e Ask your neighbour the following questions.

eg What number do you dial if you want the police? You dial 999.

1 Do the 3 emergency services all have the same number?
2 What are the number(s) for the emergency services in your country?
3 In what situations would you ring for the fire brigade?
4 In what situations would you ring for the police?
5 In what situations would you ring for an ambulance?

f Look at the information on telephone rates and ask your neighbour the following questions.

eg When is cheap rate? It's from 8pm - 8am

1 When is peak rate?
2 How much are long distance calls per minute cheap rate?
3 How much are local calls per minute peak rate?
4 How much are long distance calls per minute peak rate?
5 How much are local calls per minute cheap rate?

Telephone Rates

Peak rate times   8am - 8pm
Cheap rate times   8pm - 8am

Local Calls
(up to 15 miles away)
Cheap rate   8p per minute
Peak rate   16p per minute

Long Distance Calls
(over 15 miles away)
Cheap rate   12p per minute
Peak rate   24p per minute

g Ask your neighbour the following questions.

1 How much is a 5 minute conversation to another country at peak times?
2 How much is a 10 minute conversation to a friend living in the same village at 10.30am?
3 How much is the same conversation at 10.30pm?
4 How much is a 20 minute conversation with a business colleague in another town 50 miles away at 9.45am?
5 How much is a 30 minute conversation with a relative in another town 20 miles away at 8.30pm?

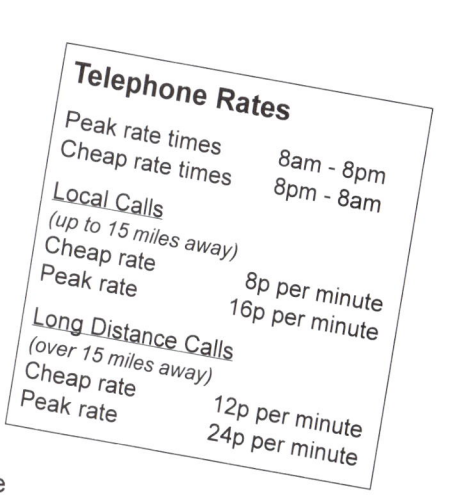

2 a You are on holiday in London. Look at the information below and ask your neighbour 5 questions.

eg   *What's the area code for Cork? It's 21.*

Area Dialling Codes

- UK -				- Republic of Ireland -			
Bath	01225	London - central	0171	Athlone	902	Roscommon	903
Birmingham	0121	London - outer	0181	Cork	21	Shannon	61
Blackpool	01253	Manchester	0114	Donegal	73	Sligo	71
Cardiff	01222	Oxford	01865	Dublin	0001	Tipperary	62
Edinburgh	0112	Portsmouth	01705	Galway	91	Waterford	51
Glasgow	0116	Southampton	01703	Kildare	45	Wexford	53
Harrogate	01423	York	01904	Limerick	61	Wicklow	404
Liverpool	0117						

International Codes

To call overseas:

1 Dial the international code 00.
2 Dial the code of the country you require.
3 Dial the area code, remembering to omit the first 0 (or in the case of Spain, 9).
4 Dial the telephone number you wish.

Australia	61	India	91
Belgium	32	Republic of Ireland	353
Denmark	45	Japan	81
France	33	Spain	34
Germany	49	Taiwan	886
Greece	30	Turkey	90
Hong Kong	852	USA	1

b Ask your neighbour.

eg   *How do I make an international call?*

c Fill in the following.

What's your area code? _____

What's your telephone number? _____

What's your number from the UK? _____

Telephone Numbers

Kevin Thompson *Central London*	2298566
Linda Dooley *Cork, Ireland*	32990
José Gonzalez *Spain*	(937) 25614
Pierre Lafayette *France*	(0623) 943211
Bob Thornton *Glasgow*	2913214
Barbara Grundmann *Germany*	(0201) 259432
Susi Kerr *USA*	(0971) 3949527
Hiromi Suzuki *Japan*	(0332) 4933215
Tania Connor *Outer London*	8922599
Daniel O'Neill *Sligo, Ireland*	49156

d Use the page from the address book and write the number you would call from Glasgow.

eg   *Kevin Thompson (0171) 2298566*

1 Bob Thornton _____
2 Linda Dooley _____
3 Barbara Grundmann _____
4 José Gonzalez _____
5 Tania Connor _____
6 Susi Kerr _____
7 Hiromi Suzuki _____

e Ask your neighbour.

eg   *What is Kevin Thompson's number? It's 0171 double 2 985 double 6.*

Now ask your neighbour about the other people.

f Ask 5 other people about their telephone numbers.

3   **a**   Look at photograph sequence 4 'Making a Phone Call' on the next pages. Describe the lady to your neighbour.

   b   **Ask your neighbour.**

eg   *What's Mrs Jackson doing in picture 1? She's opening the door of the phone box. What's she going to do next? She's going to step inside the phone box.*

1   What's she doing in picture 2? What's she going to do next?
2   What's she doing in picture 3? What's she going to do next?
3   What's she doing in picture 4? What's she going to do next?
4   What's she doing in picture 5? What's she going to do next?
5   What's she doing in picture 6? What's she going to do next?

   c   **Tell your neighbour about Mrs Jackson.**

eg   *In picture 1 she's opening the door of the phone box. She's going to step inside it next because she's going to make a phone call.*

   d   **Mrs Jackson is telephoning Susi's Hair Salon. Listen to the cassette and make notes.**

✍ Notes Mrs Jackson	Susi's Hair Salon

   e   **Which of these phrases did you hear? Listen again and tick the phrases you hear.**

☐ Hello.
☐ Can I help you?
☐ I have an appointment for Thursday.
☐ I'd like to change it.
☐ Would 3pm suit you?
☐ That's fine.
☐ Goodbye.

   f   **Practise telephoning with your neighbour. Use the following situations.**

1   You ring up a restaurant to make a reservation for yourself and some friends this evening.
2   You ring an estate agent to make an appointment to see a house and arrange a meeting place.
3   You ring a shopping centre to find out what time they close tonight.
4   You ring the railway station to reserve a seat on a train to London tomorrow. You need to be in London by 10.30am at the latest.
5   You have an appointment with Dr Giles at 10.30am next Tuesday. You would like to change it to 11.15am on Friday. Ring the surgery and rearrange the appointment.

Making a Phone Call (Photograph Sequence 4)

1

2

3

110

111

4 a Translate the following.

Vocabulary

receiver _____
coin slot _____
returned coins slot _____
to listen for _____
dialling tone _____
to lift up _____
to dial _____
to replace _____
to insert _____
to speak _____
ringing tone _____
emergency services _____
fire brigade _____
police _____
ambulance _____
telephone rates _____

peak rate _____
cheap rate _____
local call _____
long distance call _____
business colleague _____
relative _____
20 miles away _____
dialling codes _____
to call _____
overseas _____
international code _____
country code _____
area code _____
to remember _____
to omit _____
wish _____

Structures

What's this? _____
It's the receiver. _____
What do you do with it? _____
You speak into it. _____
First you lift up the receiver. _____
What number do you dial if you want the police? _____
You dial 999. _____
When is cheap rate? _____
It's from 8pm - 8am. _____
What's the area code for Cork? _____
It's 21. _____
How do I make an international call? _____
What is Kevin Thompson's number? _____
It's 0-1-7-1-double-2-9-8-5-double-6. _____
What's Mrs Jackson doing? _____
She's opening the door of the phone box. _____
What's she going to do next? _____
She's going to step inside the phone box. _____

UNIT 27

Do you have a driving licence?

1 a Ask your neighbour the following questions.

1. Do you have a driving licence?
2. Do you have a car?
3. What kind of fuel does it take?
4. Where do you normally get petrol?
5. Why do you normally go to this petrol station?

b Look at photograph sequence 5 'Filling up with Petrol' on the next pages and answer the following questions.

1. Which photograph do you think is first in the sequence? _____

2. Which photograph do you think is second in the sequence? _____

3. Which photograph do you think is third in the sequence? _____

4. Which photograph do you think is fourth in the sequence? _____

5. Which photograph do you think is fifth in the sequence? _____

c Tell your teacher about the photograph sequence.

eg I think the first photograph in the sequence is photograph C because the car is coming into the garage. I think the second photograph is...

d Ask your neighbour.

1. What is happening in photograph A?
2. What is happening in photograph B?
3. What is happening in photograph C?
4. What is happening in photograph D?
5. What is happening in photograph E?

e Ask your neighbour about the pictures.

eg How much is diesel per litre? It's 52.9 pence per litre.

1. What is the car registration number?
2. How much is unleaded petrol?
3. What is the man wearing?
4. Can you pay by credit card at this garage?
5. What is the woman wearing?

f Discuss the following questions with 2 neighbours.

1. Is petrol cheaper or more expensive in your country than in Britain?
2. Are most petrol stations self-service in your country?
3. What information does the registration plate in your country give?
4. Can you buy alcohol and/or sweets at petrol stations in your country?
5. Do you pay before or after you fill up in your country?

Filling up with Petrol (Photograph Sequence 5)

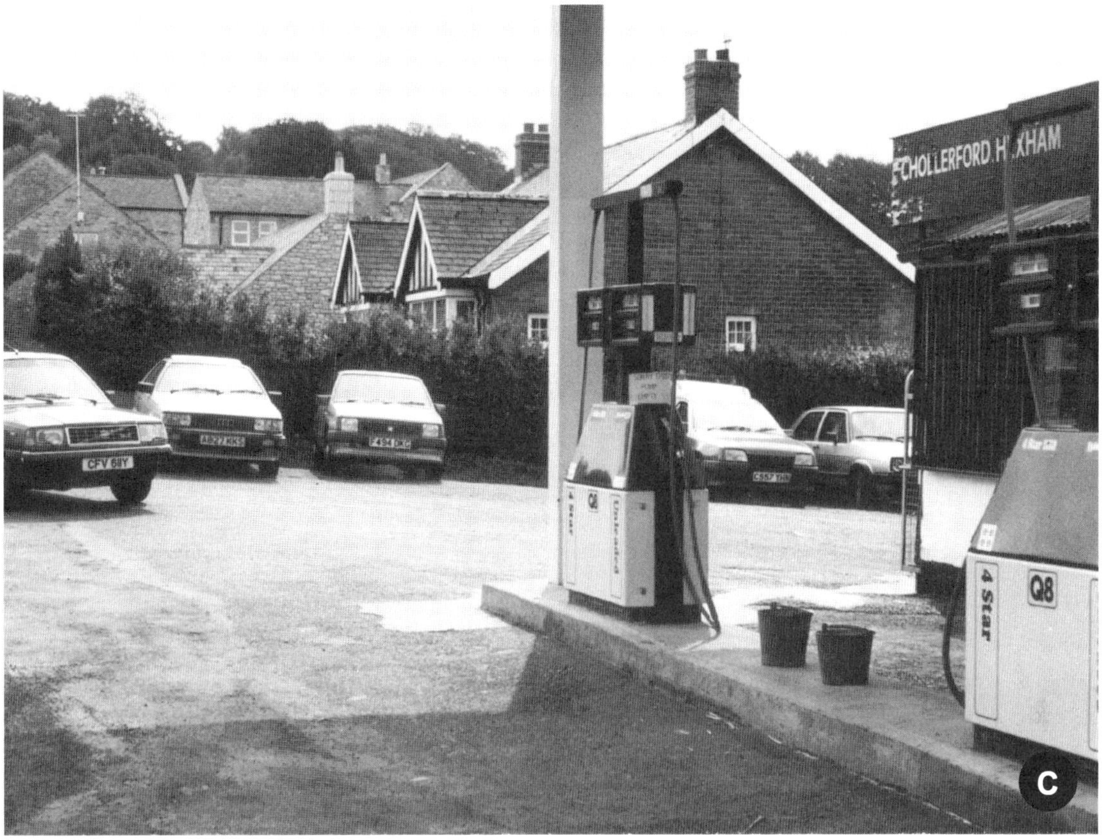
CHOLLERFORD
Q8
4 Star
C

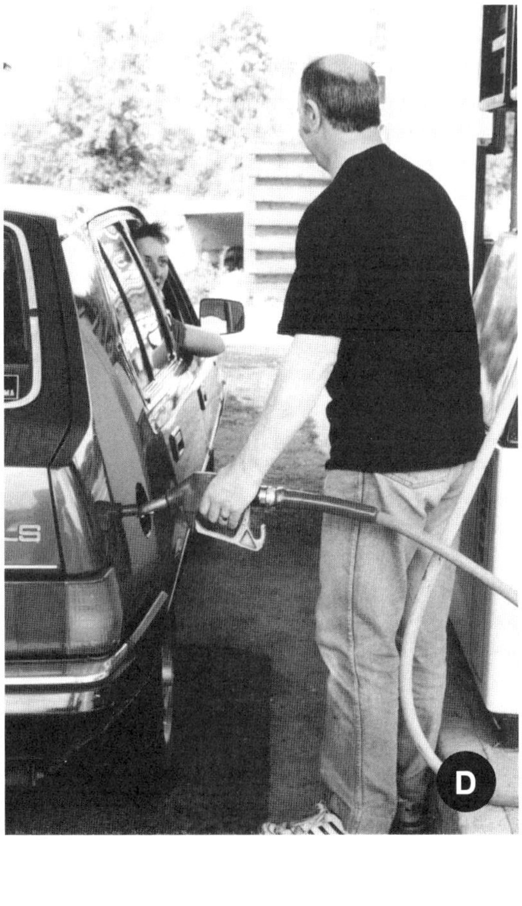
GLS
D

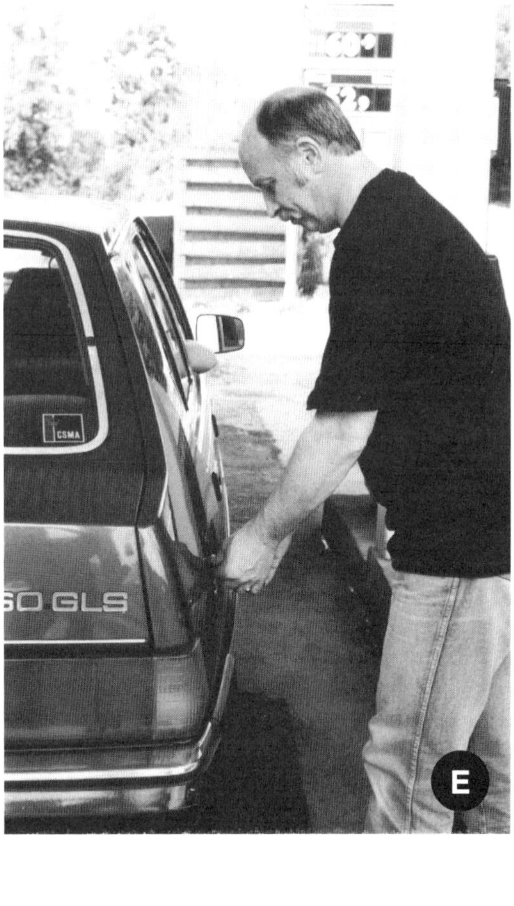
CSMA
GLS
E

2 **a** Which services do you think post offices in the UK provide? Put a tick (✓) next to the ones you know they definitely provide, a cross (x) next to the ones you know they definitely don't provide, and a question mark (?) next to the ones you're not sure about.

___ sell stamps
___ issue driving licences
___ deliver letters
___ sell phonecards
___ issue passports
___ have savings accounts
___ sell lottery tickets
___ issue TV licences
___ issue gun licences
___ change foreign currencies
___ pay pensions

Check with your teacher.

b **Write 5 sentences.**

eg *I didn't know that post offices in Britain sold phonecards.*

1 _____.
2 _____.
3 _____.
4 _____.
5 _____.

c **Discuss this with your neighbour.**

eg *I didn't know that post offices in Britain sold phonecards, did you? In our country they don't.*

d **Fill in the following. Which licences do you need in your country?**

gun licence	_____	dog licence	_____
TV licence	_____	radio licence	_____
driving licence	_____	trading licence	_____

e **Discuss with your neighbour.**

eg *In our country we need a gun licence, don't we? I don't think we need a dog licence...*

Where would you get these licences from?

f **Tell your teacher.**

3 **a** **Read the following situations and tell your neighbour what you would do.**

1. You are lying in bed one night. It's 3am and very dark outside. You suddenly hear a scream.
2. You are driving along the road. A car pulls out of a side street and crashes into the side of your car. Nobody is hurt.
3. You return home from a party at 11pm. You get your key out to open your door. The door is unlocked and a light is on inside. You had locked the door before you left.
4. You are walking along a street. You see a small bag lying on the floor. You pick it up and find it is full of money.
5. You finish work one evening. You go outside to the car park and go to where you left your car. It is not there.
6. You are walking home one evening. You notice a man climbing out of a window of a house. The house is in darkness. He is carrying something.

b **Look at the following and tick the box (✓) if you would go to the police if it happened to you.**

Somebody has broken into your house and has stolen your TV.	❏
Somebody has stolen your passport.	❏
Somebody has broken a window in your car but has not stolen anything.	❏
Somebody is playing loud music at 3am on a Wednesday morning.	❏

c **Tell your neighbour why you would go to the police.**

d **Imagine one of the situations in 3a has happened to you. Tell your neighbour what happened.**

eg *I was driving along the road, concentrating and watching the other cars. Suddenly a car pulled out of a side street and crashed into the side of my car. Nobody was hurt. I was getting out of the car when the other car drove off. I grabbed a piece of paper and a pen and while he was driving away, I wrote down the car number. I went to the police and told them about the accident. They looked in their computer and said that the car had been stolen. They told me to write to my insurance company so I wrote to them and explained what had happened.*

e **Look at the pictures for 30 seconds and then cover the page. Try to remember where the person was, what he/she was wearing and what he/she was doing.**

eg *He was in a library. He was wearing a dark suit and sunglasses, and he was sitting at a table reading a book...*

4 a Translate the following.

Vocabulary

fuel _____	pensions _____
diesel _____	dog licence _____
per litre _____	radio licence _____
car registration number _____	trading licence _____
unleaded _____	to hear _____
number plate _____	scream _____
credit card _____	side street _____
4 star petrol _____	to crash into _____
lead _____	nobody _____
registration plate _____	hurt _____
alcohol _____	to return home _____
petrol station _____	unlocked _____
to sell _____	to lock _____
stamps _____	to notice _____
to issue _____	to climb out of _____
driving licences _____	darkness _____
to deliver _____	to break into _____
letters _____	to steal _____
phone cards _____	to break _____
savings accounts _____	to concentrate _____
passports _____	to drive off _____
lottery tickets _____	to grab _____
TV licences _____	accident _____
gun licences _____	insurance company _____
to change _____	to explain _____
foreign currencies _____	

Structures

I think the first photograph is C because the car is coming into the garage. _____
How much is diesel per litre? _____
It's 52.9p per litre. _____
I didn't know that post offices in Britain sold phone cards, did you? _____
In our country, they don't. _____
In our country we need a gun licence, don't we? _____
I don't think we need a dog licence. _____
I was driving along the road. _____
I was getting out of the car. _____
While he was driving away I wrote down the car number. _____
He was in a library. _____
He was wearing a dark suit and sunglasses. _____
He was sitting at a table reading a book. _____

UNIT 28

Who do you bank with?

1 a Now read the following information.

"I bank with Lloyd's bank. I've been with them since I left school and got my first job, where I was paid by cheque every Thursday. After work I took my cheque to the bank and paid it in. I only had a deposit account then, so I had no cheques or cash cards. At the same time as I paid my cheque in I took most of my wages out, so I had some money for the weekend. Now I have a current account, so I have a cheque book and cheque card. The cheque card can be used in cash machines, so I can get money wherever and whenever I want. I get a salary every month which is paid into this account. I still have my deposit account and I try to save a little bit each month, so I can go somewhere nice for my summer holidays, but it's too easy to spend it now."

b Say whether the following statements are true (T) or false (F).

eg   *John banks with Lloyds.*   T.

1 He was paid in cash in his first job.   F
2 He was paid weekly in his first job.   T
3 His first account was a current account.   F
4 Now he has two accounts.   F
5 Now he is paid monthly.   T

Check with your neighbour.

c Fill in the questionnaire about yourself.

Banking Questionnaire

1 Who do you bank with? _Volksbank Heiden_
2 How many accounts do you have? _I have one Account_
3 Which of the following do you have?
   current account ☒   deposit account ☐   other ☐
4 Do you have a ...?
   cheque book ☒   cash/cheque card ☒   cash card ☒   cheque card ☒
5 Are you paid ...?
   hourly ☐   weekly ☐   monthly ☒
6 Are you paid / is your salary paid ...?
   in cash ☒   by cheque ☐   into your account ☐

d Tell your neighbour about yourself.

eg   *I bank with Lloyd's bank.*

2

a Ask your neighbour the following questions.

1. What is the man in the picture doing? He took money from a cash machine
2. How often do you use these machines? I use the machine every week
3. Why do you use them? I use money
4. Do you prefer using them to going into the bank? Yes.
5. Do you have to pay for the card? No
6. When was the last time you used one? Last saturday
7. Why did you use that cash machine? I took money for the weekend
8. What did you do with the money? We visit a ve steen vent
9. Did you get a receipt? No
10. Do you think cash machines are a good idea? Why (not)? Yes, they are

b How to use a cash machine. Put the instructions in the correct order.

- _2_ Key in your Personal Identification Number (PIN).
- _7_ Take your card.
- _3_ Request which service you would like.
- _1_ Insert your card.
- _4_ Key in the amount you wish to withdraw.
- _6_ Take your money.
- _5_ Wait while your request is being processed.

Check with your neighbour.

c Ask your neighbour the following questions.

eg *What do I do first? Insert your card.*

1. Do I key in the service I want or the amount I want first? The service
2. When do I key in my PIN number? After insert the card
3. Why do I have to wait? While the request is being processed
4. Do I take my card or my money first? You take the money first
5. What's the last thing I do? You take your card

d Close your books and ask your neighbour how to use a cash machine.

eg *What do I do first? First you insert your card.*

3 **a** Look at photograph sequence 6 'Changing Money' on the next pages. Describe the man and tell your neighbour what the photograph sequence is about.

b Ask your neighbour.

1. Where do you think these photos were taken? *These where taken from a Bank*
2. Why does the man go to the foreign enquiries counter? *He wants to change money*
3. Why would you go to this desk? *To take money*
4. What time of day do you think it is? Why? *Evening. Enquiries are closed*
5. What do you think he's holding in his hand? *travelled form*

c A bank clerk is talking to a customer. Listen to the cassette and fill in the missing information. (B = Bank Clerk / C = Customer)

B Good afternoon. Can I help you?

C Yes please. I want to change some _____ into _____.

B Certainly. How much would you like to change?

C _____ German Marks.

B Can I see your _____ please?

C Yes of course. Here you are.

B Thank you. Can you _____ this form here please? Thank you. That's_____.

C Thank you. Goodbye.

d Here are some phrases you can use in a bank. Read them through and then practise the dialogue with your neighbour.

1. I want to change some French Francs.
2. I want to order some traveller's cheques.
3. I want to pay a cheque in.
4. I want to take some money out.
5. I want to order a new cheque book.

e Now complete the following sentences.

eg *I want to change some German Marks.*
    He said he wanted to change some German Marks.

1. I want to change some French Francs.
   He said *he wanted to change some French Francs*

2. I want to order some traveller's cheques.
   He said *he wanted to order some traveller cheques*

3. I want to pay a cheque in.
   He said *he wanted to pay a cheque in*

4. I want to take some money out.
   He said *he wanted to take some money out*

5. I want to order a new cheque book.
   He said *he wanted to order a new cheque book*

f Now ask your neighbour these questions.

1. Have you ever changed money? Where? Why?
2. Have you ever ordered traveller's cheques. When? Why?
3. When you go on holiday, do you take cheques or cash? Why?

Changing Money (Photograph Sequence 6)

FOREIGN ENQUIRIES
4

LLOYDS BANK
PLC
HEXHAM BRANCH
SMALL
BUSINESS
CENTRE
5

4 a Translate the following.

Vocabulary

by cheque	mit Scheck
to pay in	einzahlen
deposit account	Sparbuch
cash card	Geld-Karte
to take out	auszahlen / herausnehmen
wages	
current account	laufendes Konto
cheque book	Scheckbuch
cheque card	Scheckkarte
salary	Lohn / Eingeld
to spend	geben
in cash	in Bar
weekly	wöchentlich
account	Zugang
hourly	stündlich
Personal Identification Number (PIN)	Geheimzahl
to request	Anfrage
service	Leistung
to withdraw	
to wait	warten
to be processed	wird bearbeitet
counter	Zeile
to change money	Geld wechseln
passport	Ausweis
to sign	unterschreiben
form	
signature	Unterschrift
to order	bestellen
traveller's cheques	Reiseschecks

Structures

I bank with Lloyd's bank. _Meine Hausbank ist Lloyds_
I have a current account. _Ich habe ein laufendes Konto_
I have a cheque book and cheque card. _Ich habe_
I get a salary every month. _Ich bekomme monatlich_
My salary is paid into my account. _Mein Lohn wird eingezahlt in_
John banks with Lloyd's bank. _John's Hausbank ist_
What do I do first? _Was muss ich zuerst tun_
First you insert your card. _Zuerst musst du die Karte reinstecken_
Can I help you? _Kann ich ihnen helfen_
I want to change some German Marks into pounds. _Ich möchte DM in Pfund wechseln_
Can I see your passport please? _Kann ich ihren Ausweis sehen_
Can you sign this form please? _Können sie dieses Formular ausfüllen_
I want to change some French Francs. _Ich möchte Francs wechseln_
I want to order some traveller's cheques. _Ich möchte Schecks bestellen_
I want to pay a cheque in. _Ich möchte einen Scheck einzahlen_
I want to take some money out. _Ich möchte Geld abheben_
I want to order a new cheque book. _Ich möchte ein neues_
I want to change some German Marks. _Ich möchte DM wechseln_
He said he wanted to change some German Marks. _Er sagt, er möchte deutsches Geld wechseln_

124 biodegradable = abbaubar kompostierbar ist
can bank = Dosencontainer   shopping kart = Einkaufswagen
trolly

UNIT 29

Where's the nearest car park?

1 a Answer the questions below.

1. **Which of these do you have in your town?**
   ___ a tourist information office ___ public toilets ___ car parks ___ a library
   ___ a swimming pool ___ recycling banks ___ cinemas ___ a park

2. **Who pays for these services?** _____

3. **Who pays for new roads?** _____
   rubbish collection? _____
   street cleaning? _____
   playgrounds? _____
   litter bins? _____

4. **Which of these do you have in your town?**
   restaurants _____ a taxi service _____ an old people's home _____

5. **Do you need a licence for these? If so, who do you get it from?**
   _____

6. **If you want to build a house, do you need permission? Who from?**
   _____

7. **If you want to build a factory, do you need permission? Who from?**
   _____

8. **Do you have cheap accommodation for old people?**
   _____

9. **If you eat in a restaurant and get food poisoning, who can you complain to?**
   _____

10. **Who maintains parks, grass areas, trees?**
    _____

b Tell your teacher.

c Read the following information.

In Britain many of these services are provided by the local council. The public elect councillors who serve for 4 years and a chairman is elected to chair council meetings. Their aims are to provide efficient services to residents and visitors in their district. Most meetings are open to the public.

Tourist information offices, libraries, recycling banks and public toilets are provided by the local council. Some car parks and swimming pools are provided by the council, although many are privately owned. New roads, sewers and playgrounds are planned, paid for, and maintained by the local council, who also provide rubbish collection and street cleaning. If you want to open a cinema, taxi service, pub, restaurant or kennels you need a licence and you apply for this licence to the local council. You cannot build a house or a factory, or alter your house if you do not have permission from the local council. If you are an old aged pensioner (OAP) you can apply for a cheaper flat from the council. There are sometimes waiting lists. And if you have food poisoning you will, of course, complain to the restaurant but you can also complain to the council. They will then check the restaurant. The local council also maintains parks, grass areas and trees.

These are just some of the services the local council provide. This all costs a lot of money and so the residents have to pay a council tax. The amount you pay is different in different areas.

2 a Look at the diagram below.

Local Council - Departments and Sections

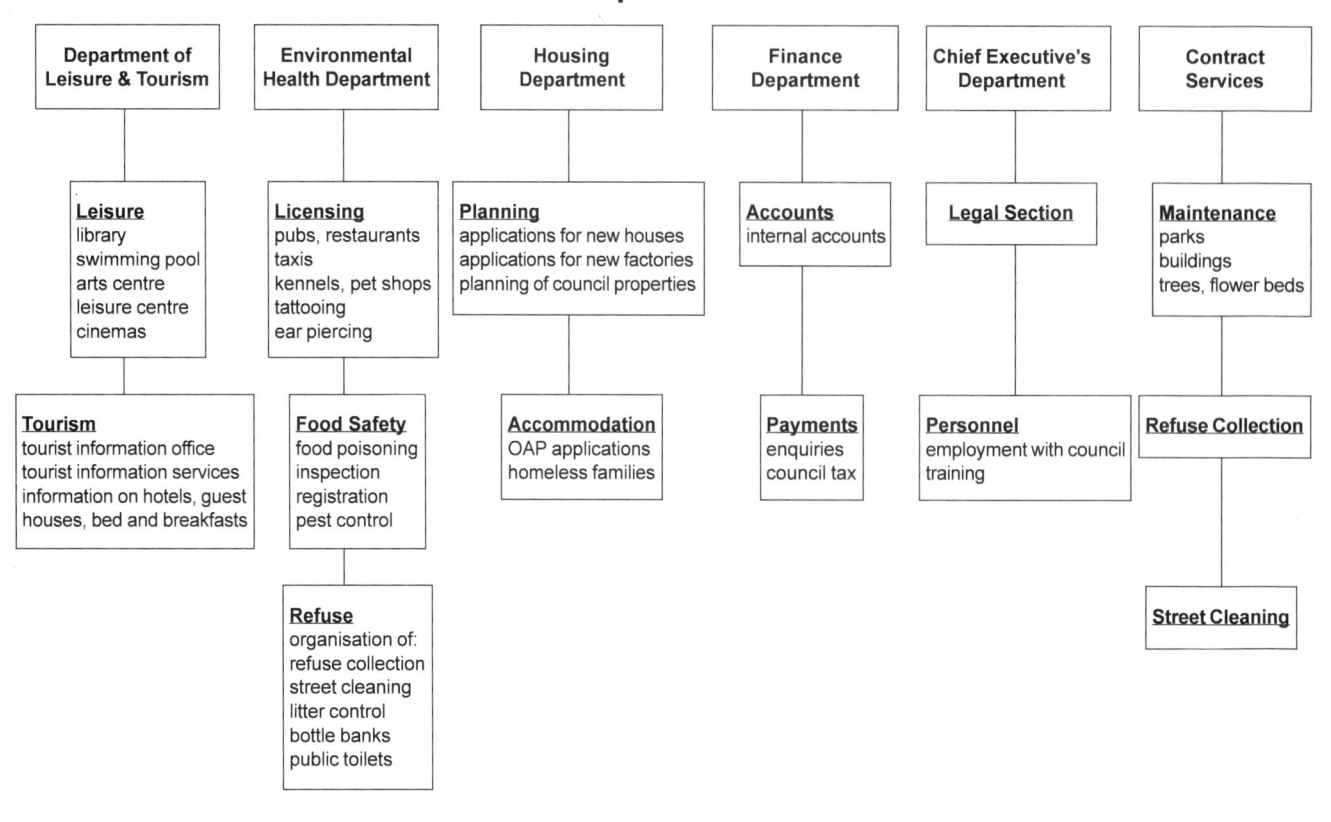

Department of Leisure & Tourism
- **Leisure**: library, swimming pool, arts centre, leisure centre, cinemas
- **Tourism**: tourist information office, tourist information services, information on hotels, guest houses, bed and breakfasts

Environmental Health Department
- **Licensing**: pubs, restaurants, taxis, kennels, pet shops, tattooing, ear piercing
- **Food Safety**: food poisoning, inspection, registration, pest control
- **Refuse**: organisation of: refuse collection, street cleaning, litter control, bottle banks, public toilets

Housing Department
- **Planning**: applications for new houses, applications for new factories, planning of council properties
- **Accommodation**: OAP applications, homeless families

Finance Department
- **Accounts**: internal accounts
- **Payments**: enquiries, council tax

Chief Executive's Department
- **Legal Section**
- **Personnel**: employment with council, training

Contract Services
- **Maintenance**: parks, buildings, trees, flower beds
- **Refuse Collection**
- **Street Cleaning**

b Now answer these questions.

eg Where should you go if you want to open a restaurant?
You should go to the licensing section in the Environmental Health Department.

1 Where should you go if you want to find a good hotel? _____
2 Where should you go if you have had food poisoning? _____
3 Where should you go if you want to pay your council tax? _____
4 Where should you go if you want a job? _____
5 Where should you go if you want to build a factory? _____

c Listen to the cassette and make notes. You will hear a recorded message giving telephone numbers.

Housing Department
Planning
Accommodation

Finance Department
Accounts
Payments

Department of Leisure and Tourism
Tourism
Leisure

Environmental Health Department
Licensing
Food Safety
Refuse

Chief Executive's Department
Personnel
Legal

Contract Services Department

d Ask your neighbour questions.

eg What's the number for the Housing Department? It's 251.

Tynedale Council
How to Get in Touch

By Phone

Ring (01434) 604011 and ask for the department you require. If you are not sure who to contact, explain briefly to the switchboard, who will transfer you to the correct department and section.

In Person

The main departments are located in Hexham and are marked on the map.

Office Hours

8am - 5pm

In case of emergency please contact (0831) 580888

Important changes

Please note the following changes:

Main Council - old   604022
Tel No   new 652448

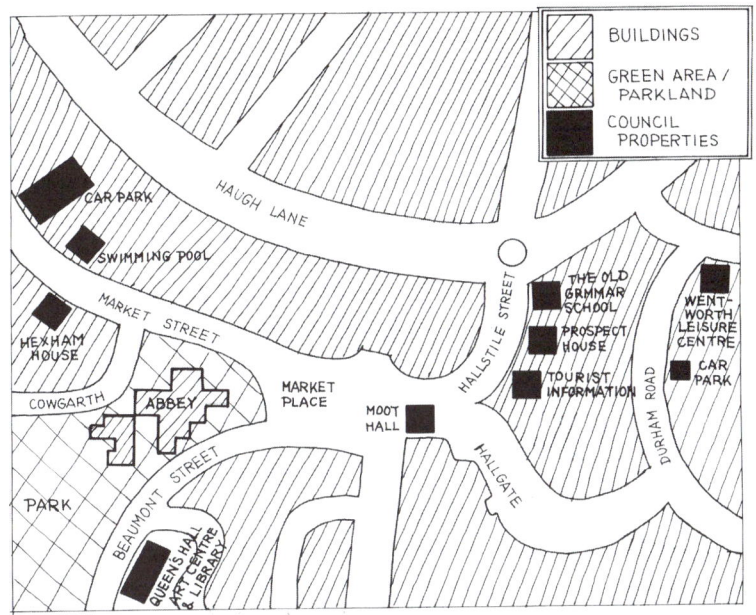

Hexham House — Chief Executive's Department and Finance Department
Prospect House — Housing Department and Department of Leisure and Tourism
The Old Grammar School — Environmental Health Department
Moot Hall — Contract Services Department

3 **a** **Ask your neighbour the following questions.**

eg *What time do the council offices close? At 5pm.*

1 What time do the council offices open?
2 When would I ring (0831) 580888?
3 Where is the Finance Department?
4 Which departments are in Prospect House?
5 Which is the number for the main council?

b **Answer the following questions.**

eg *Where is Hexham House? It's in Market Street opposite the swimming pool.*

1 Where is the tourist information office? _____ .
2 Where is the swimming pool? _____ .
3 Where is the leisure centre? _____ .
4 Where is Prospect House? _____ .
5 Where is the Queen's Hall Arts Centre? _____ .

c **Ask your neighbour for directions to 5 places.**

eg *How do you get from the swimming pool to the library? You come out of the swimming pool and turn left. You go along Market Street and turn right at the Market Place. You go along Beaumont Street past the Abbey on your right and the library is on the left opposite the park.*

d **Ask your neighbour the following questions.**

eg *Where is the Housing Department? It's in Prospect House in Hallstile Street.*

1 Where is the Finance Department?
2 Where is the Contract Services Department?
3 Where is the Department of Leisure and Tourism?
4 Where is the Environmental Health Department?
5 Where is the Chief Executive's Department?

4 a Translate the following.

Vocabulary

public toilets	to apply for
new roads	to alter your house
rubbish collection	old age pensioner (OAP)
street cleaning	waiting lists
playgrounds	council tax
litter bins	department of leisure and tourism
taxi service	environmental health
old people's home	housing
licence	finance
permission	chief executive
factory	contract services
food poisoning	kennels
to complain to	pet shops
to maintain	tattooing
park	ear piercing
local council	inspection
councillors	registration
to elect	pest control
chairman	refuse
to chair	litter control
council meetings	property
public	homeless
aims	payments
to provide	personnel
efficient	employment
residents	training
district	buildings
privately owned	flower beds
planned	switchboard
maintained	

Structures

Where should you go to if you want to open a restaurant? _____
You should go to the licensing section of the Environmental Health Department. _____
What's the number for the Housing Department? _____
It's 251. _____
What time do the council offices close? _____
At 5pm. _____
Where is Hexham House? _____
It's in Market Street opposite the swimming pool. _____
How do you get from the swimming pool to the library? _____
You come out of the swimming pool and turn left. _____
You go along Market Street and turn right at the Market Place. _____
You go along Beaumont Street past the Abbey on your right and the library is on the left opposite the park. _____

Where is the Housing Department? _____
It's in Prospect House in Hallstile Street. _____

UNIT 30

Revision

1 a What do you buy in the following containers? Work with your neighbour and see how many items you can think of.

eg   packet - cigarettes, dog food, tissues, cereals.

1 jar   2 bottle   3 box   4 tin   5 aerosol can   6 carton

b Ask your neighbour these questions.

1. What do you do with your empty bottles?
2. What do you do with your old newspapers?
3. What do you do with your empty tins?
4. What do you do with your plastic bags?
5. What do you do with your old clothes?

c Tell your neighbour what you would use these objects for.

1. a plaster
2. string
3. hairspray
4. fly spray
5. wall paper

d Discuss these sentences with your neighbour.

1. I don't buy products if the packaging is not nice.
2. I think supermarkets should charge for plastic bags.
3. I buy brand products because they're better quality.
4. I don't think packaging is important.
5. I always buy refillable containers if I can.

2 a Can you name 3 things you would buy in these shops?

1. Jeweller's   _____   _____   _____
2. Newsagent's   _____   _____   _____
3. Stationer's   _____   _____   _____
4. Chemist's   _____   _____   _____
5. Electrical Shop _____   _____   _____

b Which of these would you give to a friend, or relation as a present? Put a tick (✓) next to the ones you would give, and a cross (x) next to the ones you wouldn't give as a present. When you're finished, tell your neighbour who you would give your presents to.

1 flowers   ___   6 a map   ___
2 socks   ___   7 perfume   ___
3 sticky tape ___   8 envelopes   ___
4 belt   ___   9 chocolate   ___
5 petrol   ___   10 hairdryer   ___

c Tell your neighbour about the last time you gave somebody a present. What was it? Who did you give it to? Why did you give the person a present?

3 a   Ask your neighbour these questions.

1   When was the last time you bought something in a sale?
2   What was it?
3   Was it something you needed or did you buy it because it was a special offer?
4   Was it good value for money?
5   "You get what you pay for." Do you agree with this statement?

4 a   Jamie is going shopping this afternoon. Here is his shopping list. Read it through and then complete the sentences.

1   He's going to buy some eggs.
2   He isn't going to buy any potatoes.
3   _____ mushrooms.
4   _____ toothpaste.
5   _____ oil.
6   _____ garlic.
7   _____ toilet rolls.
8   _____ mince.
9   _____ tomatoes.
10 _____ apples.

Jamie's Shopping List

eggs
onions
milk
sugar
mince
tomatoes
garlic
toothpaste

b   Ask your neighbour these questions.

1   Have you got a TV?
2   How did you pay for it?
3   Do you prefer to pay when you buy something, or later? Why?
4   Do you think it is cheaper paying monthly? Why (not)?
5   What monthly instalments do you pay?

5 a   Match up the following and compare with your neighbour.

1   a packet of   ___ flowers
2   a bunch of   ___ coffee
3   a loaf   _1_ dog food
4   a pair of   ___ pens
5   a cup of   ___ earrings
6   a bottle of   ___ whisky
7   a set of   ___ bread

b   Ask your neighbour these questions.

1   Is there a department store in your town?
2   What is it called?
3   Where is it?
4   How often do you go there?
5   Is it cheaper or more expensive that other shops?

5 c Name 3 things you would buy in the following departments.

1. furniture department _____ _____ _____
2. stationery department _____ _____ _____
3. men's fashion department _____ _____ _____
4. electrical department _____ _____ _____
5. ladies' fashion department _____ _____ _____

d Which department would you go to if...

1. ... you wanted to change your hair style? _____
2. ... you wanted to exchange a jumper? _____
3. ... you wanted to buy some cat food? _____
4. ... you wanted to pay a bill? _____
5. ... you wanted to buy a pillow? _____

6 a Explain to your neighbour how to make a phone call from a public phone box. Your neighbour will do the actions as you explain them.

eg *First you open the door and go into the phone box.*

b Ask your neighbour these questions.

1. What are the number(s) for the emergency services in your country?
2. In what situations would you ring for the fire brigade?
3. In what situations would you ring for the police?
4. In what situations would you ring for an ambulance?
5. Have you ever telephoned the emergency services? When? Why?

c Write down the names and telephone numbers of 5 people you know in 'your telephone book'.

your telephone book	your neighbour's telephone book
1	1 ....
2	2 ....
3	3 ....
4	4 ....
5	5 ....

Your neighbour will now give you his/her 5 names and numbers. Listen and write down the names and numbers in 'your neighbour's telephone book'. Compare your work with your neighbour.

7 a Ask your neighbour these questions.

1. Do you have a car?
2. How old is it?
3. What make is it?
4. What kind of fuel does it take?
5. Where do you normally get petrol?

7 b **Can you name 3 services which post offices in Britain provide and 3 services which post offices in your own country provide? Work with your neighbour.**

c **What would you do? Read these situations and then tell your neighbour what you would do.**

1 You lend a friend your car while his is in the garage. He rings you next morning to say he drank too much last night and crashed the car while he was driving home.

2 You are on holiday in Britain and go to a restaurant for lunch. When you want to pay you find that somebody has stolen your purse.

3 You go shopping one Saturday afternoon. When you return to the car park, the window in your car is broken and the radio has been stolen.

4 You are lying in bed one night and hear somebody moving around in your flat.

5 You are walking home one night and you see a baby lying by the side of the road.

8 a **Ask your neighbour these questions.**

1 Who do you bank with? Why?
2 How many accounts do you have?
3 What type of account(s) do you have?
4 Have you got a cheque book?
5 Are you paid weekly or monthly?

b **Your neighbour has just received a cash card from the bank. He/she has never used a cash machine before. Explain how to use it. Remember you have to explain every stage.**

c **Ask your neighbour about their holiday. When you are on holiday in a foreign country how do you pay for:**

1 your hotel?
2 a meal in a restaurant?
3 the hire of a car?
4 shopping?
5 sun cream?

9 a **Ask your neighbour these questions about their country.**

1 How often is the street where you live cleaned? Who by?
2 Who collects your rubbish? Do you have to pay for it?
3 Who provides playgrounds and litter bins?
4 Do you have cheap accommodation for old people?
5 Do you need permission to build a house? Who from?

10 a **You are going to tell your neighbour about yourself. Try and talk for at least 5 minutes. Here are some topics you can talk about.**

- what you recycle and why
- what you think of brand names and packaging
- why you would(n't) buy things from sales
- how you pay for things (eg cars, TV's)
- shopping facilities in your town
- post office services in your country
- local council services in your town
- who you bank with and why

UNIT 31

I've got a headache.

1 a Match the words and the parts of the body.

_h_ toes	___ knee
___ fingers	___ hand
___ ankle	___ waist
___ leg	___ head
___ thumb	___ elbow
___ foot	___ chest
___ wrist	___ neck
___ arm	___ ear
___ hips	___ eye

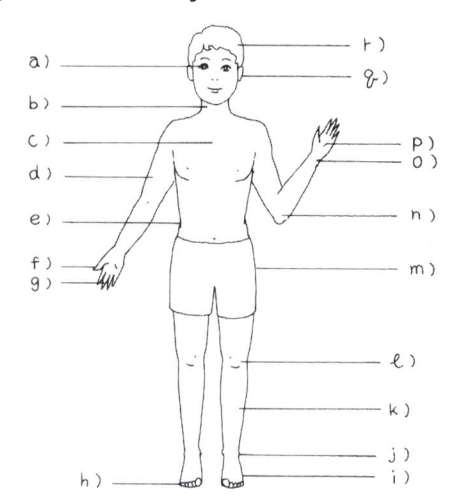

b Tell your neighbour to touch parts of his/her body.

eg Touch your left knee.

c Ask your neighbour these questions.

eg *Have you ever had toothache? Yes, I had toothache a lot when I was younger. What did you do? At first I took tablets but they didn't help, so I went to the dentist. He took two teeth out and I've had no problems since then.*

1 Have you ever had toothache? What did you do?
2 Have you ever had food poisoning? What did you do?
3 Have you ever had sunburn? What did you do?
4 Have you ever had flu? What did you do?
5 Have you ever had backache? What did you do?

d Now read these dialogues and say whether you agree or disagree with the advice given.

1 Tim: Hello Louise. You look awful. What's the matter?
   Louise: I've got terrible toothache.
   Tim: Have you taken anything for it?
   Louise: Yes, I've taken some tablets but they haven't helped.
   Tim: I think you should see a dentist.

2 Christine: What's the matter?
   Jane: I've got stomach ache.
   Christine: Have you taken anything for it?
   Jane: Yes, I've taken a tablet but it still hurts.
   Christine: I think you should lie down for a while.

3 Samantha: What's the matter Ian?
   Ian: I feel sick.
   Samantha: You look terrible. I think you should see a doctor.

e What advice would you give? Read the problems below and give your neighbour some advice.

1 I've got a headache.
2 I've got a sore throat.
3 I've got terrible backache.
4 I think I've got food poisoning.
5 I've got a cold.
6 I've got toothache.
7 I've got flu.
8 I've got stomach ache.
9 I've got sunburn.
10 I feel sick.

f You have a headache and go to the chemist's to get something for it. Read the dialogue and then practise with your neighbour.

Chemist: Hello. Can I help you?
You: Yes. I've got a terrible headache. Can you give me something for it?
Chemist: Of course. Here are some tablets. You should take 2 every 6 hours, but no more than 8 tablets in one day.
You: Thanks. How much are they?
Chemist: The 10-pack is £1.20 and the 20-pack is £1.90. Which would you like?
You: I'll take the 10-pack thanks.

2 a Look at the following information.

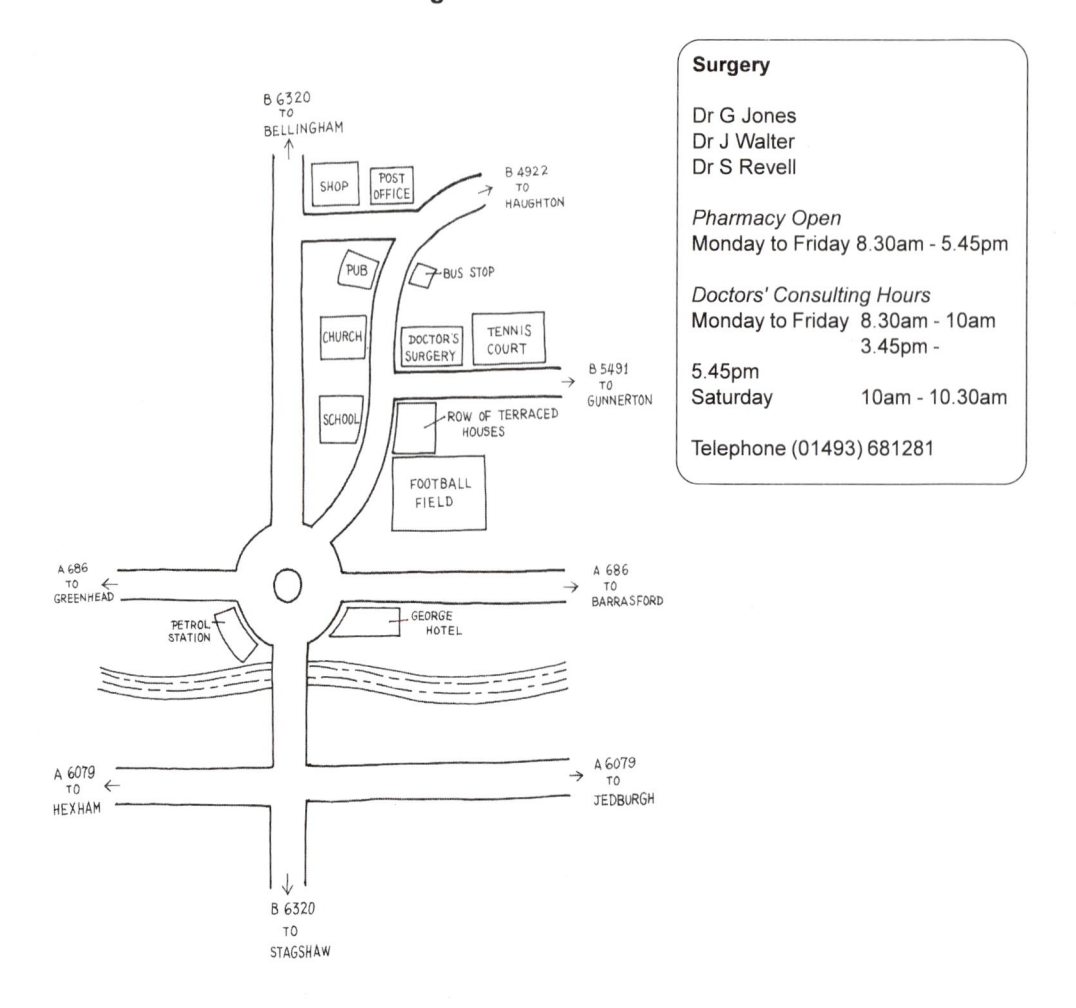

Surgery

Dr G Jones
Dr J Walter
Dr S Revell

Pharmacy Open
Monday to Friday 8.30am - 5.45pm

Doctors' Consulting Hours
Monday to Friday 8.30am - 10am
                              3.45pm - 5.45pm
Saturday   10am - 10.30am

Telephone (01493) 681281

b **Ask your neighbour the following questions.**

1 Can I see a doctor on Saturday afternoon?
2 How many doctors work at the surgery?
3 Can I collect a prescription at 2pm on Monday?
4 Can I see a doctor at 4pm on Monday?
5 What is the telephone number?

c **Here are the directions to get to the surgery from Hexham.**

> Coming from Hexham you go along the A6079 towards Jedburgh. At the crossroads you turn left towards Bellingham on the B6320. You go across the bridge, then round the roundabout and take the third exit. You go past a football field on your right, then a school on your left and some houses on your right. Take the first right turn after the row of terraced houses and the surgery is on your left - you can't miss it. It's opposite the church.

d **Now give your neighbour directions to get to the surgery from Bellingham, Barrasford, Haughton, Gunnerton and Jedburgh.**

e **You think you have food poisoning. Telephone the surgery and make an appointment to see a doctor. You usually see Dr Revell. Say which direction you are coming from and ask for directions.**

3 **a** Look at photograph sequence 7 'At the Doctor's' on the next pages and ask your neighbour the following questions.

1. What can you see in photograph 1?
2. What can you see in photograph 2?
3. What can you see in photograph 3?
4. What can you see in photograph 4?
5. What can you see in photograph 5?
6. What can you see in photograph 6?

b Now ask your neighbour these questions.

1. What do you think is the matter with the woman?
2. What do you think she is saying to the receptionist in photograph 2?
3. What do you think the doctor is saying in photograph 3?
4. What do you think the doctor is doing in photograph 4? Why?
5. What do you think the doctor is saying in photograph 5?
6. What do you think he is holding in his right hand in photograph 5?
7. What do you think the doctor is giving the lady in photograph 6?
8. What do you think he has in his pocket in photograph 6?
9. What is the lady wearing?
10. Describe the doctor.

c Give the lady a name and make up a short story, explaining why she is ill, what she tells the doctor, what advice he gives her and what she does after she leaves the surgery.

d The following signs are on the wall in the waiting room of the surgery. Look at them and ask your neighbour the questions below.

Please report to the receptionist on arrival.

Please hand any unused tablets back to your pharmacy for safe disposal.

Hypothermia Kills

Last winter 2,000 people died of hypothermia. Don't be one of them this year.

Keep warm this winter.

Prescription Charges

With effect from 1 April 1996, prescription charges have been increased to £5.75 per item.

Nurses Treatment Sessions

For: blood pressure, weight, dressings, etc.

Monday: 9.30am - 10.30am
Wednesday: 9.30am - 10.30am
              4.00pm - 5.00pm
Friday: 9.30am - 10.30am

---

1. What is the first thing you should do when you enter the surgery? _____

2. How many people died of hypothermia last winter? _____

3. If the doctor prescribes 2 items, how much do you have to pay? _____

4. What should you do with any unused tablets you have? _____

5. Can I have my blood pressure taken on Friday afternoon? _____

At the Doctor's (Photograph Sequence 7)

137

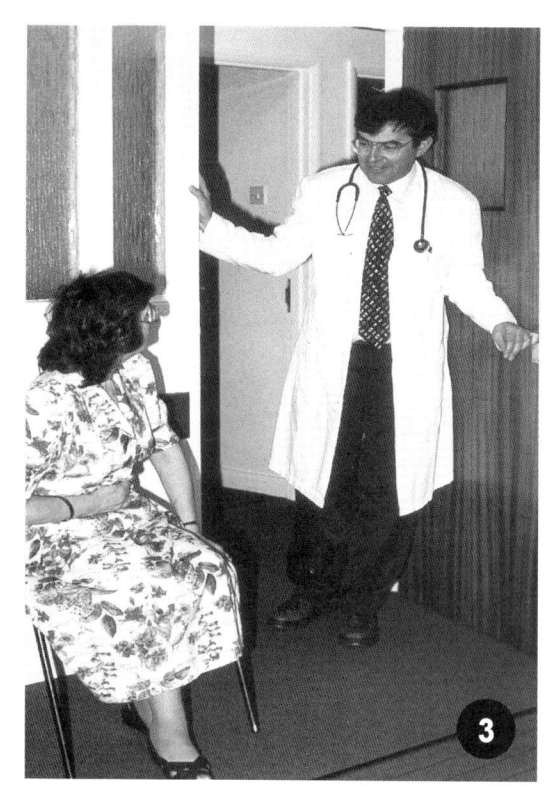

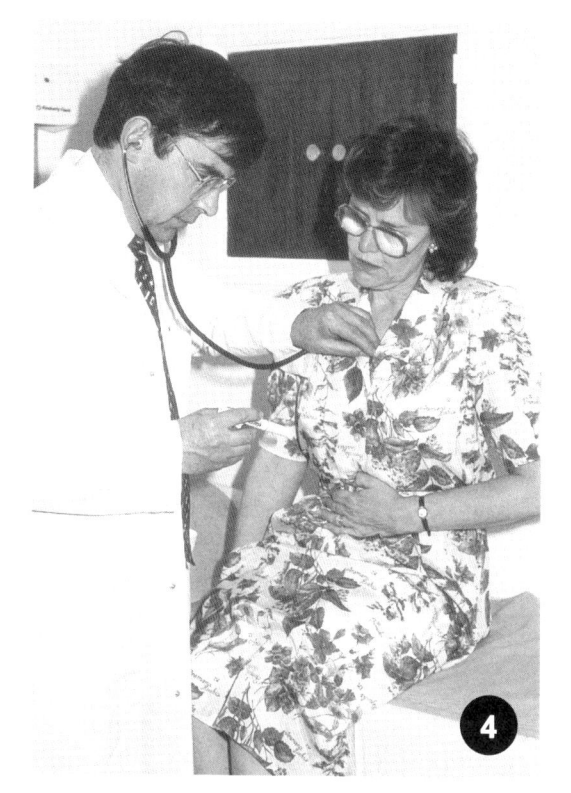

4 a Translate the following.

Vocabulary

toes _____	toothache _____
fingers _____	tablets _____
ankle _____	dentist _____
leg _____	sunburn _____
thumb _____	flu _____
foot _____	backache _____
wrist _____	awful _____
arm _____	terrible _____
hips _____	headache _____
elbow _____	sore throat _____
knee _____	surgery _____
hand _____	pharmacy _____
waist _____	prescription _____
head _____	charge _____
chest _____	nurse _____
neck _____	treatment _____
ear _____	blood pressure _____
eye _____	

Structures

Have you ever had toothache? _____

I had toothache a lot when I was younger. _____

What did you do? _____

I took tablets. _____

They didn't help. _____

So I went to the dentist. _____

He took two teeth out. _____

I've had not problems since then. _____

You look awful. _____

What's the matter? _____

I've got terrible toothache. _____

Have you taken anything for it? _____

Yes, I've taken some tablets. _____

I think you should see a dentist. _____

I've got a terrible headache. _____

Can you give me something for it? _____

You should take 2 every 6 hours. _____

UNIT 32

Rescue at Sea

1 a Read the text below and put the verbs in the correct place.

walked	saw	drove	sailed	lit	telephoned
packed	heard	put	took	parked
was	switched	shouted	helped	explained

1 Claire Haycroft is a bank clerk in Brighton. Her hobby is sailing and on May 6 she had an experience that she will never forget.

2 It was 7.15am on Saturday May 6 when Claire got into her car and _____ to the marina. She _____ on the radio and listened to the weather report. The forecast was ideal for sailing - sunshine and wind. At 7.30am she turned into the marina and _____ her car. She picked up her bag, locked her car and _____ to the boat where she met Nigel and Sarah. They _____ their supplies onto the boat and checked the safety equipment. At 8 o'clock they left the marina and sailed out to sea.

3 It was a lovely day and they _____ a long way out to sea. At 11 o'clock the weather changed. There was a strong wind and it started to rain heavily. They _____ on their waterproof clothes and brought the sails in. Suddenly a wave hit the boat and overturned it. All 3 of them were thrown into the water. Nigel swam to the surface and climbed onto the upturned boat. He saw Sarah and _____ her out of the water but he couldn't see Claire. They _____ her name again and again. She didn't reply and they thought she was dead. Nigel _____ a flare and hoped that someone would come and help.

4 After a few minutes Sarah _____ someone shouting 'help'. They looked around but couldn't see anyone. They listened again. They heard Claire shouting their names and realised that she was trapped inside the upturned boat. They were very happy that she was alive but were worried about her.

5 It was about 12 o'clock when Nigel _____ a lifeboat coming towards them. The rescue team took Sarah and Nigel to the lifeboat. Nigel _____ that Claire was trapped inside the upturned boat. A diver tried to rescue Claire but her feet were caught in the ropes and she couldn't get out. The diver came back and told the rescue team that he couldn't get her out. It was now almost 1 o'clock and Claire had been trapped for nearly 2 hours. The weather was getting worse.

6 The wind was very strong by now and it was not safe to stay there. The diver swam back to Claire with some oxygen and the rescue team started to tow the boat back to the marina. Claire _____ very frightened and was glad that the diver was with her. After an hour they arrived in the marina. It was now 3 hours since the boat had overturned and trapped Claire. One of the rescue team _____ 999 and asked for an ambulance to come to the marina.

7 In the marina the water was calm. The diver untied the ropes and freed Claire's foot. They swam through the ropes and sails and up to the surface. She _____ a deep breath of fresh air. At that moment she was the happiest person alive.

b Compare with your neighbour.

1 **c** **Match the paragraph and the summary.**

eg   7   The diver rescued Claire.

___ The lifeboat arrived.
___ Claire drove to the marina.
___ The boat overturned.
___ Nigel and Sarah realised Claire was trapped.
___ Claire's job and hobby.
___ The lifeboat towed the boat back to the marina.

d **Answer these questions.**

eg   What time did Claire leave home on Saturday May 6? She left home at 7.15am.

1 What time did she arrive at the marina? _____
2 Who did she meet at the marina? _____
3 What did they check before they left the marina? _____
4 What did they pack on to the boat? _____
5 What happened at 11 o'clock? _____

e **Now make up 5 more questions and ask your neighbour.**

eg   How long was Claire trapped for? She was trapped for 3 hours.

f **Have you ever had an experience you will never forget? Ask your neighbour.**

2 **a** **Read the following situations and discuss with your neighbour what you would do.**

1 A motorcyclist is driving along a road. A car pulls out of a pub in front of him. The motorcyclist pulls out to overtake the car. The car turns right. The motorcyclist drives into the side of the car. The motorcyclist has a broken leg. The car driver is not hurt.

   eg   What would you do in this situation? I would ring for an ambulance first, and then warn any traffic.

2 A young mother is cooking the evening meal. She takes the pan with the potatoes in it to the sink and drains the water. Her 8 year old daughter Tania wants to help. Tania reaches for the pan with the carrots in it but it is too heavy. She drops the pan and boiling water covers her legs. The mother tries to help and drops her pan of potatoes. Both are badly scalded.

3 A young couple go out for a meal one night. They ask one of the grandparents to look after their two children. They decide the two children will stay the night at the grandparents. Grandfather, the dog and the two children are playing with a ball in the garden. One of the children runs for the ball. The dog jumps for the ball at the same time. The dog misses the ball but catches the child's arm. The child has to go to hospital for stitches.

4 A couple are invited to friends for dinner. The host asks them what they would like to drink. The man asks for white wine and the lady asks for red wine. The host gives the man the white wine and the man takes it. He does not have hold of the glass properly and drops it. The glass breaks. The host picks up the pieces of glass and cuts his hand badly.

5 An old lady is cleaning her house and puts her electric fire on a chair while she is vacuuming. When she has finished vacuuming she takes out the vacuum cleaner plug and replaces the electric fire plug. She takes her vacuum cleaner to the next room and continues cleaning. The electric fire heats up and sets fire to the chair covers.

b **Ask your neighbour these questions about his/her own experience.**

1 Have you ever had an accident? What happened?
2 Have you ever been scalded? When? What happened?
3 Have you ever had stitches? Where? How many? What happened?
4 Have you ever been trapped? Where? What happened?
5 Have you ever cut yourself? Where? What happened?

3 **a** **Look at the following pictures.**

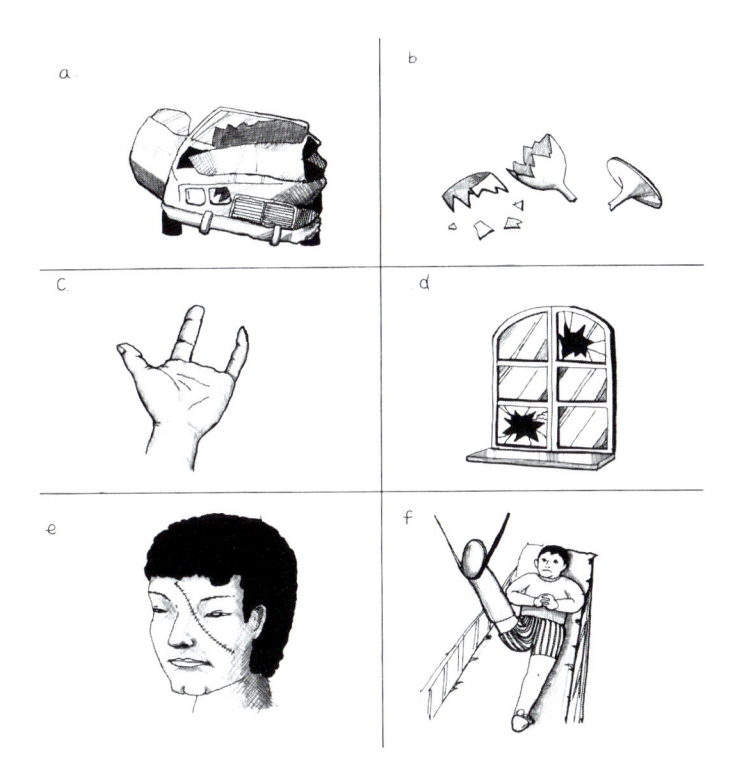

b **What do you think happened in each picture? Discuss with your neighbour.**

eg *I think somebody went to a party, had a lot to drink and while he was driving home he crashed the car.*

c **Choose one picture and make up a story about it. Tell the other people in your class.**

d **Listen to the cassette. There are 6 people saying how the situation in the picture happened. Note down which picture they are talking about and how it happened.**

person	picture	how it happened
1	_____	_____
2	_____	_____
3	_____	_____
4	_____	_____
5	_____	_____
6	_____	_____

e **Read the following sentences and underline the correct verb form.**

eg *I was driving/drove along the road when the car was skidding/skidded on some ice.*

1 I was playing/played tennis when I was slipping/slipped and broke my arm.
2 I was doing/did some shopping when I was falling/fell over.
3 I was dropping/dropped the cup while I was washing/washed up.
4 I was spraining/sprained my ankle while I was jogging/jogged.
5 I was walking/walked by the river when I was tripping/tripped and fell in.

141

4 a Translate the following.

Vocabulary

experience _____	worse _____
to forget _____	oxygen _____
marina _____	to tow _____
to switch on _____	calm _____
weather report _____	to untie _____
supplies _____	to free _____
boat _____	fresh air _____
to check _____	to pull out _____
to sail _____	to overtake _____
safety equipment _____	to drain _____
heavily _____	to drop _____
sails _____	boiling water _____
wave _____	to cover _____
to hit _____	scalded _____
to overturn _____	to jump _____
to throw _____	to miss _____
surface _____	stitches _____
to climb _____	host _____
upturned _____	to cut _____
to help _____	to vacuum _____
to shout _____	ice _____
to reply _____	to skid _____
to think _____	window _____
dead _____	scar _____
to light _____	last minute shopping _____
flare _____	to hurry _____
to hop _____	to slip _____
to realise _____	to fall _____
trapped _____	to sprain _____
alive _____	to trip _____
worried _____	to catch _____
lifeboat _____	ropes _____
rescue team _____	diver _____
to rescue _____	to tell _____

Structures

What time did Claire leave home on Saturday May 6? _____
She left home at 7.15am. _____
How long was Claire trapped? _____
She was trapped for 3 hours. _____
What would you do in this situation? _____
I would ring for an ambulance. _____
While he was driving home he crashed the car. _____
I was driving along the road when the car skidded on some ice. _____
Have you ever had an accident? _____
What happened? _____

UNIT 33

Do you live a healthy life?

1 a Put the words/phrases in the column you think suitable.

- a exercising every day
- c smoking
- a living in the country
- b dairy products
- b alcohol
- vegetarian food
- dieting
- working outside
- fried food
- b meat
- body building
- fresh fruit
- 8 hours sleep a night
- living in a town
- jogging
- eating raw fish

healthy	not sure/it depends	unhealthy
a	b	c

b Explain to your neighbour why you put the words and phrases in each column.

eg I put exercising every day in the healthy column because I think it's very important to keep fit. Where did you put it? I put it in the same column for the same reason.

c Now discuss with another neighbour.

*eg I think that exercising every day is healthy. What do you think?
I disagree with you. I think that exercising every day is unhealthy. It's too much. Your body needs to rest. I think exercising four times a week is healthy.
Yes, I suppose you're right.*

d Complete the questions using 'a lot' or 'a lot of'.

		you		your neighbour	
		yes	no	yes	no
1	Do you smoke ....?	....	....	....	....
2	Do you exercise ....?	....	....	....	....
3	Do you live in the country?	....	....	....	....
4	Do you eat .... dairy products?	....	....	....	....
5	Do you drink .... alcohol?	....	....	....	....
6	Do you eat .... vegetarian food?	....	....	....	....
7	Do you diet ....?	....	....	....	....
8	Do you work outside ....?	....	....	....	....
9	Do you eat .... fried food?	....	....	....	....
10	Do you eat .... meat?	....	....	....	....
11	Do you do .... body building?	....	....	....	....
12	Do you eat .... fresh fruit?	....	....	....	....
13	Do you sleep for 8 hours a day?	....	....	....	....
14	Do you live in a town?	....	....	....	....
15	Do you go jogging ....?	....	....	....	....
16	Do you eat .... raw fish?	....	....	....	....

e Answer the questions about yourself then ask your neighbour the questions. Who do you think is the healthiest - you or your neighbour?

2 a   Are you fit? Discuss these questions with your neighbour.

1   What is physical fitness?
2   How can you improve your level of physical fitness?
3   How can you measure physical fitness?
4   What factors affect your level of physical fitness?
5   Do you think you are fit? Why (not)?

b   Now read the text below.

The American Academy of Physical Education recently described fitness as a person who can carry out daily tasks efficiently and have plenty of energy to take part in leisure time activities. Physical fitness can be measured by 4 criteria: strength, endurance, coordination and flexibility. Fitness can be improved by regular exercise. Swimming, running, jogging, cycling, energetic dancing, and walking are good examples. There are many places which offer the facilities to do these: schools, gymnasiums, clinics, sports centres. It is important that the instructor is fully trained and qualified and can give you an individual programme. People with health problems eg diabetes, high blood pressure should see a doctor before beginning a programme of physical exercise. However, exercise alone will not guarantee physical fitness, healthy eating is also important. A bad diet will cause a drop in fitness levels. People who are underweight, overweight or weak will have a lower than average level of physical fitness.

c   Read the following questions and tick the appropriate box in the column marked 'you' ....

		you			your neighbour		
		yes	no	sometimes	yes	no	sometimes
1	Do you sleep badly at night?						
2	Do you find it difficult to relax?						
3	Do you feel there is not enough time to do everything?						
4	Do you lose your temper easily?						
5	Do you often rush things to get everything finished?						
6	Do you often take work home with you?						
7	Do you ever have bad dreams?						
8	Do you find it difficult to concentrate for a long time?						
9	Do you ever think that everybody else is an idiot?						
10	Do you make mistakes in your work?						

d   Before you ask your neighbour, fill in the answers you think he/she will give ....

e   Ask your neighbour and see if you were correct.

3

a   Read the following questions and discuss them with your neighbour.

1   Do you know what AIDS stands for?
2   Do you know what the symptoms of AIDS are?
3   Do you know when or where the first case of AIDS was identified?
4   Do you know what the connection between HIV and AIDS is?
5   How many cases of AIDS do you think there were world-wide between 1979 and 1989?

b   What do you know about AIDS? Make a few notes in the boxes below.

things I know	things I've heard but am not sure of

c   Now read this text about AIDS.

Acquired Immune Deficiency Syndrome, also known as AIDS, is a disease of the body's immune system. Symptoms include weight loss and tiredness. The first known case of AIDS was in New York in 1979. The disease comes from a virus known as HIV (Human Immunodeficiency Virus). This virus was first identified in 1983-84 by scientists at the National Cancer Institute in the United States. AIDS is passed on through blood and sexual contact. Needles used by drug-abusers are a major means of transmitting the disease. The disease was passed on through blood transfusions at first, but now all blood donations are tested for AIDS. Once the body has the virus it may be up to 10 years before the AIDS symptoms appear. In 1990 the World Health Organisation (WHO) reported over 203,599 known cases of AIDS so far world-wide, but say the actual number is nearer 600,000.

d   Ask your neighbour these questions about AIDS.

1   Can you name one symptom of AIDS?
2   Where was the virus first identified?
3   What is a major means of transmitting the disease among drug-abusers?
4   Can you have the virus but not have any symptoms of AIDS?
5   What does WHO stand for?

e   Here are some notes about influenza. Read them through and then write a short article about influenza.

influenza	- also known as flu
disease	- of the body's breathing system
symptoms	- dry cough, sore throat, blocked or runny nose, burning of eyes, fever, headache, aching muscles and joints
first case	- England - 16th Century
cause	- These are 3 types of virus: Virus A identified in 1993; Virus B identified in 1940 and Virus C identified in 1950
transmission	- by breathing in contaminated air
symptoms appear	- 2-3 weeks
number of cases	- 20 million known - actual 25 million (WHO 1987)

4 a Translate the following.

Vocabulary

unhealthy _____	to sleep badly _____
exercising _____	difficult _____
vegetarian food _____	to relax _____
dieting _____	to lose your temper _____
fried food _____	easily _____
body building _____	to rush things _____
jogging _____	bad dreams _____
raw fish _____	to make mistakes _____
physical education _____	AIDS _____
to carry out _____	symptoms _____
daily tasks _____	case _____
efficiently _____	to identify _____
energy _____	HIV _____
to take part in _____	disease _____
leisure time _____	immune system _____
criteria _____	weight loss _____
strength _____	tiredness _____
endurance _____	virus _____
coordination _____	scientists _____
flexibility _____	to transmit _____
to improve _____	blood _____
level _____	sexual contact _____
energetic _____	needles _____
facilities _____	drug-abusers _____
clinics _____	blood donations _____
instructor _____	blood transfusions _____
fully trained _____	actual _____
qualified _____	dry cough _____
health problems _____	blocked nose _____
diabetes _____	runny nose _____
bad diet _____	fever _____
underweight _____	aching _____
overweight _____	muscles _____
weak _____	joints _____

Structures

Do you live a healthy life? _____
I think that exercising every day is healthy. _____
What do you think? _____
I disagree with you. _____
I think that exercising every day is unhealthy. _____
Yes, I suppose you're right. _____
Do you smoke a lot? _____
Do you exercise a lot? _____
Do you eat a lot of dairy products? _____
Do you drink a lot of alcohol? _____

UNIT 34

Do you have medical insurance?

1 a What do you know about medical care in Britain? Read the following statements and put a tick in the appropriate column.

	true	false	don't know
1 Medical care is provided by the government.	.....	....	....
2 Prescriptions are free.	.....	....	....
3 If you choose private medical insurance, you still have to pay for state insurance.	.....	....	....
4 Not many people take out private medical insurance.	.....	....	....
5 One disadvantage of the NHS is that you may have to wait for an operation.	.....	....	....

b Now read the text below and see if you are correct.

The NHS

In Britain there is a National Health Service (NHS). Everybody pays a small amount from their wages to the government and in return the government provides medical care, free of charge, for everybody.

If you have a problem and you see a doctor, there is no charge. If you have an operation, there is no charge. However, if your doctor gives you a prescription, you have to pay for this.

The advantages of the service are that everybody has medical care, whether they are unemployed, homeless or working. The disadvantages are that you may have to wait for a long time to get an appointment with a doctor or for an operation. Or you may be in a ward with 20 other people after an operation. You may decide to take out private medical insurance. If you do this, you still have to pay towards the National Health Service. Many people do it because they say the service is better.

c Explain to your neighbour about the health service in your country. Use the following questions to help.

1 Is medical care private?
2 Is medical care provided by the state?
3 Can you choose your own health insurance?
4 Can you choose which doctor you see?
5 Who pays for prescriptions? Operations?

d Discuss the advantages and disadvantages of private medical care.

eg *I think one of the advantages is that you don't have to wait.*

2 a **Match the words and the pictures.**

_3_	safety pin
___	scissors
___	bandage
___	plaster
___	plastic gloves
___	triangular bandage

b   Which of these items would you use if you had to treat a cut or a sprained wrist? Tell your neighbour.

c   If you were going on holiday to another country (eg India, Japan, Africa), what first aid equipment would you take and why? Would you go to a doctor before you went? Why? Discuss this with your neighbour.

d   The following pictures show what to do in different situations. Match the pictures and what you should do.

1   What to do if somebody cuts him/herself.   _____
2   What to do if somebody faints.   _____
3   What to do if somebody has a nose bleed.   _____
4   What to do if somebody stops breathing.   _____
5   What to do if somebody has a cardiac arrest.   _____

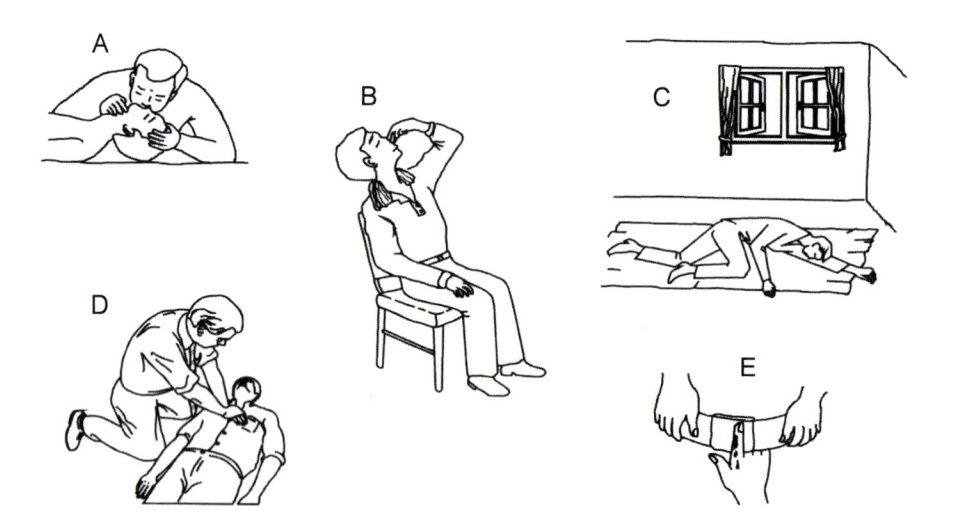

e   **Now ask your neighbour these questions.**

eg   *I had first aid training when I was at school. It was only two days but it was useful. I learnt what to do if somebody has a cardiac arrest or if somebody stops breathing. I've never given first aid treatment but I know what to do and it may save a life.*

1   Have you ever had first aid training? When? Where? Why?
2   Do you have a first aid kit in your house? What is in it? Have you ever used it? When? Why?
3   Have you ever needed first aid help?
4   Have you ever given somebody first aid help? When?
5   Do you think it is important to have first aid training? Why (not)?

3 a Look at the following plan of a hospital.

WARD A	WARD B	WARD G	OPERATING THEATRE 1	
			OPERATING THEATRE 2	
WARD C	WARD D	WARD H	OPERATING THEATRE 3	EMERGENCY VEHICLES ONLY
			X-RAY ROOM	
WARD E	WARD F	WARD I	WAITING ROOM	
				CASUALTY ENTRANCE
HALL				
STORES	WC	RECEPTION & SEATING AREA	TREATMENT ROOMS 1 2 3 4 5	
VISITORS CAR PARK		MAIN ENTRANCE		
		STAFF CAR PARK		

b Answer the following questions.

1 Where is the X-ray room? _____

2 How many treatment rooms are there? _____

3 Which entrance would be used for an emergency? _____

4 Which entrance do visitors use? _____

5 How would you get from the X-ray room to ward B? _____
_____

c Listen to the cassette and make notes. You will hear it twice.

✎ **Notes**

d Compare your notes with your neighbour. What other information can you remember?

4 a Translate the following.

Vocabulary

National Health Service _____
government _____
in return _____
medical care _____
no charge _____
operation _____
advantages _____
ward _____
private medical insurance _____
bandage _____
plastic gloves _____
triangular bandage _____
cut _____
sprained wrist _____
first aid _____
to cut yourself _____
to faint _____
nose bleed _____
to stop breathing _____
cardiac arrest _____
operating theatre _____
X-ray room _____
casualties _____
treatment rooms _____
stores _____
main entrance _____
regulations _____
emergency vehicle _____
staff car park _____

Structures

I think one of the advantages is... _____
I think one of the disadvantages is.... _____
I think the advantages are... _____
I think the disadvantages are... _____
If somebody faints you should... _____
I had first aid training when I was at school. _____
It was only two days but it was useful. _____
I learnt what to di if somebody faints. _____
I've never given first aid treatment. _____
But I know what to do and it may save a life. _____

UNIT 35

What do you do for a living?

1 a Match the pictures and the job titles. *eg* *f* shop assistant.

___ policeman   ___ chef   ___ DJ (disc jockey)
___ teacher   ___ receptionist ___ company salesman
___ housewife   ___ bus driver   ___ nurse

a b c d
e f g
h i j

b Match the job description and the title.

1 I wear a uniform to work. I drive around my area to see that everything is all right or I do administration work in the police station. The hours are not regular - Friday and Saturday nights are always busy when the pubs close.

2 I get up first in the morning and wake the children. I help them to get washed and dressed. I wake my husband and then I make breakfast. We eat breakfast together then the kids go off to school and my husband goes to work. I go shopping, clean the house, tidy up and prepare the evening meal.

3 I work in a school. I have to do a lot of preparation for my lessons. I teach geography to 12 and 13 year olds. I like my pupils. It's quite well paid and I get long holidays.

4 I work in the evenings but not every evening. On Friday and Saturday evenings I always work in the same club. I start at 7pm and finish at 1am. It takes an hour to put all my equipment in the van again. I play music so that people can dance all evening.

5 I work regular hours. I drive to work by car and then get into my bus. I drive the same route every day and I see the same people quite a lot. I work 8 hours a day and then I go home.

6 I work for a company which sells steel plate. I have to go to trade fairs and make contact with new customers. We sell a lot to car factories so I have a lot of regular customers, who I have to visit quite often.

7 I work behind a counter all day. I start at 9am and finish at 5pm and I have one hour lunch break from 12pm - 1pm. When customers come in I say "Hello. Can I help you?" When they have everything they need I take the money, put it in the till and give the customer a receipt.   *f*

8 I work in the kitchen of a big hotel. You don't normally see me but I'm very important. I prepare food and cook dishes that are good enough for a king.

9 I work in a ward in a hospital. I work very long hours and often it's hard work. I look after the patients in my ward - they all have back problems and there are 27 of them in the ward. It's not very well paid.

10 I work in a hotel. I'm normally the first person the guests speak to. I find rooms for them, ask them to fill out registration cards and take payment from them.

Check with your neighbour.

c Point at the pictures and tell your neighbour about the people.

eg She's a shop assistant. She works behind a counter all day. She starts at 9am and...

Unit 35   151

2 a Fill in the following questionnaire about yourself. Put a tick (✓) in the relevant boxes.

Your Name: _____

Your Address: _____

1 **Where do you work?**

factory ❑   office ❑   shop ❑   hotel/restaurant ❑

school ❑   hospital ❑   other ❑ _____

Name of Work: _____

Address of Work: _____

2 **When do you work?**   yes   no

Do you start work at the same time every day?   ❑   ❑

Do you finish work at the same time every day? ❑   ❑

Do you work the same number of hours every day? ❑   ❑

Do you ever work in the evening?   ❑   ❑

Do you ever work on Saturdays?   ❑   ❑

Do you ever work on Sundays?   ❑   ❑

3 **Which field do you work in?**

production ❑   education ❑   services ❑   research ❑

administration ❑   sales ❑   other ❑ _____

4 **Which of these activities does your work involve?**

working on a computer ❑   giving presentations ❑

travelling on business ❑   writing letters ❑

speaking on the telephone ❑   using a calculator ❑

working at home ❑   going to meetings ❑

going to trade fairs ❑   wearing a uniform ❑

working behind a counter ❑   taking payment from people ❑

asking people to fill forms out ❑   other ❑

5 **What's your position?**

(in your language) _____

(in English) _____

---

b Ask your neighbour the questions.

c Tell your teacher about yourself.

3 **a** Look at photograph sequence 8 'At Work' on the next pages and find the following objects. When you've found them, ask your neighbour where they are.

| filing cabinet | folder | mug | drawer | tray | box file |

b Match the question and the answers.

eg *What has she just done? She has just taken out a folder.*

1 What has she just done?   ___ She was reading the information in the folder.
2 What is she doing?   _1_ She has just taken out a folder.
3 What do you think she'll do next?   ___ I think she'll put the folder back in the filing cabinet.
4 What did she do first?   ___ She had opened the drawer.
5 What was she doing while she was telephoning?   ___ She opened the drawer and took out a folder.
6 What had she done before that?   ___ She's telephoning.

c Ask your neighbour the following questions about the woman in the photographs.

1 What is she doing in photograph 1?   Why do you think she's doing this?
    What had she done before this?   What is she going to do next?

2 What is she doing in photograph 2?   Why do you think she's doing this?
    What had she done before this?   What is she going to do next?

3 What is she doing in photograph 3?   Why do you think she's doing this?
    What had she done before this?   What is she going to do next?

4 What is she doing in photograph 4?   Why do you think she's doing this?
    What had she done before this?   What is she going to do next?

5 What is she doing in photograph 5?   Why do you think she's doing this?
    What had she done before this?   What is she going to do next?

d Now ask your neighbour these questions.

1 What does the woman look like?
2 What is she wearing?
3 What time of day do you think it is? Why?
4 What kind of company do you think she works for? Why?
5 Which department do you think she works in? Why?
6 What do you think her job is? Why?
7 Who do you think she's telephoning? Why?
8 Why does she go to the filing cabinet before she makes the phone call?
9 Why does she put her glasses on?
10 What do you think she does after the phone call?

e Make up a story about the photographs and tell your neighbour.

eg *The photographs show a lady at work. I know that she's at work because there's a desk, a filing cabinet and lots of box files. She's wearing smart clothes, too. I think she's a Sales Manager in a large company. She's going to make an important telephone call to one of her customers. Before she makes the phone call she goes to the filing cabinet to get out a folder. She looks at the folder to check that it's the right one and then...*

At Work (Photograph Sequence 8)

154

155

4 a Translate the following.

Vocabulary

shop assistant _____
policeman _____
teacher _____
housewife _____
chef _____
bus driver _____
disc jockey _____
company salesman _____
uniform _____
police station _____
to wake _____
to tidy up _____
evening meal _____
to teach _____
lesson _____
geography _____
12 year olds _____
pupils _____
well paid _____
equipment _____
van _____
to work regular hours _____
route _____
company _____
steel plate _____
to make contacts _____
customers _____

car factories _____
till _____
receipt _____
important _____
king _____
to work long hours _____
hard work _____
back problems _____
guests _____
to fill out _____
registration cards _____
to take payment _____
production _____
education _____
services _____
administration _____
sales _____
research _____
trade fairs _____
presentations _____
position _____
filing cabinet _____
folder _____
mug _____
drawer _____
tray _____
box file _____

Structures

What does she do? _____
She's a shop assistant. _____
She works behind a counter all day. _____
What has she just done? _____
What is she doing? _____
What do you think she'll do next? _____
What did she do first? _____
What was she doing while she was telephoning? _____
What had she done before that? _____
She was reading. _____
She has just taken the folder out of the filing cabinet. _____
I think she'll put it back in the filing cabinet. _____
She had opened the drawer. _____
She opened the drawer and took the folder out. _____
She's telephoning. _____
What is she doing in picture 1? _____
What had she done before this? _____
What is she going to do next? _____

UNIT 36

Applying for a job.

1 a Look at the following job vacancies.

Secretary	Computer Programmer	Sales Assistant
International Company is looking for a hard working and ambitious person. Must have computer experience. Typewriting and shorthand skills required. Knowledge of French preferred.	Graduate required with 3 years computing experience.	Part time sales assistant required for electrical goods shop. Sales experience required. 3 days a week and every second Saturday.
£13 K p.a.	Contract for 18 months.	£3.50 per hour.
Apply in writing to:	£17 K p.a.	Send CV to:
ILC International	CV's to	The Manager
19-23 Port Road	Intact Computing Ltd	Robsons Electrical Shop
Truro	13 Fordway	29-33 Pool Street
	London W3 2BR	Durham DH3 49P
The Independent 29.04.96	*The Times 29.04.96*	*The Guardian 29.04.96*

b Ask your neighbour these questions.

1. Which advert appeared in the Independent newspaper?
2. Which job was advertised in the Times?
3. How much is the salary for the position as secretary?
4. How much experience do you need for the job as computer programmer?
5. What should you do if you decide to apply for the position as sales assistant?

---

49 Garden Road
Penzance
PE5 3PH

30 April 1996

ILC International
19-23 Port Road
Truro

Dear Sirs

Position of Secretary

I saw your advertisement for the above position in the Independent newspaper (29.04.96) and would like to apply for this position.

I am 26 years old and am a qualified secretary with over 5 years experience. I speak conversational French and Italian, and have excellent computing, typing and shorthand skills.

At present I am working for a small company in Penzance. I have been employed there as a secretary since I finished my secretarial training in 1990.

I am interested in working with an international company so that I can broaden my experience and use my languages.

I enclose a CV and photograph and am available for interview at any time.

I look forward to hearing from you.

Yours faithfully

Sharon Olsen

Sharon Olsen

---

c Read the letter which was sent to ILC in reply to their advert, then ask your neighbour the following questions.

1. Where does Sharon Olsen live?
2. Which job is she applying for?
3. Can she speak French?
4. Why is she applying for the job?
5. How old is she?
6. What is her present job?
7. Can she type?
8. When can she come for interview?
9. How many years experience has she got?
10. Has she sent anything else with the letter?

d Which job would you apply for? Write a letter like Sharon's for one of the jobs in 1a.

e When you are finished, work in groups. Look at your letters and decide who would be the best for each job. Tell the rest of the class who you have chosen and why.

2 a Look at the plan of ILC International and ask your neighbour questions.

eg   *Where's Room 111? It's between the WC and Room 112.*

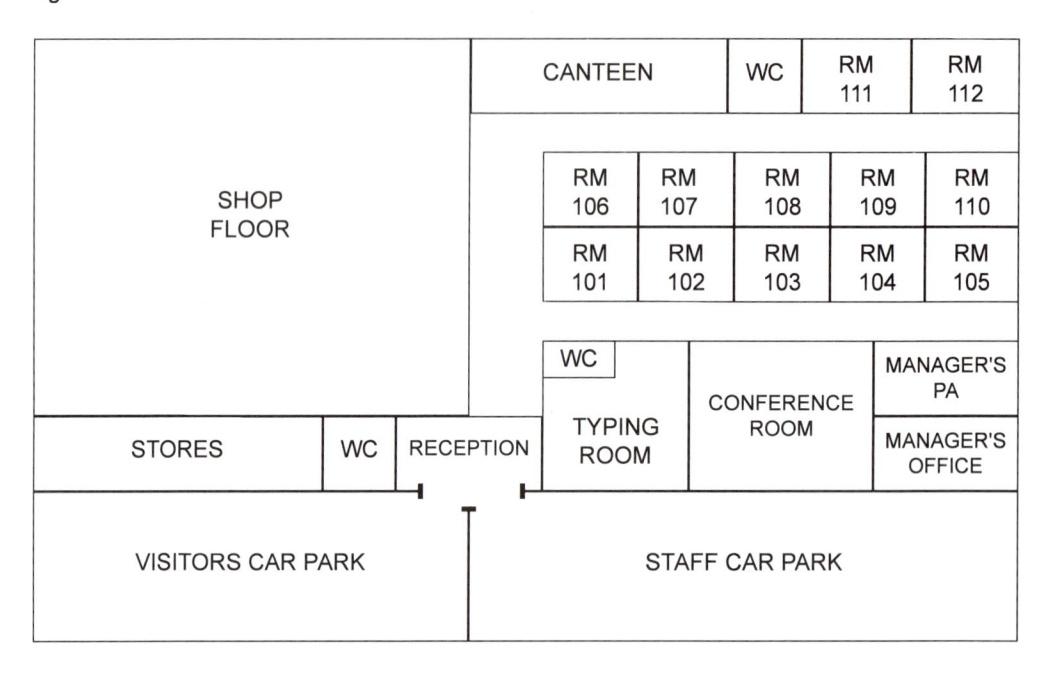

			CANTEEN	WC	RM 111	RM 112
SHOP FLOOR		RM 106	RM 107	RM 108	RM 109	RM 110
		RM 101	RM 102	RM 103	RM 104	RM 105
		WC		CONFERENCE ROOM	MANAGER'S PA	
STORES	WC	RECEPTION	TYPING ROOM		MANAGER'S OFFICE	
VISITORS CAR PARK			STAFF CAR PARK			

b   You are going to hear a telephone conversation between Sharon Olsen and Mike Bell, Personnel Manager at ILC. You will hear the cassette twice. Make notes while you are listening.

✎ Notes Sharon Olsen	Mike Bell

c   Compare your notes with your neighbour.

d   Ask your neighbour these questions.

1   Can you remember your first job interview?
2   Before the interview, did you find out information about the company?
3   Before the interview, did you practise what you would say?
4   Before the interview, did you think what kind of questions the interviewer would ask?
5   Did you practise your interviewing techniques with anyone?
6   During the interview, did you say anything you regretted?
7   During the interview, did you ask any questions?
8   Did you learn anything from the interview?
9   Did you get the job?
10   If you got the job, are you still in the same job now?

e   Tell your teacher about yourself.

3 **a** You are going to order some items for your office. Look at the price list for Armstrong's Stationery and fill in the details on order form A.

Armstrong's Stationery
Catalogue and Price List
25 George Street, Cheltenham
(tel 01242 262632)

Order No	Description	Colour	Price
SL001	scissors, large	red	£2.50 for set of 3
SS002	scissors, small	black	£2.00 for set of 3
PCL001	pencils	red	£2.00 for 20
PCL002	pencils	black	£2.00 for 20
PN001	pens	red	£3.00 for 20
PN002	pens	black	£3.00 for 20
EB001	elastic bands, large	-	£2.50 per 1000
EB002	elastic bands, small	-	£2.00 per 1000
PCS001	paper clips	-	£1.99 per 1000
FR001	fax roll	-	£8 each
RR001	ruler	clear	20p each

Order Form A

Customer Name _____

Customer Address _____

_____

Date _____

Order No	Description	Quantity	Price

Total ....

+ VAT @ 17½% ....

Grand Total ....

Order Form B

Customer Name _____

Customer Address _____

_____

Date _____

Order No	Description	Quantity	Price

Total ....

+ VAT @ 17½% ....

Grand Total ....

b Now phone your neighbour who works at Armstrong's to give him/her your order. Sit back to back and your neighbour will note down your order on form B. You start the phone call.

eg *Hello, this is..., I'd like to order the following goods.*

c **Compare with your neighbour.**

4 a Translate the following.

Vocabulary

hard working _____	Manager's Office _____
ambitious _____	PA (Personal Assistant) _____
computer experience _____	administration area _____
skills _____	catalogue _____
required _____	price list _____
knowledge of _____	elastic bands _____
preferred _____	paper clips _____
£13 K p.a. _____	fax roll _____
to apply _____	ruler _____
in writing _____	clear _____
Computer Programmer _____	customer name _____
graduate _____	customer address _____
contract _____	date _____
part time _____	order no _____
per hour _____	description _____
above _____	quantity _____
to broaden _____	total _____
to enclose _____	+ VAT @ 17½% _____
shop floor _____	grand total _____

Structures

Dear Sirs _____

I saw your advertisement for the above position in the ... _____

I would like to apply for this position. _____

I am ... years old. _____

I am a qualified ... with over 5 years experience. _____

I speak conversational French. _____

I have excellent ... skills. _____

At present I am working for ... _____

I have been employed there as ... since ... _____

I am interested in working with ... so that I can ... _____

I enclose a ... _____

I am available for interview ... _____

I look forward to hearing from you. _____

Yours faithfully. _____

UNIT 37

Who do you work for?

1 a Look at the names in the box below. Ask your teacher to say any which you can't pronounce, then repeat them. Listen to the cassette and match the names and the people in the photograph.

1. Mary Allinson
2. Colin Reed
3. Nicola Laker
4. Michael Buchanan
5. Mel Roberts
6. George Fraser
7. Scott Hamilton
8. Jo Walker
9. David Young
10. Angus Oliver

Listen again and check.

b Now listen again and write the names of the people under their position. When you've finished, check with your neighbour by asking questions.

eg *Who's the Production Manager?*
What's Angus Oliver's position?

```
                    Managing Director
                    Scott Hamilton
     ┌──────────────┬──────────────┬──────────────┐
Production      Financial        Marketing      Personnel
Manager         Manager          Manager        Manager
   │          ┌────┴────┐        ┌───┴────┐         │
Foreman   Customer    Wages    Sales   Advertising  Recruitment and
          Accounts   Section  Manager   Manager    Training Officer
          Manager     Head
   │          │         │        │         │            │
Shop Floor  Accounts  Wages   Sales   Advertising   Personnel Department
Workers     Clerks    Clerks   Team   Assistants    Staff
```

c Here are some numbers which were on the cassette. Listen again and note down what they refer to.

eg 10 = 10th anniversary last summer. Photo was taken then.

1) 5   2) 90   3) 60   4) 5   5) 28

2 **a** Look at the following five business cards.

Ian McLeary
Sales Assistant

The Computer Superstore

Computer Superstores Ltd
Unit 55 Retail World
Team Valley
Gateshead
NE11 OLP

Tel: 0191 491323
Fax: 0191 491444

Robson's Electricentre

68 Commercial Street
Dundee
DD1 2AB
Tel 01382 26437
Fax 01382 26451

Tony Robson
Managing Director

Far End Bookshop
99 Harcourt Street
DUBLIN 2

Tel 01-5716554
Fax 01-5715923

Mark Rickwood
Sales Manager

Sheila Kerr
Training Officer

4122 West Avenue 5
Anaheim
CA 92804
USA
Tel 0714 7729201
Fax 0714 7729132

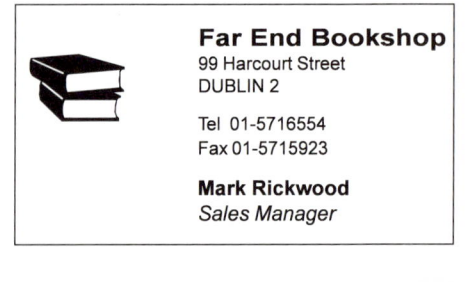

AT
Telephone
International

---

6 Davy Way
Llay
Wrexham
Clywd   LL12 0PG
Tel 01978 242424 / Fax 01978 255552

PCL Software Solutions

Bridget Heale
Financial Manager

---

b Ask your neighbour these 5 questions.

1 Which company does Sheila Kerr work for?
2 What's the address of the Computer Superstore?
3 Who is the Financial Manager of PCL Software Solutions?
4 What's Ian McLeary's position?
5 If I want to speak to Tony Robson, which number should I ring?

c Now make up another 5 questions about the business cards and ask your neighbour these.

d Fill in your details on business card A.

A
company name _____
your name _____
your position _____
your company address _____
_____
your company tel no _____
your company fax no _____

B

C

D

e Ask 3 other neighbours about their work and fill in their details on business cards B - D.

3 **a** You are at the opening of a customer's new premises. You hear the following dialogues. Read them and decide if the people know each other or if they are meeting for the first time.

1. Hi Rob. It's good to see you again.
   It's good to see you too, Tom. How are you?
   I'm very well. And you?
   I'm fine.

2. Hello. I'm Peter Richter. You must be Jeff Shaw.
   Yes that's right. Nice to meet you.

3. Hello. I don't think we've met. I'm Janice Ellis.
   Nice to meet you. My name's Renate Kennedy, but you can call me Renny.

4. Hello. I'm Patricia Nelson. What's your name?
   My name's Alice Barda. Pleased to meet you Patricia.

5. It's Frances Cooper isn't it?
   Yes that's right and you're Ben Hutchinson aren't you?
   Yes. It's nice to see you again. How are you?

b At the opening Patricia Nelson introduces herself to you. What would you say? What would you say after that? Here are some questions you could use. Match the questions and the answers.

1	Do you work for this company?	*j*	a	Yes, it's because of the rail strike.
2	Have you come far?		b	Machinery for recycling plants.
3	Who do you work for?		c	They're very light and spacious.
4	It's a lovely day, isn't it?		d	Atraverda Ceramics Ltd.
5	What line of business are you in?		e	Yes, dreadful for the time of year.
6	Terrible weather at the moment, isn't it?		f	No, my company is just around the corner.
7	What do you think of the new premises?		g	The Production Department.
8	Which department do you work in?		h	I'm a Production Manager.
9	The traffic is bad today, isn't it?		i	Yes, wonderful.
10	What do you do?		j	No I don't.

c It's now 10.50am and people are starting to leave. You have to be back in your office for 11.15am. Here are some phrases which you can use to say goodbye. Practise the dialogues with your neighbour.

1. A It's been a pleasure talking to you. Goodbye.
   B Goodbye.

2. A I'm afraid I have to leave. I have a meeting at 11.15am. Do you have a card?
   B Of course. Here you are.
   A Thank you. Goodbye.
   B Bye.

3. A It was nice meeting you. Here's my card.
   B Thank you.
   A Goodbye.
   B Goodbye.

4. A Why don't you call me next week. Here's my card.
   B I certainly will. Thank you.
   A Bye.
   B Bye.

5. A If you'll excuse me, I must dash. I hope we meet again some time.
   B I'm sure we will. Goodbye.
   A Bye.

d Now work in groups of 6. You are at the opening of a customer's new premises. Introduce yourself, ask a few of the questions and then say goodbye.

4 a Translate the following.

Vocabulary

Managing Director _____	Advertising Assistants _____
Production Manager _____	Recruitment and Training Officer _____
Financial Manager _____	Personnel Department Staff _____
Marketing Manager _____	business card _____
Personnel Manager _____	customer _____
Foreman _____	premises _____
shop floor worker _____	rail strike _____
Customer Accounts Manager _____	machinery _____
Accounts Clerks _____	recycling plants _____
Wages Section Head _____	light _____
Wages Clerks _____	spacious _____
Sales Manager _____	dreadful _____
Sales Team _____	bye _____
Advertising Manager _____	goodbye _____

Structures

It's good to see you again. _____
How are you? _____
I'm very well. And you? _____
You must be Jeff Shaw. _____
Nice to meet you. _____
I don't think we've met. _____
You can call me Renny. _____
Pleased to meet you. _____
Do you work for this company? _____
Have you come far? _____
Who do you work for? _____
It's a lovely day isn't it? _____
What line of business are you in? _____
Terrible weather at the moment, isn't it? _____
What do you think of the new premises? _____
Which department do you work in? _____
The traffic is bad today, isn't it? _____
What do you do? _____
It's been a pleasure talking to you. _____
I'm afraid I have to leave. _____
I have a meeting at 11.15am. _____
Do you have a card? _____
It was nice meeting you. _____
Here's my card. _____
Why don't you call me next week. _____
I certainly will. _____
If you'll excuse me, I must dash. _____
I hope we meet again some time. _____
I'm sure we will. _____

UNIT 38

What happens to your waste paper?

1 a The sequence of photographs on the next page shows the process of recycling waste paper. Look at the photographs then read the paragraphs below and match the photograph and the description.

☐ 1 Next the waste paper is sorted into bleached (white) paper and coloured paper/cardboard. It is tied together and then stacked in a fenced area. The bleached paper is stacked on the left, and the coloured paper/cardboard on the right.

☐ 2 The sheet of recycled paper is wound onto a roll at the end of the drying machine. When the roll is full, it is taken away and a new roll is started.

☐ 3 The waste paper is collected from the paper banks and delivered to the mill by lorry, where it is emptied into the yard.

☐ 4 The waste paper is mixed with water and left for 24 hours. The mixture is then fed through a machine where the water is squeezed out and the sheet of recycled paper is carried along a conveyor belt. Hot air is blown on it and the recycled paper is dried.

☐ 5 The roll of recycled paper is weighed, then wrapped and loaded onto pallets. It is then ready to be despatched.

b Complete the sentences using the phrases below.

is sorted	is mixed	is left	is started	is emptied
is squeezed	is weighed	is carried	is dried	is loaded

1 The waste paper _____ into bleached paper and coloured paper.

2 When the roll is full, it is taken away and a new roll _____.

3 The roll of recycled paper _____.

4 The waste paper _____ with water.

5 Hot air is blown on it and the paper _____.

6 The waste paper _____ into the yard.

7 The water _____ out.

8 The recycled paper _____ along a conveyor belt.

9 The waste paper _____ for 24 hours.

10 The roll of recycled paper _____ onto pallets.

c Look at photograph sequence 9 'Recycling Waste Paper' on the next pages and explain what happens to the waste paper when it is delivered to the factory.

Recycling Waste Paper (Photograph Sequence 9)

C

D

E

2 a You have written a letter to your penfriend in Hong Kong. What happens to the letter? Put the sentences in the correct order.

eg   _1_   The letter is weighed.

___ The letter is put into the post box.
___ The letters are sorted.
___ The letters are sent to Hong Kong.
___ The stamps are stuck on.
___ The post box is emptied.
___ The letters are taken to the sorting room.
___ The letter is delivered to your penfriend.

b **Work with someone who has travelled by plane. What happens to your luggage after you check in?**

eg   *My luggage is put on the scales and weighed.*

c **Answer these questions about your place of work.**

eg   *Is anything emptied regularly in your office? Yes, the bins are emptied every day.*

1 Is anything delivered to your office?
2 Is anything collected from your office?
3 Is anything weighed in your office?
4 Is anything wrapped in your office?
5 Is anything cleaned in your office?

d **Can you think of anything else in your place of work...**

1 which is sorted?
2 which is tied together?
3 which is taken away?
4 which is filed away?
5 which is checked?

3 **a** You are on a business trip to Britain. You have been invited to visit Fourstones Paper Mill. Look at the information below and answer these questions.

1. When was Fourstones Paper Mill established?
2. Where is the mill located?
3. What is brought from all over the country to the mill?
4. What happens to the waste paper at the mill?
5. What happens to the recycled paper?

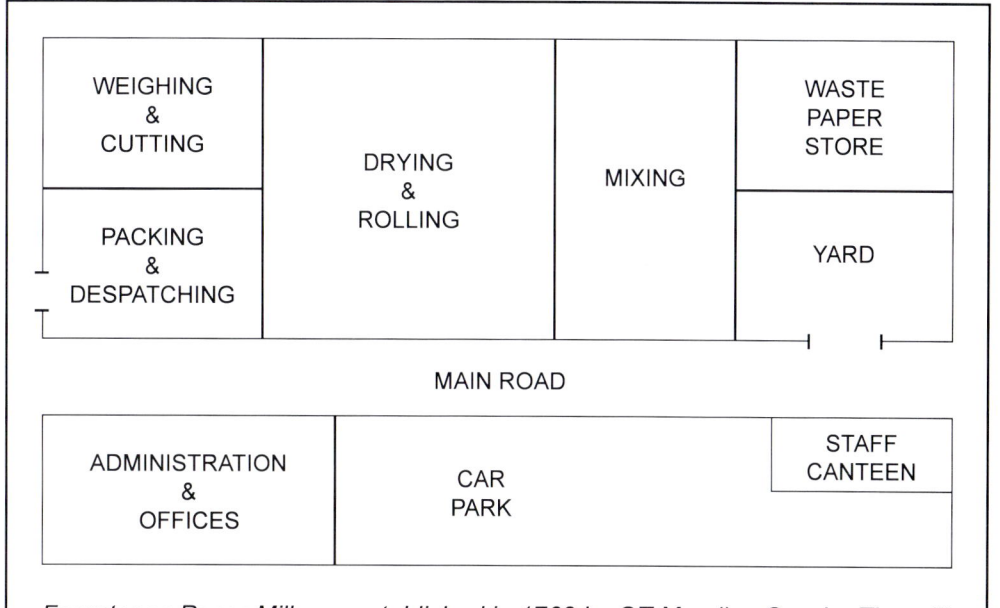

WEIGHING & CUTTING	DRYING & ROLLING	MIXING	WASTE PAPER STORE
PACKING & DESPATCHING			YARD

MAIN ROAD

ADMINISTRATION & OFFICES	CAR PARK	STAFF CANTEEN

Fourstones Paper Mill was established in 1763 by GT Mandl, a Czech. The mill is located in the heart of Northumbria and has excellent connections by road and rail. Waste paper from all over the country is brought to Fourstones paper mill where it is recycled and the recycled paper is supplied to companies worldwide. Fourstones Paper Mill is committed to the protection of the environment and is working towards a better future.

b While you are at the paper mill you will be given a guided tour of the factory and a presentation of the company's current markets. The guided tour is about to begin and the guide is going to give you some information before you start. What information do you think he will give you? Put a tick (✓) next to the information you think you will hear.

___ the name of the guide
___ where you are now
___ when the company was established
___ where the tour will start
___ what the bleached paper is used for
___ how many people work in the factory
___ where the Marketing Manager will give his presentation
___ the name of the Managing Director
___ the time now
___ how long the tour will take
___ what time you'll be taken back to your hotel

c Now listen to the cassette and see if you were correct. Listen a second time and make some more notes, compare your notes with your neighbour.

4 a Translate the following.

Vocabulary

process _____
waste paper _____
to sort _____
bleached _____
cardboard _____
to tie _____
to stack _____
fenced _____
sheet _____
to wind _____
to take away _____
by lorry _____
to empty _____
yard _____
to mix _____
mixture _____
to feed through _____
to squeeze out _____

recycled paper _____
conveyor belt _____
hot air _____
to blow _____
to dry _____
to weigh _____
to wrap _____
to load _____
to file away _____
pallet _____
to despatch _____
to supply _____
worldwide _____
to produce _____
wide range _____
products _____
protection _____
future _____

Structures

The waste paper is sorted. _____
It is tied together. _____
It is stacked. _____
It is wound onto a roll. _____
It is taken away. _____
A new roll is started. _____
Waste paper is delivered. _____
It is emptied into the yard. _____
It is mixed with water. _____
The mixture is fed through a machine. _____
The water is squeezed out. _____
Hot air is blown on it. _____
The paper is dried. _____
The paper is weighed. _____
The paper is wrapped and loaded onto pallets. _____
It is ready to be despatched. _____
The letters are sorted every morning. _____
The waste paper bins are emptied every evening. _____
The rubbish is taken away. _____
It was established in 1763. _____
It was established by ... _____
It is located in... _____

UNIT 39

At Work

1 a Read the following questions, then try to find the answers in the text below as quickly as possible.

eg   What is the woman's name?   *Jilly Wright.*

1   What is her occupation? *television presenter*
2   How old was she when she left school? *16*
3   What happened when she was 22? *start training new employees*
4   When did she start working as a TV presenter? *29*
5   What time does she go 'on air'? *6.15am*
6   What happens at 3.30pm?
7   What time does she go to bed?
8   How much does she earn a year?
9   What is her ambition?
10 How much does she spend on clothes per month?

Name: Jilly Wright
Age: 30
Occupation: Television Presenter

Route to Job

Jilly left school at 16 and worked as a typist for a small company for 3 years. When she was 19 she did a secretarial course which lasted for one year. Her next job was with an international company where she worked as a secretary in the training section of the Personnel Department. When she was 22 she became a trainer and started to train new employees. After another 3 years she left the company to work for a small company who produce training videos. A year ago she started working part time as a TV presenter on one of the cable channels and now she works there full time.

Jilly's Day

I normally get up at 4.30am and go jogging for an hour. I have a quick shower, get dressed for work and have some breakfast - fresh fruit, cereal and orange juice. As I'm a presenter on breakfast television I have to leave home at 5.45am. It takes me about 10 minutes to travel to the television studio, if there are no traffic jams. I arrive there just before 6am. Luckily I have my own parking space so I don't have to worry about that. As soon as I walk in I'm given a cup of strong black coffee and a list of the themes on today's programme. I know all of this because I have to find out information about the themes before the show so I can talk about them or interview people. If there are any last minute questions, for example, how to pronounce someone's name correctly, this is my last chance. At 6.15 am I go 'on air'. I normally start with the news and the weather and then I look at the headlines in all the national newspapers. If something important has happened the producer tries to get experts in to discuss why or what it means, but usually we just have well known faces talking about current affairs. I come 'off air' at 10.30am and grab a sandwich and another coffee. Then I go to the information centre in the TV studio to find out information for tomorrow's programme or practise what I'm going to say tomorrow. I leave the studio about 3.30pm and go to the gym for an hour, then go home and have something to eat. In the evening I watch TV or meet friends, but I'm always in bed by 10pm

Salary: approximately £25,000 p.a.
Monthly Spendings: £500 mortgage / £200 make-up, hair / £50 gym fees / £200 clothes
Ambition: To have my own chat show.

b Now read the text again and make notes about her day. When you have finished, use your notes to tell your neighbour about Jilly. Do you both have the same information?

✎ **Notes**

1 c Ask your neighbour.

1 Would you like to be a TV presenter on breakfast TV? Why (not)?
2 Do you think she earns a lot of money? Why (not)?
3 Do you think her job is easy? Why (not)?
4 Do you think her job is interesting? Why (not)?
5 Do you think she should have been trained to be a presenter? Why (not)?

2 a Other members of the class are going to interview you. They will ask you about your occupation, your work experience and your normal day. Make notes on the form below so you can prepare what you're going to say. Do not use full sentences.

Name _____	✎ **Notes**	**A Normal Day**
Age _____		
Occupation _____	Before Work	
Past Jobs:		
	At Work	
	After Work	

b You will also be interviewing other members of your class about their occupation, work experience and normal day. Write down 10 questions you can ask them.

1 _____ ?
2 _____ ?
3 _____ ?
4 _____ ?
5 _____ ?
6 _____ ?
7 _____ ?
8 _____ ?
9 _____ ?
10 _____ ?

c Now ask 3 neighbours your questions. If you need more information, you'll have to think up more questions. Make brief notes of the answers so you can tell your teacher about one of your neighbours.

3 a   Janice Goulding is receptionist at ABC Office Supplies. Look at the notes she has made in her diary and ask your neighbour questions.

eg   *Who is at Head Office all morning?*

	Thursday 10 March			
	Mike Smith	**Simon Parker**	**Mandy Wardle**	**John Banks**
9.30		9.30 - 10 Meeting		sick all day
10.00	At Head		10-10.30 Meeting	
10.30	Office all	10.30 - 11.30		
11.00	morning	Meeting		
11.30			11.30-12 Meeting	

b   Between 10 and 10.30 Janice has 5 phone calls. What do you think she says to each caller? Match the questions and replies below.

1   Hello. Can I speak to Mike Smith please?   ___   Hold the line please. I'll put you through.
2   Hello. Can I speak to Janice Goulding please?   ___   She's in a meeting at the moment. Can I ask her to call you back?
3   Hello. Can you put me through to Simon Parker please?   ___   I'm afraid he's not here at the moment. Can I take a message?
4   Hello. Can I speak to Mandy Wardle please?   ___   I'm afraid he's off sick today. Can I take a message?
5   Hello. Can you put me through to John Banks please?   ___   Speaking.

c   Janice Goulding is on her coffee break between 11 and 11.15. Your neighbour answers the phone while she is on her break. Telephone your neighbour and ask to speak to different people.

d   Later Simon Parker receives a call from Nigel Adinall. Practise the dialogue with your neighbour.

Simon Parker	Nigel Adinall
Simon Parker speaking	Hello Simon. This is Nigel Adinall from ATV. How are you?
Fine thanks. How are you?	Very well. Look Simon I have a small problem with our meeting this afternoon.
Oh, what's that?	Well my car's broken down and I have to take it to the garage. Could we rearrange the meeting for Friday morning?
Yes that's fine. How about 9 o'clock?	9 o'clock's fine by me. Thanks a lot.
No problem. See you then.	Okay. Bye.

e   Here are some more useful phrases for telephoning. When would you say them?

1   Could you repeat that please?   ___   When the person is speaking too quickly.
2   Could you speak more slowly please?   ___   When the person is speaking too quietly.
3   Could you speak a bit louder please?   ___   When you want to note something down.
4   Could you hold on while I get a pencil?   ___   When you want the person to say something a second time.
5   Could you spell that please?   ___   When you want to write something down letter by letter.

f   You are going to make some phone calls now. Read the situations and think about what you are going to say and which phrases you are going to use before you begin.

1   You have a meeting at 10.30am tomorrow with Dawn Anderson, Marketing Manager at Aztec Fabrics Ltd. Unfortunately you can't make it as there is a rail strike. Ring her up, explain the situation and rearrange the meeting.

2   You have received a translation of your company brochure to check. You notice that the address is wrong. It reads Normad Exports, 52 Rue de le Victoire, 7509 Paris. It should read Normand Exports, 52 Rue de la Victoire, 75009 Paris. Ring Isabelle Meyer at Intertrans to explain the situation.

3   You have been invited to visit one of your customers, John MacLean at IT Tools. Ring him to let him know the exact time and date you will arrive.

4   You have seen an advert in a magazine which is very interesting. Ring the company (Envirotec) and see if they can send you some general information, a catalogue and a price list.

5   Julian Armitage had an appointment with you at 10 o'clock. He didn't come. Ring him and find out why not.

4 a Translate the following.

Vocabulary

television presenter _____	'on air' _____
typist _____	headlines _____
to last _____	producer _____
trainer _____	experts _____
to train _____	well known faces _____
employees _____	current affairs _____
training videos _____	'off air' _____
cable channels _____	gym _____
full time _____	spending _____
breakfast television _____	mortgage _____
television studio _____	make up _____
as soon as _____	gym fees _____
themes _____	ambition _____
programme _____	chat show _____
to interview _____	translation _____
last minute questions _____	brochure _____
to pronounce _____	

Structures

Hello. Can I speak to Mike Smith please? _____
Hold the line please. _____
I'll put you through. _____
She's in a meeting at the moment. _____
Can I ask her to call you back? _____
I'm afraid he's not here at the moment. _____
Can I take a message? _____
I'm afraid he's off sick today. _____
Simon Parker speaking. _____
Hello Simon. This is Nigel Adinall from ATV. _____
Look Simon, I have a small problem with our meeting this afternoon. _____
_____
Could we rearrange the meeting for Friday? _____
Yes that's fine. _____
How about 9 o'clock? _____
No problem. _____
See you then. _____
Could you repeat that please? _____
Could you speak more slowly please? _____
Could you speak a bit louder please? _____
Could you hold on while I get a pencil? _____
Could you spell that please? _____

UNIT 40

Revision

1 a Here are the names of some parts of the body. Point at each one and tell your neighbour what it is

eg   This is my ankle. These are my toes.

elbow	wrist	arm	chest	thumb	leg	waist	head
fingers	hips	hand	neck	ear	foot	eye	knee

b Here are some common problems. What advice would you give?

I've got flu   I've got backache   I feel sick
I've got toothache   I've got a sore throat   I've got a headache

c What do you do when you want to see a doctor in your country? Discuss these questions with your neighbour. Do you have to make an appointment? Do you have to go to the doctor, or does he come to you? How long do you have to wait for an appointment? How much does it cost?

2 a Work with your neighbour and make up a short story using at least 5 of the words below. Make notes and when you're ready, tell your story to the rest of the class.

started	helped	drove	checked	shouted	saw	sailed
came	thrown	locked	thought	heard	met	explained
freed	arrived	trapped	packed	telephoned	was	tried

b Look at these situations and say what you would do.

1   Your boss has invited you and your girlfriend/boyfriend out for a meal. The evening is going well and the atmosphere is good. Suddenly your girlfriend/ boyfriend coughs and knocks over a glass of red wine. The red wine runs across the table and on to your boss's best suit.

2   You are looking after a friend's pet dog while they are on holiday. One morning when you go to feed it, you find that it is lying in its basket. It is very ill.

3   You had a job interview last week. This morning you received a letter informing you that you did not get the job. You know that you were the most suitable and best qualified for the job. You also know that you were the oldest.

4   Your partner doesn't come home one night.

5   You take your boyfriend/girlfriend out to a restaurant. At the end of the meal you ask for the bill and give the waiter your credit card. After a few minutes, he returns and tells you that it has not been accepted.

c Read these sentences and underline the correct form.

1   The sun was shining/shone when I was arriving/arrived in Hawaii.
2   While I was shopping/shopped, someone was shouting/shouted my name.
3   I was lying/lay in the bath when the telephone was ringing/rang.
4   While I was walking/walked home, someone was screaming/screamed.
5   I was running/ran through the woods when I was tripping/tripped over.

3 a Do you live a healthy life? Ask your neighbour these questions.

1. Do you exercise regularly?
2. Do you eat healthy food?
3. Do you sleep well?
4. Do you find it easy to relax?
5. Do you enjoy life?

b Read these statements and tell your neighbour whether you agree with them or not. Explain why.

1. Eating meat is unhealthy.
2. Too much exercise is bad for you.
3. Fresh fruit is bad for old people.
4. Dairy products are good for children.
5. Vegetarians find it difficult to concentrate for long.

4 a Explain the following words to your neighbour by describing what you use them for: safety pin - scissors - bandage - plastic gloves

b What would you take with you if you were going on holiday to India. You are allowed 10 things in your suitcase. When you've made your list, compare it with your neighbour's. Explain why you need all 10 items on your list.

1. _____
2. _____
3. _____
4. _____
5. _____
6. _____
7. _____
8. _____
9. _____
10. _____

5 a What do you do for a living? Ask your neighbour to explain briefly what the following people do for a living: nurse - teacher - chef - receptionist - policeman

b Now ask your neighbour these questions.

1. What do you do for a living?
2. Which branch do you work in?
3. Do you ever have to work at weekends?
4. Do you work in a factory?
5. What activities does your work involve?

6 a Here are 3 job adverts.

Secretary	Computer Programmer	Sales Assistant
International Company is looking for a hard working and ambitious person. Must have computer experience. Typewriting and shorthand skills required. Knowledge of French preferred. £13 K p.a. Apply in writing to: ILC International 19-23 Port Road Truro *The Independent 29.04.96*	Graduate required with 3 years computing experience. Contract for 18 months. £17 K p.a. CV's to Intact Computing Ltd 13 Fordway London W3 2BR *The Times 29.04.96*	Part time sales assistant required for electrical goods shop. Sales experience required. 3 days a week and every second Saturday. £3.50 per hour. Send CV to: The Manager Robsons Electrical Shop 29-33 Pool Street Durham DH3 49P *The Guardian 29.04.96*

Your neighbour has applied to you for one of the jobs and you are going to interview him/her. Before you start, think about the questions you will ask and the information you need to know. Here are a few ideas.

languages - skills - work experience - education - own transport - possible overtime

6 b You need some items for your office. Decide what you need and fill in order form A. (Make up the details). When you are finished, ring your neighbour and place your order. Write down your neighbour's order on form B and then compare your work.

Order Form A

Customer Name _____

Customer Address _____

_____

Date _____

Order No	Description	Quantity	Price

Total ....

+ VAT @ 17½% ....

Grand Total ....

Order Form B

Customer Name _____

Customer Address _____

_____

Date _____

Order No	Description	Quantity	Price

Total ....

+ VAT @ 17½% ....

Grand Total ....

Robson's Electricentre

68 Commercial Street
Dundee
DD1 2AB
Tel 01382 26437
Fax 01382 26451

Tony Robson
Managing Director

7 a Here are 3 business cards. Ask your neighbour at least 5 questions about them.

Far End Bookshop
99 Harcourt Street
DUBLIN 2

Tel 01-5716554
Fax 01-5715923

Mark Rickwood
Sales Manager

PCL Software Solutions

6 Davy Way
Llay
Wrexham
Clydd   LL12 0PG
Tel 01978 242424 / Fax 01978 255552

Bridget Heale
Financial Manager

b You have been invited to the opening of a customer's new premises. Work in groups of 6. You have to socialise with the others. If you have any business cards with you, use them and give them to the people when you are introducing yourself.

8 **a** Work with your neighbour. You want to send a parcel to your penfriend in England. What happens to the parcel after you take it to the post office?

Here are some words which may help:

delivered   weighed   stacked   sorted
tied together   emptied   loaded   taken away

b Can you think of anything in your place of work...

1 which is emptied?
2 which is collected?
3 which is sorted?
4 which is weighed?
5 which is cleaned?
6 which is checked?
7 which is filed away?
8 which is wrapped?
9 which is tied together?
10 which is delivered?

9 **a** Read the following situations. You are going to make a telephone call to your neighbour, so sit back to back.

1 *You have received the translation of your company brochure to check, but there are several mistakes. Telephone the company and explain the mistakes. The post code should read NH5 2LP, not NH5 2LB. The telephone area code should have a '1' in front of it, so should be (01978). The address is 19a, not 19, and your surname is also wrongly spelt.*

2 *You are arranging some interviews for next week for a position in your company. Your neighbour has applied for the job. Ring him/her and arrange a time, place and date. You will probably have to give directions.*

3 *You have a meeting with Simon Parker tomorrow but your car has broken down. Telephone him and explain the situation and rearrange the meeting.*

4 *You have just received a delivery from Armstrong's Stationery. There are several mistakes in the order including 500 red pens which you didn't order, fax rolls which are the wrong size, as well as incorrect quantities. Ring your neighbour and complain. Find out when you can expect the missing articles.*

5 *Your boss has just informed you that you will have to work late tonight. You had arranged to go out for a meal with your boyfriend/girlfriend. Ring your boyfriend/girlfriend and explain the situation.*

10 **a** You are going to tell your neighbour about yourself. See if you can talk for at least 5 minutes. Here are some topics to help you.

- the medical service in your country
- common illnesses, what advice you should give and why
- health and healthy living
- what you do for a living
- your ideal job
- your work experience

UNIT 41

What was your favourite subject at school?

1 a Which subjects did you learn at school? Look at the subjects listed below and put a tick (✓) next to the subjects you learnt at school.

Biology ☐	Geography ☐	English ☐	Business Studies ☐
French ☐	Economics ☐	Maths ☐	Religious Studies ☐
History ☐	Law ☐	Sport ☐	Swimming ☐
Spanish ☐	Typing ☐	Chemistry ☐	Metalwork ☐
Psychology ☐	Computing ☐	Physics ☐	Politics ☐
Music ☐	Art ☐	Cookery ☐	Technical Drawing ☐
Woodwork ☐	Sewing ☐	Shorthand ☐	Astronomy ☐

b Ask your neighbour and then complete the following sentences.

We both learnt _____ at school.

Neither of us learnt _____ at school.

I learnt _____ , but my neighbour didn't.

My neighbour learnt _____ , but I didn't.

c Answer the following questions in note form, then ask your neighbour.

1. Which was your favourite subject at school? _____ .
2. Why was this your favourite subject? _____ .
3. Which was your least favourite subject? _____ .
4. Why was this your least favourite subject? _____ .
5. Who was the best teacher you have ever had? _____ .
6. Why was he/she the best teacher you have ever had? _____ .
7. Who was the worst teacher you have ever had? _____ .
8. Why was he/she the worst teacher you have ever had? _____ .
9. Which subjects did you study for your school leaving examinations? _____ .
10. What time did school start and finish? _____ .

d Jacqueline is 15 and is a schoolgirl. Her mum, Lilian, is 42 and works in a supermarket. Look at the sentences below. Who do you think is speaking, Jacqueline or Lilian?

1. I learnt history and physics at school.
2. I'm going to do french and maths next year.
3. I went to school for 10 years.
4. School started at 9am and finished at 3.30pm.
5. My least favourite subject was chemistry.
6. I'm learning biology.
7. I've been going to school for 10 years.
8. We don't have school on Saturdays.
9. I didn't do economics.
10. My favourite subject at school is maths.

2 a   Here is the weekly timetable for class 5b. You are going to hear a cassette informing you of some changes. Before you listen to the cassette ask your neighbour these questions and then make up 5 more questions.

eg   What do 5b have at 1310 on Friday? English in Room 21.

1   What time is French on Wednesday?
2   What is first two on Friday?
3   Who teaches history?
4   When is Mrs Wheeler teaching?
5   Which room is computing in?

Now listen to the cassette and make the changes.

	TIMETABLE CLASS 5b				
	MON	**TUE**	**WED**	**THUR**	**FRI**
09:10 - 09:45	English Room 21 Miss Fisher	Biology Room 35 Mrs Lambard	French Room 17 Mr Normand	Maths Room 10 Mrs Wheeler	Swimming Pool Miss Brown
09:45 - 10:20	English Room 21 Miss Fisher	Biology Room 35 Mrs Lambard	Geography Room 06 Miss Crosfield	Computing Room 09 Mr Graham	Swimming Pool Miss Brown
10:20 - 10:35	**B**	**R**	**E**	**A**	**K**
10:35 - 11:10	Computing Room 09 Mr Graham	French Room 17 Mr Normand	Maths Room 10 Mrs Wheeler	History Room 12 Mr Bell	French Room 17 Mr Normand
11:10 - 11:45	Maths Room 10 Mrs Wheeler	Computing Room 09 Mr Graham	English Room 21 Miss Fisher	Geography Room 06 Miss Crosfield	Maths Room 10 Mrs Wheeler
11:45 - 13:10	**L**	**U**	**N**	**C**	**H**
13:10 - 13:45	French Room 17 Mr Normand	Physics Room 32 Mr Middleton	Sport Hall Mr Johnson	Chemistry Room 33 Mr Marshall	English Room 21 Miss Fisher
13:45 - 14:20	History Room 12 Mr Bell	Physics Room 32 Mr Middleton	Sport Hall Mr Johnson	Chemistry Room 33 Mr Marshall	Computing Room 09 Mr Graham
14:20 - 14:55	Chemistry Room 33 Mr Marshall	Geography Room 06 Miss Crosfield	Physics Room 32 Mr Middleton	Music Room 29 Miss Reid	History Room 12 Mr Bell
14:55 - 15:30	Chemistry Room 33 Mr Marshall	Geography Room 06 Miss Crosfield	Physics Room 32 Mr Middleton	Music Room 29 Miss Reid	History Room 12 Mr Bell

b   Read these words and phrases. Would you say them when you agree(✓), when you're unsure (?), or when you disagree (x)? Compare with your neighbour.

___ I don't think so   ___ of course   ___ perhaps   ___ it depends   ___ definitely
___ of course not   ___ certainly not   ___ I agree   ___ I suppose so   ___ definitely not
___ I think so   ___ certainly   ___ I'm not sure   ___ I don't agree ___ sometimes

c   Work in groups of 3. Look at the statements and ask your neighbour.

eg   *Do you think that all children should learn English at school?*
       Yes definitely. I think it's important to be able to speak English.
       I agree with you. It's much harder to learn a language when you're working.

1   All children should learn English in school.
2   All children should learn maths in school.
3   Naughty children should be smacked.
4   It's easier to teach 10 year olds than to teach 16 year olds.
5   Bad exam results are because of bad teaching.
6   Children should be able to choose which classes they go to.
7   Teachers should be paid more.
8   Parents should be able to choose which school their children go to.
9   Classes should be no more than 15 pupils.
10 Education should be free.

3 a Listen to the cassette and fill in the missing information on the CV.

C V

Surname _____			**First Name** _____	
Address 27 Park Avenue			**Tel No** _____	
Blackpool _____			**Date of Birth** October 12 _____	

Education

Name and Address of Institute	From	To	Qualifications
Fylde Primary School, Blackpool	1965	____	
Queen Elizabeth Middle School, St Annes	____	1972	
Fylde High School, Blackpool	1972	____	____ 'O' Levels and
			3 'A' Levels _____
Leeds University, Leeds	____	1981	BSc _____

Work Experience

Name and Address of Employer	From	To	Position
Holdsworth Electronics, Skipton	1981	____	_____
Holdsworth Electronics, Skipton	____	1988	Sales Manager
Strathdale Systems, Halifax	____	now	General Manager

Skills and Languages _____

Hobbies and Interests Skiing _____

---

b Now fill in one of the forms below about yourself. When you've finished ask your neighbour and fill in the details on the other form.

Surname _____	First Name _____	
Address _____	Tel No _____	
_____	Date of Birth _____	
_____		

Education

Name/Address of Institute	From	To	Qualifications

Work Experience

Name/Address of Employer	From	To	Position

Skills and Languages _____

Hobbies and Interests _____

Surname _____	First Name _____	
Address _____	Tel No _____	
_____	Date of Birth _____	
_____		

Education

Name/Address of Institute	From	To	Qualifications

Work Experience

Name/Address of Employer	From	To	Position

Skills and Languages _____

Hobbies and Interests _____

4 a Translate the following.

Vocabulary

biology _____
history _____
psychology _____
woodwork _____
economics _____
law _____
typing _____
computing _____
art _____
maths _____
chemistry _____
physics _____
shorthand _____
business studies _____
religious studies _____
swimming _____
metalwork _____
politics _____
technical drawing _____
astronomy _____
favourite _____
least favourite _____
best _____
worst _____

certainly not _____
I suppose so _____
I'm not sure _____
I agree _____
certainly _____
I don't agree _____
of course _____
perhaps _____
definitely _____
definitely not _____
I don't think so _____
of course not _____
I think so _____
naughty _____
to be smacked _____
results _____
surname _____
date of birth _____
institute _____
qualifications _____
work experience _____
manager _____
languages _____

Structures

We both learnt biology, chemistry and maths. _____
Neither of us learnt woodwork. _____
I learnt economics but my neighbour didn't. _____
My neighbour learnt technical drawing but I didn't. _____
What do 5b have at 1310 on Friday? _____
English in Room 21. _____
Do you think that all children should learn English at school? _____
Yes definitely. _____
It's very important to be able to speak English. _____
I agree with you. _____
It's much harder to learn a language when you're working. _____

UNIT 42

How long have you been learning English?

1 **a** Look at the questionnaire below. Fill in your details.

Language Learning Background

1 **Did you learn English at school?** No ☐ Yes ☐
How many years of English did you have? _____

2 **Since leaving school have you taken part in any English courses?** No ☐ Yes ☐
Name of Institute(s) _____
Number of hours of course _____
Qualification _____

3 **Have you ever been on holiday to an English speaking country?** No ☐ Yes ☐
How often? _____
Which country(ies)? _____
How long did you stay? _____
When was the last time? _____

4 **Do you have any English speaking penfriends?** No ☐ Yes ☐
How many? _____
What nationality are they? _____
How often do you write? _____

5 **Do you have any English speaking friends?** No ☐ Yes ☐
How often do you speak with them? _____

6 **Do you ever listen to music in English?** No ☐ Yes ☐
What is your favourite group? _____

7 **Do you ever listen to English radio?** No ☐ Yes ☐
Which radio station? _____

8 **Do you ever watch TV or films in English?** No ☐ Yes ☐
How often? _____

9 **Are you a member of any English speaking society?** No ☐ Yes ☐
How often do you meet? _____
How long have you been a member? _____

10 **What do you think is the best way of learning English?**
living in an English speaking country ☐   going to language school in your country ☐
other ☐

---

b Now ask your neighbour about his/her English background.

c Tell your teacher about yourself.

d Complete the following sentence about yourself and then ask your neighbour.

eg *How long have you been learning English?*
I've been learning English for .... years.

2 a You are spending a year abroad at Nottingham University to improve your English. Look at the map of the campus opposite and ask your neighbour these questions.

1 Which hall is on my right when I come in from the West Entrance?
2 Which is the best entrance if I want to go to the computing centre?
3 How do you get from the sports centre to the arts centre?
4 How many book shops are there and where are they?
5 Which residential hall is nearest to the library?

b Now ask your neighbour 5 more questions.

eg Where is Derby Hall?
    It's on Beeston Lane between Sherwood Hall and Lincoln Hall.

c Today is your first day at Nottingham University and the foreign student coordinator is about to give you some information. Tick (✓) the information you think you will hear.

- [ ] The name of the foreign student coordinator.
- [ ] The telephone number of the foreign student coordinator.
- [ ] How to register with the University Administration Department.
- [ ] How to register with the Students' Union.
- [ ] Which hall you are staying in.
- [ ] How to meet people.
- [ ] Which bus to take into Nottingham city centre.
- [ ] How to register at the library.
- [ ] How to register at the health centre.
- [ ] Opening times of the sports centre.
- [ ] Opening times of the computing centre.
- [ ] Days and times of your lectures.
- [ ] Where and when your next meeting will take place.

d Listen to the cassette. Did you hear what you expected?

e Listen again and make notes and then tell your neighbour.

eg I heard the number 251 but I'm not sure what it was for.

✎ **Notes**

f Ask your neighbour these questions.

1 Where is the University Administration Department?
2 What do I need £10 for?
3 When is the library open?
4 What do I need to take with me to the health centre?
5 Where am I ringing if I dial 273?

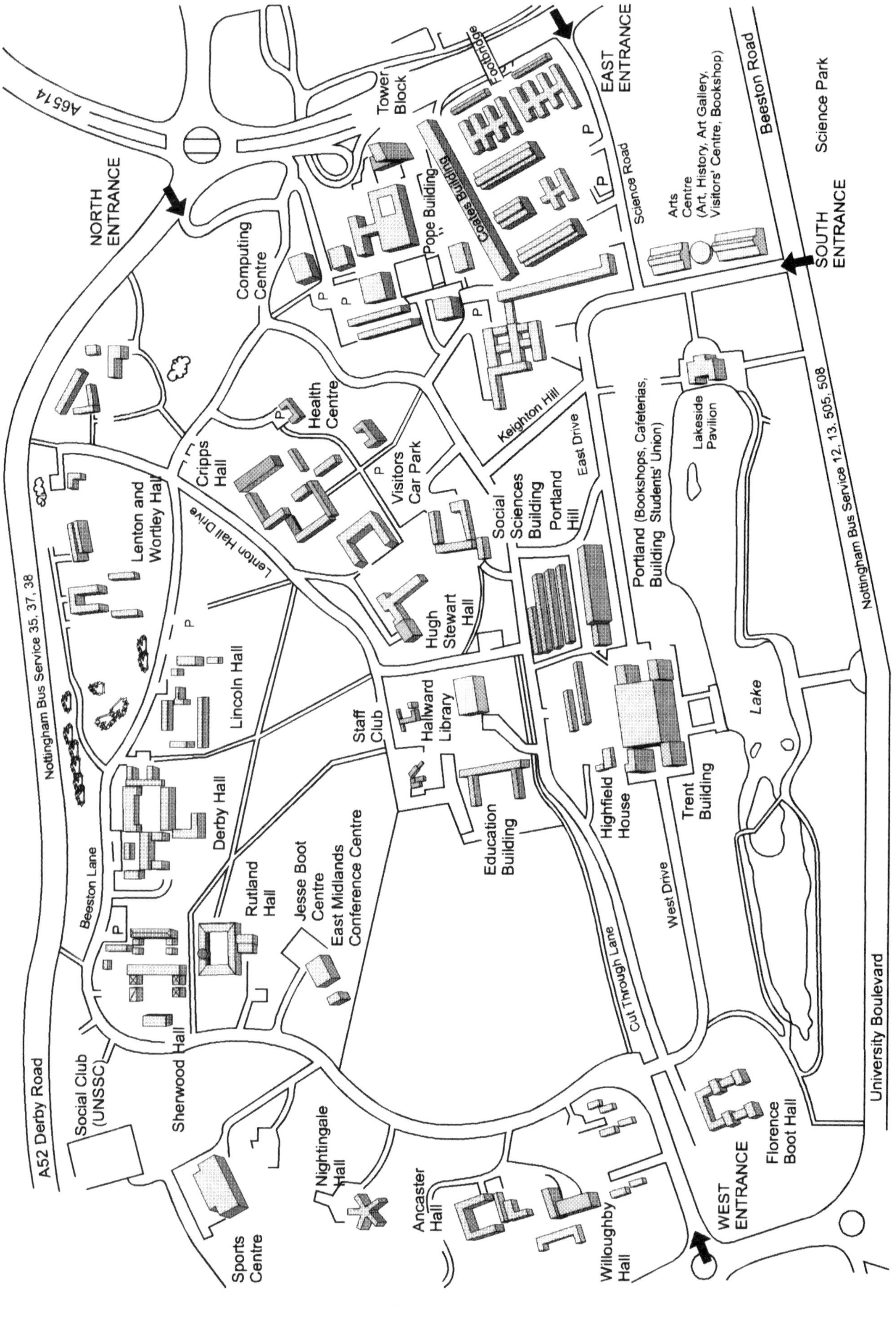
A52 Derby Road
Nottingham Bus Service 35, 37, 38
A6514
NORTH ENTRANCE
Social Club (UNSSC)
Beeston Lane
Lenton and Wortley Hall
Sherwood Hall
Derby Hall
Lincoln Hall
Sports Centre
Rutland Hall
Lenton Hall Drive
Cripps Hall
Computing Centre
Jesse Boot Centre
East Midlands Conference Centre
Nightingale Hall
Health Centre
Staff Club
Visitors Car Park
Tower Block
Ancaster Hall
Hallward Library
Hugh Stewart Hall
Pope Building
Coates Building
Education Building
Social Sciences Building
Keighton Hill
Footbridge
Portland Hill
East Drive
Willoughby Hall
Highfield House
Cut Through Lane
EAST ENTRANCE
Science Road
Portland Building (Bookshops, Cafeterias, Students' Union)
West Drive
Trent Building
Lakeside Pavilion
Arts Centre (Art, History, Art Gallery, Visitors' Centre, Bookshop)
WEST ENTRANCE
Lake
Florence Boot Hall
Beeston Road
SOUTH ENTRANCE
Science Park
Nottingham Bus Service 12, 13, 505, 508
University Boulevard
P

3 **a** You are on a full time training course which has a 3 month work experience placement. You would like to do your work experience placement in the UK. Read the questions and find the answers in the information below as quickly as possible.

eg *What is the name of the company? European Language Skills.*

1. Can I write my letter of application in French? _____
2. Who do European Language Skills bank with? _____
3. How many copies of my CV do I have to send? _____
4. What size do the photographs have to be? _____
5. How much do I have to send with the registration form? _____
6. Do I have to send a letter of application? _____
7. What language do the details of my current training programme have to be in? _____
8. When does the company have to receive all my details? _____
9. What is the bank account number of the company? _____
10. How much do I have to pay 21 days before I start my work placement? _____

Application for Work Experience in the UK

Introduction

European Language Skills is a London based training organisation servicing the European and International business communities in the field of UK Work Experience Placements, Language Learning and Commercial and Cultural Orientation.

In the area of Work Experience Placements, we enjoy official recognition from several key organisations including the London Chamber of Commerce and Industry, of which we are a registered examinations centre, and the Conseil Régional Ile de France.

Over the years we have developed a highly professional service that seeks to satisfy the specific demands of trainees in their search for challenging on the job assignments at an international level. Close attention is paid to individual needs, to the business activity for which trainees are being prepared, and to the sector of industry or commerce in which they would wish to put to good use their newly acquired skills.

For our part, and in order to satisfy all these needs, trainees are encouraged to put their placement dossier together in a very precise and professional manner. Guidelines on how this may be achieved are provided opposite.

Your Dossier

In order to process your application effectively, our Placement Officers need to receive the following items from you **at least 8 weeks** prior to commencement of the placement:

1. **A comprehensive CV** (4 copies) We enclose a *model CV* which will serve as a guide when elaborating your own. This should be as detailed as possible. The more we know about your education, training, English language ability and professional experience, the easier it is to find you a **tailor-made** placement.

2. **A passport size photograph** (x 4) Please look smart and don't forget to say *cheese*!

3. **A letter of application** This should be in English and should briefly describe (a) the training programme you are currently attending, (b) what you hope to achieve while on placement in a UK company, and (c) your professional aspirations for the future.

4. **Details of your current training programme** Your training organisation, college or university will provide you with a programme syllabus. UK companies will require a brief summary, **in English**, of this syllabus.

With this four-fold contribution, we can help to ensure that your placement period in the UK is a worthwhile and satisfying experience.

Placement Fees

1. Our placement fee is **£260**. This is paid in two instalments.
   i. Placement Administration Fee £60 (non refundable). This sum should be sent with your Placement Registration Form.
   ii. **£200** is due **21 days** before the commencement of your work experience placement.

Payment should be made by direct transfer to: **European Language Skills**

Details for direct bank transfer of fees.   Account Number 19815573
Sorting Code 60-50-09
National Westminster Bank, 50 Ilford Hill, Ilford, IG1 2AP, ESSEX, England

3   **b**   Now ask your neighbour for his/her details and fill in the application form.

European Language Skills Roman House 9/10 College Terrace LONDON E3 5AN	
PLACEMENT REGISTRATION FORM	
Trainee's Name:	
Address:	
Post Code:	
Tel No:	
Training Organisation:	
Address:	
Post Code:	
Tel No:	
When Would You Like to Train?	
From: To:	
In Which Field/Sector Would You Like to Train?	

Accommodation	
	Yes/No
Do you require family accommodation?	
Hotel	
Guest House	

Registration Check List	
Before returning this registration form, together with all the documents requested for your placement please complete the following check list by ticking (✓) the appropriate box.	
4 copies of CV	
4 photographs (passport size)	
Letter of Application	
Details of your current Training Programme	
Placement Administration Fee: £60 (non-refundable)	
This Registration Form	

   c   Look at the following questions and discuss your answers with your neighbour.

1   Have you ever worked abroad? If so, where, when and why?
2   Would you like to work abroad? Why (not)?
3   In which country would you like to work? Why?
4   In which country wouldn't you like to work? Why?
5   If you worked abroad for 3 months, what do you think you would miss most?

4 a Translate the following.

Vocabulary

questionnaire _____	surfing _____
English speaking _____	playing chess _____
penfriend _____	debating _____
group _____	student card _____
radio station _____	health centre _____
member _____	health insurance _____
society _____	squash courts _____
foreign student _____	badminton courts _____
coordinator _____	fitness rooms _____
to register _____	essay _____
administration department _____	print-out _____
Students' Union _____	training course _____
registration fees _____	placement _____
noticeboards _____	dossier _____
societies _____	placement fee _____
clubs _____	

Structures

How long have you been learning English? _____

I've been learning English for 10 years. _____

Did you learn English at school? _____

Yes I did. _____

No I didn't. _____

Since leaving school have you taken part in any English courses? _____

Yes I have. _____

No I haven't. _____

Do you have any English speaking pen friends? _____

Yes I do. _____

No I don't. _____

Are you a member of any English speaking society? _____

Yes I am. _____

No I'm not. _____

I heard the number 251 but I'm not sure what it was for. _____

What is the name of the company? _____

UNIT 43

Why are you learning English?

1   **a**   Fill in the questionnaire below about yourself.

Needs Analysis - You

1. **Why are you learning English?**
   - ☐ for my job   ☐ for pleasure   ☐ other

2. **Put the following skills in order of importance:**
   (1 = I need this the most / 4 = I need this the least)
   - ☐ speaking   ☐ listening   ☐ reading   ☐ writing

3. **Put the following in order of difficulty:**
   (1 = I find this the most difficult / 4 = I find this the easiest)
   - ☐ speaking   ☐ listening   ☐ reading   ☐ writing

4. **Speaking Skills. Put a tick in any boxes where you have to speak English.**
   - ☐ face-to-face (with one other person)
   - ☐ face-to-face (with a group of people)
   - ☐ on the telephone

5. **Listening Skills. Put a tick in any boxes where you need to listen to English.**
   - ☐ face-to-face (with one other person)   ☐ face-to-face (with a group of people)
   - ☐ on the telephone   ☐ cassettes/videos   ☐ radio programmes

6. **Reading Skills. Put a tick in any box where you have to read English texts.**
   - ☐ letters/faxes   ☐ notices   ☐ books/newspapers

7. **Writing Skills. Put a tick in any box where you have to write in English.**
   - ☐ forms   ☐ letters/faxes   ☐ notes/memos

8. **Which of the following describes you best?**
   - ☐ I speak English slowly but the grammar is correct.
   - ☐ I speak English quickly but I make mistakes in grammar.

9. **Which of the following is true for you?**
   - ☐ I find it easier to speak English to classmates than to other people.
   - ☐ I find it easier to speak English to other people than to classmates.

10. **How will you continue learning English after this course?** _____
    _____
    _____
    _____

---

b   Tell your teacher about yourself.

eg   *I'm learning English for my job.*
Speaking is the most important skill for me.
Writing is the least important.

2 a Now find out about your neighbour and fill in the needs analysis below.

Needs Analysis - Your Neighbour

1. **Why are you learning English?**
   ☐ for my job   ☐ for pleasure   ☐ other

2. **Put the following skills in order of importance:**
   (1 = I need this the most / 4 = I need this the least)
   ☐ speaking   ☐ listening   ☐ reading   ☐ writing

3. **Put the following in order of difficulty:**
   (1 = I find this the most difficult / 4 = I find this the easiest)
   ☐ speaking   ☐ listening   ☐ reading   ☐ writing

4. **Speaking Skills.** Put a tick in any boxes where you have to speak English.
   ☐ face-to-face (with one other person)
   ☐ face-to-face (with a group of people)
   ☐ on the telephone

5. **Listening Skills.** Put a tick in any boxes where you need to listen to English.
   ☐ face-to-face (with one other person)   ☐ face-to-face (with a group of people)
   ☐ on the telephone   ☐ cassettes/videos   ☐ radio programmes

6. **Reading Skills.** Put a tick in any box where you have to read English texts.
   ☐ letters/faxes   ☐ notices   ☐ books/newspapers

7. **Writing Skills.** Put a tick in any box where you have to write in English.
   ☐ forms   ☐ letters/faxes   ☐ notes/memos

8. **Which of the following describes you best?**
   ☐ I speak English slowly but the grammar is correct.
   ☐ I speak English quickly but I make mistakes in grammar.

9. **Which of the following is true for you?**
   ☐ I find it easier to speak English to classmates than to other people.
   ☐ I find it easier to speak English to other people than to classmates.

10. **How will you continue learning English after this course?** _____
    _____
    _____
    _____

---

b Tell your teacher about your neighbour.

eg *She's learning English because she's going on holiday to the USA.
Speaking and listening are the most important so she can ask for things.
She finds listening the most difficult because people speak so quickly.
She may have to speak on the phone and she'll definitely have to speak with people face-to-face.*

3 a You want to improve your English and have decided to do a language course in your summer holidays. Look at the adverts below and answer these questions.

1. What is the name of the company in Ireland?
2. Where is Perthshire?
3. Where does Mr Lord work?
4. What is the telephone number for the Maraid Language Institute?
5. Who do I stay with in Ireland?
6. Who do I stay with in Scotland?
7. Who offers English for Communication?
8. Who offers English for Special Purposes?
9. What is the address to write to in Ireland?
10. What social activities are offered in Scotland?

Learn English in the Heart of the Highlands

Why not improve your English and enjoy yourself at the same time. We put together a programme of formal study tailored to your needs and offer a programme of activities allowing you to enjoy the natural beauty of the Highlands and practise socialising in English at the same time.

- one-to-one tuition
- English for Special Purposes
- tailored programme
- qualified teacher
- living in the teacher's house
- golf
- visit to whisky distillery
- trip to Highland Games
- evening in a pub
- walking
- traditional food

For more information, contact: *Mr A Lord, Balloch House Language School, Pitlochry, PL24 9ZJ, Perthshire, Scotland*

Come to Ireland

- 2 and 3-week language courses.
- English language
- English for Communication
- English for Special Purposes
- Anglo-Irish literature

Small classes ☆ Practical Courses

Social Programmes ☆ Host Family ☆ All Levels

Maraid Language Institute
25 Donnybrook Road
Donnybrook
Dublin 4
Tel 353 1 6605522
Fax 353 1 6605523

---

b Which course do you think is better for you? Why? Tell your neighbour.

eg I think the course in Ireland is better for me because I want to learn in a class.

c Read the letter below and underline the correct verb form.

Dear Sirs

I saw/have seen your advertisement for 2 and 3-week language courses in the Times yesterday.

I work/worked for a large, international company and I need/needed English in my job. I regularly have to go to meetings where English is speaking/spoken and I find that I do not understood/understand everything. I also feel/felt that I am making/make a lot of mistakes in grammar when I am speaking/I speak.

I am very interested in the 'English for Communication' course advertised and would like to do a 2 week course from 17 August to 28 August.

I learnt/have been learning English in school for 8 years when I was younger and learn/have been learning in an evening class for the last 6 months.

Please could you send me information and prices for the above course.

I look forward to hearing from you.

Yours faithfully

A J Faisel

AJ Faisel (Mr)

---

d Write a letter in reply to one of the advertisements asking for information about their courses.

4 a Translate the following.

Vocabulary

needs analysis _____

for pleasure _____

speaking _____

listening _____

reading _____

writing _____

face-to-face _____

faxes _____

notices _____

forms _____

heart _____

Highlands _____

to enjoy yourself _____

formal study _____

tailored _____

activities _____

natural _____

beauty _____

socialising _____

one-to-one tuition _____

English for Special Purposes _____

qualified teacher _____

small classes _____

social programme _____

host family _____

all levels _____

prices _____

Structures

Why are you learning English? _____

I'm learning English for my job. _____

Speaking is the most important skill for me. _____

Writing is the least important skill for me. _____

She's learning English because she's going on holiday to the USA. _____

Speaking and listening are the most important. _____

She finds listening the most difficult. _____

People speak too quickly. _____

She may have to speak on the phone. _____

She'll definitely have to speak to people face-to-face. _____

Which do you think is better, and why? _____

I think the course in Ireland is better for me. _____

Dear Sirs _____

Please could you send me information. _____

I look forward to hearing from you. _____

Yours faithfully _____

UNIT 44

I don't have time to learn vocabulary.

1 a Read the following statements and put a 'T' next to them if you think they are true for you, or an 'F' if you think they are false.

1 I like working with my neighbour and testing each other on new vocabulary. ___
2 I write down new words again and again until I can remember them. ___
3 I say the words aloud when I'm learning them. ___
4 I put the words in a sentence and try to remember full sentences. ___
5 I write down how to say new words (eg through = thru). ___
6 I can remember short words better than long words. ___
7 There are some words which I can never remember ___
   (tell your neighbour what they are, if you can).
8 I try to categorise new vocabulary with groups of words I already know. ___
9 I record words and sentences on to a cassette and listen to them in the car. ___
10 I don't have time to learn vocabulary. ___

b Compare your answers with 4 or 5 other neighbours. Who put 'T' next to the same statements as you? Do you have other ways of learning vocabulary? Who do most people think learns vocabulary the easiest? How does he/she learn vocabulary?

c Look at the words in box A. You can group the words into furniture (chair, bed, cupboard), languages (Spanish, English, French), and animals (horse, cat, rabbit). You can also group the words into words with one syllable (chair, bed, French, horse, cat) and words with two syllables (cupboard, Spanish, English, rabbit). You can also group the words into words containing the letter 'e' (bed, English, French, horse) and words containing the letter 'a' (chair, cupboard, Spanish, cat, rabbit). Look at the words in boxes B-E and see how many groups of words you can make.

A	chair bed Spanish horse English cat rabbit French cupboard
B	tin Denmark cabbage onions Belgium England apples packet jar
C	apple black advert boat car accident coat bag catch
D	easy boring interesting empty difficult black full tall white short
E	kettle bedroom bathroom ferry saucepan taxi hall bus pot

Compare your categories with your neighbour.

d Look at the words in box A and write down 3 other words which you associate with them. Do the same for the words in boxes B - E.

A	next year
B	work
C	happy
D	doctor
E	English

e Now tell your neighbour why you chose these words.

f Close your book and see how many words you can remember from exercise c. Compare with your neighbour. See if you can remember the words your neighbour always forgets.

2 a The following 5 people are all learning English. What do you think motivates them? What do you think they want to learn? Do you think that speaking, listening, reading, or writing is most important for them? What kind of vocabulary and phrases do you think they will need? Discuss your answers with your neighbour.

1 A 15 year old girl going on an exchange visit to Britain.
2 A business man representing his company in meetings abroad.
3 A 65 year old man who wants to visit his English speaking grandchildren.
4 A traffic controller at Mexico City Airport.
5 A doctor who is going to an international conference.

b Do you have a grammar book which explains English grammar in your language? What's it called? Which grammar books do other students have? Which do you find easiest to use?

c Now look at the following sentences and underline the correct form.

1 I telephoned/have telephoned him yesterday.
2 I went not/didn't go to the cinema last night.
3 He work/works every day.
4 She is talking/talks on the phone at the moment.
5 She is going/goes to see the doctor tomorrow.

d This time you have to produce the correct form.

1 I (work) _____ here since 1967.
2 In 1992 I (get) _____ a new job.
3 He (get up) _____ at 6 o'clock every morning.
4 She (not watch) _____ TV last night.
5 We (speak) _____ English now.

e Now put the correct preposition in the space (on, in or at).

1 _____ Tuesday
2 _____ 10 August
3 _____ 3 o'clock
4 _____ 24 October
5 _____ September

f Look at the sentences and tell your neighbour the negative form and the question form.

eg I work on Saturdays. I don't work on Saturdays. Do you work on Saturdays?

1 He plays football.
2 I go swimming on Saturdays.
3 We learn English on Wednesday evenings.
4 I drink coffee with milk.
5 She likes pizza.

g Ask your neighbour what he/she normally does on a Saturday. Make notes and then tell your teacher.

h Look at the picture and tell your neighbour about Jack using the notes below.

> Jack - works at Smedley's Supermarket, plays football every Sunday morning, goes to the cinema every Sunday evening, girlfriend's name is Karen.

i Look back through this book and discuss the following questions with your neighbour.

1 Which Unit did you find the most interesting? Why?
2 Which activity did you find the most interesting? Why?
3 Which Unit did you find the most boring? Why?
4 Which activity did you find the most boring? Why?
5 Which Units did you find the most difficult? Why?

3 a Heidi Fetzer took part in an English course last summer in London. Look at her diary and tell your neighbour about her week in London.

	Sun May 29	Monday	Tuesday	Wednesday	Thursday	Friday	Saturday
Morning	Arrived Heathrow 1030. Bus to hotel "Park View" - nice hotel.	First day of course - 10 people in my class.	Roleplays in the morning.	Everybody gave presentation - very interesting - lots of ideas to learn English better.	Made video in class.	Visited Madame Tussauds.	Went shopping - expensive!
Afternoon	Roast beef, carrots and potatoes for tea.	Practised Introductions - watched a video.	Played quiz-game in the afternoon.	Trip into London.	Showed our video to other classes and watched theirs.	Did a test and was given a certificate.	
Evening	Phoned home to say all okay.	After school - coffee with people from course - did homework.	Homework - prepare for presentation "What I do to improve my English".	Theatre - Cats. Enjoyed it very much.	Giovanni's birthday - went to restaurant 'Hollywood Planet' to celebrate - late to bed.	End of course party.	17:30 leave Heathrow - Flight BA 572 home. Mum and Dad collected me.

eg Heidi arrived in Heathrow on Sunday May 29 at 1030. She took the bus from Heathrow to her hotel. The hotel was called 'Park View' and she thought it was a nice hotel.

b Ask your neighbour about Heidi's week.

eg What did she do on Friday morning? She visited Madame Tussaud's with the rest of her class.

c What do you do to improve your English between lessons? Discuss with your neighbour and make a list of 3 things you both do to improve your English. Tell the rest of the class.

d When Heidi was back in Austria she started going to an evening class. At first she didn't think that she was improving so she started to keep records. Here is a card she filled out. Ask your neighbour questions.

eg Was the lesson on Tuesday November 14 a good lesson? Yes. It was a good lesson, probably because she was in a good mood.

DATE *Tuesday November 14*

1 Hello Heidi. How are you feeling today? ☑ I'm in a good mood   ☐ I'm in a bad mood
2 How was your English lesson? ☑ good   ☐ bad
3 Why was it good/bad? *I prepared the lesson so I understood everything and spoke a lot.*
4 Which skills did you practise? ☑ listening   ☑ speaking   ☑ reading   ☐ writing
5 What can you do better now? *My listening skills are improving.*
6 What can you do now that you couldn't before? *Tell the chemist what's the matter with me.*
7 When are you going to do your homework? *I'll try to do it on Thursday.*
8 What are you going to do before the next lesson?
   ☑ listen to the cassette again   ☑ learn vocabulary from this lesson
   ☐ learn structures from this lesson   ☐ listen to English radio
   ☐ read English newspapers   ☑ meet classmates to practise
9 When are you going to review this? *Sunday afternoon.*
10 When are you going to prepare for the next lesson? *Probably Tuesday afternoon.*

---

e Ask your neighbour the questions and then make some cards for yourself. Fill them out at the end of each lesson and keep a record of your improvement.

4 a Translate the following.

Vocabulary

to test _____	to represent _____
to say aloud _____	abroad _____
to categorise _____	traffic controller _____
exchange visit _____	activity _____
businessman _____	mood _____

Structures

Which Unit did you find the most interesting? _____

I found Unit 32 the most interesting because I like sailing. _____

Which activity did you find the most interesting? _____

I found writing a CV the most interesting because I need a CV in English. _____

Which Unit did you find the most boring? _____

I found Unit 32 the most boring because I don't like sailing. _____

Which activity did you find the most boring? _____

Heidi arrived in Heathrow on Sunday May 29 at 1030. _____

She took the bus from Heathrow to her hotel. _____

The hotel was called 'Park View'. _____

She thought it was a nice hotel. _____

What did she do on Friday morning? _____

She visited Madame Tussauds. _____

How are you feeling today? _____

How was your English lesson? _____

Why was it good/bad? _____

Which skills did you practise? _____

What can you do better now? _____

What can you do that you couldn't do before? _____

When are you going to do your homework? _____

What are you going to do before the next lesson? _____

When are you going to review this Unit? _____

When are you going to look up the vocabulary for the next lesson? _____

UNIT 45

What do you do in your spare time?

1 a Look at the pictures and describe the people to your neighbour. What do you think they like doing in their spare time?

Andy

Freda

Sandra

b Read the following sentences. Is the second person agreeing (✓) or disagreeing (x) or uncertain (?). Compare with your neighbour.

1	I think Andy likes sailing.	I don't.
2	I don't think Andy likes cooking.	Neither do I.
3	I think Freda enjoys going shopping.	Hmm, maybe.
4	I think Freda likes knitting.	So do I.
5	I don't think Sandra likes knitting.	Oh, I do.
6	I think Andy enjoys keeping fit.	I don't.
7	I think Sandra enjoys keeping fit.	So do I.
8	I think Sandra enjoys learning English.	Oh, I don't.
9	I don't think Freda enjoys walking.	Neither do I.
10	I don't think Andy enjoys going shopping.	Oh, I do.

c Read these sentences about the people and say whether you agree or disagree using 'I do', 'I don't', 'so do I' or 'neither do I'.

1 I think Sandra likes going to discos. _____ .
2 I don't think Freda likes going to discos. _____ .
3 I think Andy enjoys going out with friends. _____ .
4 I think Freda enjoys reading. _____ .
5 I don't think Sandra likes cooking. _____ .

d Make up 3 sentences about each person. Your neighbour will tell you his/her sentences. Reply using the phrases above.

2 a Look at the hobbies and interests listed below and say whether you like them (✓) or whether you don't like them (x).

☐ skiing	☐ cooking	☐ jogging	☐ knitting
☐ going out with friends	☐ keeping fit	☐ collecting stamps	☐ walking
☐ gliding	☐ playing the guitar	☐ going shopping	☐ going to pop concerts
☐ painting	☐ playing chess	☐ reading	☐ swimming
☐ taking photographs	☐ bird watching	☐ sewing	☐ learning English
☐ walking	☐ gardening	☐ sailing	☐ going to the theatre

b Tell your neighbour.

eg   I like jogging. I don't like sewing.

What else do you like doing in your spare time?

c Fill in the following.

1   How many hours are there in a day? _____
2   How many hours do you work a day? _____
3   How many hours do you sleep a day? _____.
4   How many hours do you spend travelling every day? _____.
5   How many hours do you spend eating every day? _____.
6   How many hours do you spend watching TV a day? _____.
7   How much spare time do you have left every day? _____.

d You're going to hear Joanne talking about her hobby. Before you hear the cassette, read the statements below. While you're listening, put a (✓) true, or (x) false in the box.

1   ☐ Her hobby is playing the piano.
2   ☐ She bought the piano second-hand.
3   ☐ The piano cost over £400.
4   ☐ She has 3 half-hour lessons a week.
5   ☐ She finds it very relaxing.

Listen again and check, then compare with your neighbour.

e Fill in the following about your favourite hobby.

What is your favourite hobby? _____.
When did you start this hobby? _____.
What equipment do you need? Have you bought all the equipment? _____.
Is it an expensive hobby? _____.
Are you in a club? _____.
How much time a week do you spend on your hobby? _____.
Would you like to spend more time on your hobby? _____.

f Ask your neighbour about his/her hobby.

3 a Here are 5 ways of expressing reaction to a statement.

1. I think that's correct.
2. Well, I suppose it could be true.
3. I agree completely with that.
4. I disagree totally with that.
5. I don't think there's much truth in that.

b Now read through these statements. What is your reaction to the statement? Write the number of the phrase in the box.

| eg Reading is bad for your eyes. | 5 |

Going to the theatre is expensive.

Knitting can reduce stress.

Playing the guitar is easy.

Smoking is good for you.

Walking is good for your heart.

Skiing is dangerous.

Drinking water is good for you.

Learning English is fun.

Jogging is bad for your knees.

Eating chocolates is healthy.

Collecting stamps is boring.

Playing the piano is difficult.

Bird watching is interesting.

c Your neighbour will read the statements to you. Tell him/her what you think.

d Now make up 5 more statements. Read them to your neighbour and ask what he/she thinks.

4 a Translate the following.

Vocabulary

cooking _____

shopping _____

knitting _____

keeping fit _____

collecting stamps _____

sewing _____

painting _____

going to pop concerts _____

taking photographs _____

bird watching _____

gardening _____

gliding _____

Structures

I think Sandra likes cooking. _____

So do I. _____

I don't. _____

I don't think Sandra likes cooking. _____

Neither do I. _____

Oh, I do. _____

Maybe. _____

I like jogging. _____

I don't like sailing. _____

I think that's correct. _____

Well, I suppose it could be true. _____

I agree completely with that. _____

I disagree totally with that. _____

I don't think there's much truth in that. _____

Reading is bad for your eyes. _____

Do you agree with that? _____

Walking is good for your heart. _____

UNIT 46

Going Swimming

1 a Look at photograph sequence 10 'Going Swimming' on the next pages and match these questions and answers about photograph 1.

1 Where is the girl? ☐ She'll go to the changing rooms and get changed.
2 What is she doing? ☐ She's in a swimming pool foyer.
3 Why is she doing this? ☐ She's buying a ticket.
4 What is she wearing? ☐ Because she wants to go swimming.
5 What will she do next? ☐ She's wearing a T-shirt, leggings, socks and trainers.

b Ask your neighbour these questions about each of the other photographs.

1 Where is the girl?
2 What is she doing?
3 Why is she doing this?
4 What is she wearing?
5 What will she do next?

c Work with your neighbour and answer questions about the photograph sequence and then check with your teacher.

1 What is in her bag in photograph 1?
2 What is she saying to the assistant in photograph 1?
3 What will the assistant give her?
4 What will she do with the ticket?
5 What is she wearing on her left wrist in photograph 2?
6 What has she done with her clothes? Why?
7 Why is she wearing a swimming costume?
8 Do you think the water is warm or cold in photograph 3? Why?
9 What is she holding in her hands in photograph 4?
10 What time of year do you think it is? Why?

d Make up some information about the girl and then tell your neighbour. Here are some questions to help you.

1 What is her name? How old is she?
2 What does she do - schoolgirl? shop assistant?
3 Why is she going swimming on her own?
4 Does she like swimming? How often does she go swimming?
5 What do you think her ambitions are? Why?

e Ask your neighbour these questions.

1 Can you swim?
2 When/where did you learn to swim?
3 Do you like swimming?
4 When/where was the last time you went swimming?
5 Do you think everybody should learn to swim? Why (not)?

Going Swimming (Photograph Sequence 10)

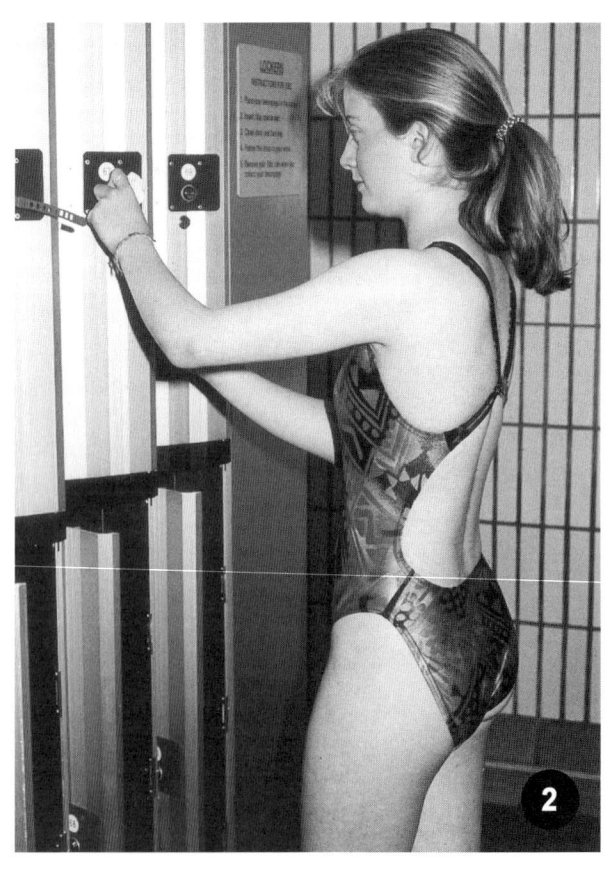

1

2

202

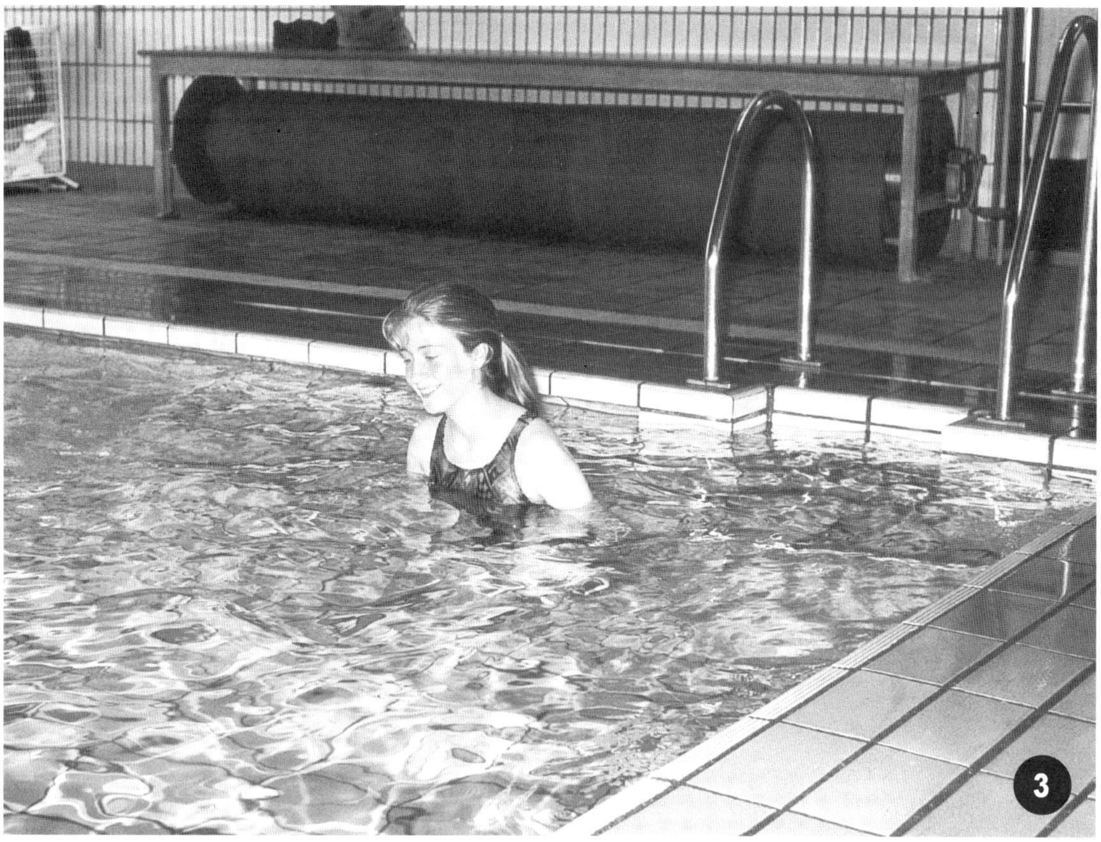
3

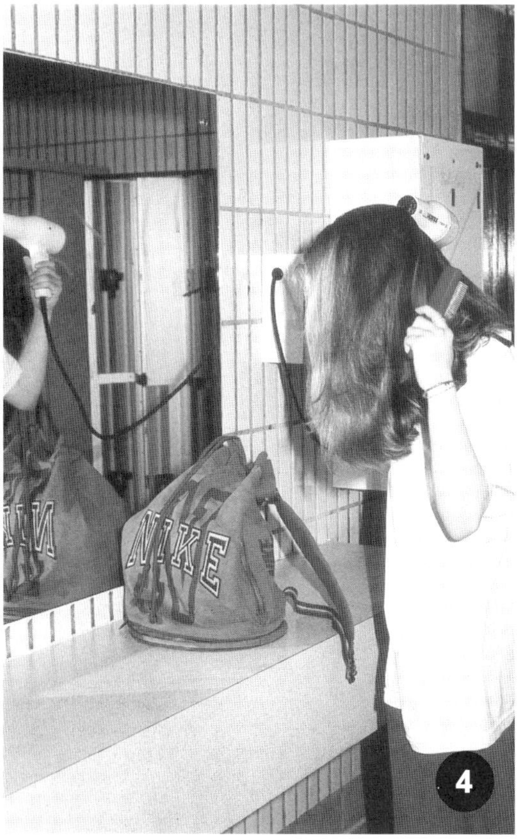
NIKE
4

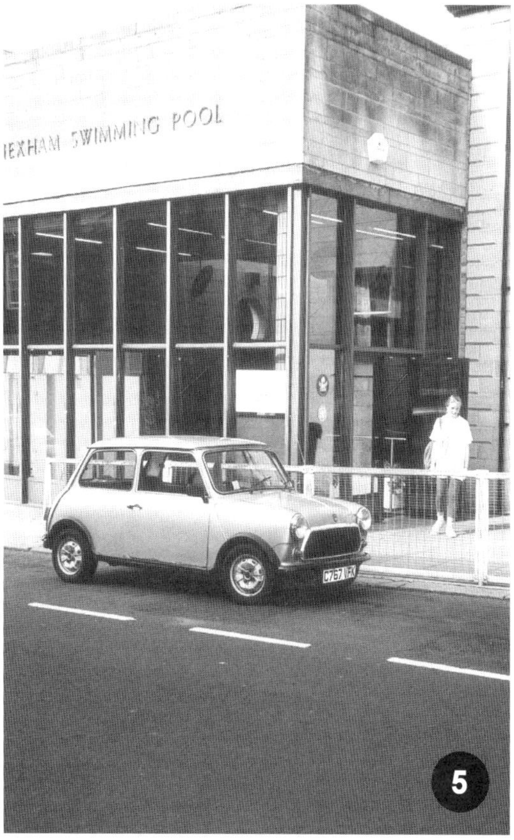
IEXHAM SWIMMING POOL
5

2 a Ask your neighbour the following questions.

1. Do you play any sports? What? How often?
2. Where do you play?
3. Are you a member of a club?
4. Do you have to pay a registration fee?
5. What do you wear? What do you do with your normal clothes? Why?

b Look at the instructions for a locker in a swimming pool and then explain to your neighbour how the locker works. Use the words: first, then, next, after that, finally.

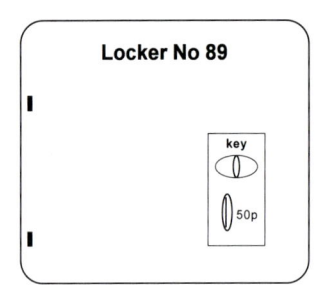

Locker No 89

Lockers

Instructions for Use

1. Place your belongings in the locker.
2. Insert 50p coin in slot.
3. Close door and turn key.
4. Fasten the key strap to your wrist.
5. Remove your 50p coin when you collect your belongings.

c Ask your neighbour these questions.

1. Where else do you find lockers?
2. Have you ever used a locker? Where? Why?

d Look at the information below.

POOL PROGRAMME
6th June - 24th July

	7	8	9	10	11	12 noon	1	2	3	4	5	6	7	8	9	9.45
MON	Early Birds		Schools			Public Swimming							Swimming Club	Over 50's	Lane Swimming	
TUE	Early Birds		Schools			Public Swimming						Women's Hour	Swimming Club	Aquarobics 8.00 - 8.40	Lane Swimming	
WED	Early Birds		Schools			Public Swimming		Parent & Toddler	Junior Lessons			Aquarobics 6.30 - 7.50		Scouts 7.50 - 8.45	Women 8.45 - 9.30	
THU	Early Birds		Schools			Aqua Babies	Public Swimming					Swimming Club			Lane Swimming	
FRI	Early Birds		Schools			Public Swimming						Inflatable Session 6.30 - 8.00			Adult Lessons	
SAT		Early Birds	Public Swimming					Fun Session	Canoe Courses			Available for Party Hire				
	7	8	9	10	11	12 noon	1	2	3	4	5	6	7	8	9	9.45

Ask your neighbour these 5 questions then make up some questions of your own.

1. What time does the pool open on Monday?
2. What time does the pool close on Wednesday?
3. When is 'Aqua Babies'?
4. When is the canoe course?
5. Can I book the pool for a party? If so, when?

3 a Look at this advertisement for skiing breaks.

❄ Ski Extravaganza Packages ❄

Aviemore Skiing Breaks

Come Skiing

You know what fun it is.
We've joined forces with the
Scottish Norwegian Ski School
and the Aviemore Ski School
to offer you some super
2, 3 or 5 day skiing packages.

Package	Adults		Children	
	Low	High	Low	High
White Lady	£250	£289	£169	£190
Ptarmigan	£73	£79	£47	£53
West Wall	£111	£120	£64	£71

Ptarmigan Package

- 1 night accommodation and breakfast
- 2 days skiing
- full area lift pass
- either equipment hire (skis, boots and poles) or four hours instruction each day

If you would like both instruction and equipment hire, please add an extra £14.

West Wall Package

- 2 nights accommodation and breakfast
- 3 days skiing
- full area lift pass
- either equipment hire (skis, boots and poles) or four hours instruction each day

If you would like both instruction and equipment hire, please add an extra £21.

Stakis Hotels Aviemore - Telephone 01479 810661

White Lady Package

This holiday includes 5 nights accommodation (Sunday to Thursday) and 5 days skiing (Monday to Friday) in the Cairngorms and is available during January, February, March and April '96 and don't forget this package comes with a "no snow" guarantee.

- welcome drinks reception
- accommodation and breakfast
- 2 table d' hote dinners, to be taken on the days of your choice
- equipment hire (skis, poles and boots)*
- transport to and from ski slopes*
- full area lift pass*
- daily ski tuition*
- best of class races*
- ASSGB international ski school test*
- prize giving ceremony for the ASSGB certificate*

Note Non-skiers who omit items marked * will receive a case of wine on departure. Please indicate on the booking form. (This offer only applies to guests over 18 years of age.)

Seasons

Low - November, December, January
High - February, March, April

All prices are per person based on two adults sharing a twin/double room. Prices for children under 16 are per child based on sharing a room with 2 adults.

All offers contained herein are subject to availability and all details are correct at the time of printing.

"No Snow" Guarantee   This guarantee is only available on the White Lady Package. If there's not enough snow for skiing on your chosen dates, we will refund £50 per skiing guest. We will also arrange a series of alternative activities which we are sure you will enjoy.

The will include a selection from:
- dry ski slope lessons (every day)
- ice skating
- mountain biking
- ski maintenance clinic
- swimming
- a distillery trip
- curling

3 b   Now ask your neighbour the following questions.

eg   *When is high season? February, March and April.*

1   Which package has 2 nights accommodation and breakfast?
2   Which package has 2 days skiing?
3   Which package has a welcome drinks reception?
4   In the Ptarmigan Package, is equipment hire and four hours instruction each day included in the price?
5   How many days skiing do I get in the West Wall Package?
6   Is an evening meal included in the West Wall Package?
7   Which package has a 'no snow' guarantee?
8   How much is the White Lady Package for one adult in high season?
9   Which package is the cheapest?
10 If I go with my wife and two children on a West Wall Package in January, how much will it cost?

c   Ask your neighbour the following questions.

1   Have you ever been skiing?
2   Where and when was the last time?
3   If you have never been skiing would you like to try it? If not, why not?
4   Do you get a lot of snow where you live?
5   What other winter sports can you think of?

4 a   Translate the following.

Vocabulary

diagram _____	a selection _____
locker _____	high season _____
to place _____	low season _____
belongings _____	equipment hire _____
to fasten _____	skies _____
strap _____	poles _____
to remove _____	ski slopes _____
coin _____	non-skier _____
skiing package _____	instructions _____
refund _____	

Structures

What is the girl wearing? _____
What is the girl doing? _____
Why do you think she is doing this? _____
What do you think she will do next? _____
What time of year do you think it is? _____
What time of day do you think it is? _____
First you place your belongings in the locker. _____
Then you... _____
Next you... _____
After that you... _____
Finally you... _____

UNIT 47

What's on?

1 **a** Look at the list of 'What's On' below and ask your neighbour 5 questions.

eg   *What's on at the Central Cinema? Rambo 5 is on from July 21 - 25.*

What's On

Antiques Fair	The Royal Hotel	July 21-23	
Painting Exhibition	Wellington Arts Centre	July 21-25	
Classical Music	High School (Main Hall)	July 22	7pm
Charity Fund Raising Parachute Jump	Catterick Airfield	July 23	
Rambo 5	Central Cinema	July 21-25	
Marathon Run	Start - Wellfield Sports Centre	July 22	11am
Treasure Hunt	Start - The Golden Lion Hotel	July 22	5.30pm
"The Future of the Planet"	High School, Lecture Theatre	July 24	7pm
Hamlet	Beaumont Theatre	July 22-24	7.30pm

---

b Answer the following questions.

1   Where do you find information about what's on in your local area?
_____

2   Is there a cinema in your town/city? What's on at the moment?
_____

3   Is there a theatre in your town/city? What's on at the moment?
_____

4   Is there a sports centre in your town/city? What's on at the moment?
_____

5   Is there an exhibition centre in your town/city? What's on at the moment?
_____

6   Is there an arts centre in your town/city? What's on at the moment?
_____

7   Where else do events take place?
_____

c Look at your local 'What's On' page. Work with your neighbour and answer the following questions.

eg   *Are there any sporting events on this week? Yes there's a football match on Saturday.*

1   Are there any sporting events? When and Where?
2   Are there any charity fund raising events? When and Where?
3   Are there any musical events? When and Where?
4   Are there any events for nature lovers? When and Where?
5   Are there any public lectures?   What about? When and Where?
6   Are there any outdoor events? When and Where?
7   Are there any crafts events? When and Where?

d Discuss with your neighbour which events you would like to go to and why.

eg   *I would like to go to the Antiques Fair because I'm very interested in antiques. It's on at the Royal Hotel from July 21 - 23. Would you like to come too?*

2 **a** **Read the following questions and answer them as quickly as possible using the TV guide opposite.**

eg   *What's on Grampian at 9.25am? He-Man.*

1   What is on BBC 2 at 4 o'clock? _____ .

2   How many films are on TV that day? _____ .

3   Which channel is the Open University on? _____ .

4   How many news broadcasts are there on BBC 1? _____ .

5   What time is 'The Bill' on Grampian? _____ .

6   What is on Channel 4 at 6.30pm? _____ .

7   What time is the film 'Beyond the Stars' on? _____ .

8   Which channel closes at 3.15am? _____ .

9   Which channel is 'True Stories' on? _____ .

10   How many channels are showing 'Golf - The Open'? _____ .

Check with your neighbour.

b **Now make up 5 more questions and ask your neighbour.**

eg   *When is 'The Big Breakfast' on? It's on Channel 4 at 7am.*

c **Now look more closely at the TV page and answer the following questions. Work with your neighbour.**

1   If you were interested in sport, which programmes would you watch?
2   If you were interested in nature, which programmes would you watch?
3   If you were interested in gardening, which programmes would you watch?
4   If you were interested in politics, which programmes would you watch?
5   If you were interested in science fiction, which programmes would you watch?

d **Work with 3 neighbours. You are flatmates and only have one TV. Find 3 programmes between 7pm and midnight which you would like to see.**

e **Now discuss what you would like to watch and decide what all 3 of you will watch.**

eg   *I'd like to watch 'The Beechgrove Garden' at 8pm. Oh, that's on at the same time as 'The Mind Field'. I wanted to see that! But you watched it last week. Well okay, we'll watch 'The Beechgrove Garden' if I can watch 'Wildlife Showcase' at 8.30pm. Okay.*

f **Ask your neighbour these questions.**

1   How many hours a day do you spend watching TV?
2   What are the advantages of having a TV?
3   What are the disadvantages of having a TV?
4   What do you watch regularly? Why?
5   When was the last time you watched TV? What did you watch?

TV Guide

1 BBC

6.00	Business Breakfast
7.00	BBC Breakfast News
9.05	The Flintstones
9.35	Lassie
10.00	News; Weather
10.05	Playdays
10.30	**The Season** - A look at Henley, one of the institutions of the British summer.
11.00	News; Weather
11.05	**Timekeepers** - Bill Dodd presents the fast-moving general knowledge quiz.
11.30	TalkAbout
12.00	News; Weather
12.05	TalkAbout
12.20	Scoundrels of Suburbia
1.00	One O'Clock News; Weather
1.30	Neighbours
1.50	Turnabout
2.15	**Golf - The Open** - Coverage of the 124th Open Golf Championship from St Andrews.
4.00	Cartoon
4.10	The Animals of Farthing Wood
4.35	Clarissa Explains it All
5.00	Cartoon
5.05	**Escape From Jupiter** - Sci-fi adventure
5.35	**Neighbours** - Annalise and Mark get a surprising reception, and the future is beginning to look a little brighter for the Kennedys.
6.00	Six O'Clock News; Weather
6.30	Reporting Scotland
7.00	Top Of The Pops
7.30	**EastEnders** - Nigel and Clare go to court, but Liam seems to be on surprisingly food form. Steve finally manages to find two more holiday candidates, and Arthur upsets Michelle while Sanjay encourages Mark.
8.00	**The Beechgrove Garden** - Gardening Magazine.
8.30	**2point4 Children** - Bill goes as far as causing a power cut to bring about an evening of culture and conversation.
9.00	Nine O'Clock News; Weather
9.30	**Till Murder Do Us Part** - A true story of a wife who goes to drastic lengths to hold on to her failing marriage. After courtroom dramas that hurt her children and leave her embittered, she feels desperate to take revenge.
11.00	**Golf - The Open** - Highlights of the 124th Open Golf Championship from St Andrews, with Steve Rider.

> **11.40 FILM: Beyond the Stars** (1989) Space adventure starring Martin Sheen, Christian Slater and Sharon Stone.

| 1.10 | Weather |
| 1.15 | Close |

2 BBC

6.20	Open University
8.00	Breakfast News
8.15	**Westminster On-Line With Andrew Nell**
9.00	Consuming Passions
9.05	**How The West Was Lost** - Last in the Series.
9.55	For The Love Of It
10.00	Age Is No Barrier
10.25	**Golf - The Open** - Live coverage from St Andrews. Introduced by Steve Rider and Peter Alliss.
12.30	Working Lunch
1.00	The Brollys
1.15	**Golf - The Open** - Continued coverage from St Andrews.
2.15	Between Two Worlds
2.45	Milestones in Science And Engineering
3.00	**News; Westminster With John Sopel**
3.55	News; Regional News; Weather
4.00	Golf - The Open
7.30	**The Business** - New Series. A look at the career of Andrew Lloyd Webber and his Really Useful Group.
8.00	**African Footsteps** - (African Summer Season) Antony Sher and Greg Dorin visit Tangier in Morocco, much visited haunt of many famous English writers and artists.
8.30	**Wildlife Showcase** - A profile of the Kea parrot.
9.00	**The Likely Lads** - Terry tries to lift Bob out of his depression by persuading him to go on a double date.
9.30	**One Foot In The Past** - Liz Dawn visits Temple Newsam House in Leeds.
10.00	Grace Under Fire
10.30	Newsnight
11.15	Gaytime TV
11.55	Weatherview
12.00	Open View
12.05	Images Of The Cosmos
12.30	**The Record** - Today's debates and exchanges in Parliament.
1.00	Close

4 CHANNEL

6.35	The Adventures of Super Mario Bros
7.00	The Big Breakfast
9.00	You Bet Your Life

> **9.30 FILM: Naughty Marietta** (1935) Amiable period operetta starring Jeanette MacDonald.

11.25	Scotland's Larder
11.55	Profiles of Nature
12.25	Who's Dragon?
12.30	Sesame Street
1.30	The Wonderful Wizard of Oz
1.55	**Haunted House** - Buster Keaton short.

> **2.15 FILM: The Mark of Zorro** (1940) Swashbuckler starring Tyrone Power and Basil Rathbone.

4.00	Jimmy's
4.30	Countdown
5.00	Ricki Lake
5.45	Terrytoons
6.00	**Home Improvement** - US sitcom.
6.30	Tour De France
7.00	Channel 4 News; Weather
7.50	The Slot
8.00	**The Mind Field** - Kwame McKenzie looks at how memory can be improved.
8.30	**The Crystal Maze** - Hosted by Ed Tudor Pole.
9.30	**True Stories** - A group of Russian mothers want to find their sons whom they believe have been captured by Chechens.
11.05	Stephen King's Golden Years
	Sci-fi drama.
12.00	Walk On The Wild Side
12.30	First Sex
1.30	Tour De France

> **2.00 FILM: Confirm Or Deny** (1941) Wartime melodrama starring Don Ameche and Joan Bennett.

| 3.15 | Close |

GRAMPIAN

6.00	GMTV
9.25	He-Man
9.50	Mission Top Secret
10.20	News
10.25	Grampian Headlines

> **10.30 FILM: Trading Hearts** (1989) An ex-baseball star and a single mother begin a tentative romance after meeting in a bar-room brawl. Starring Raul Julia and Beverly D'Angelo.

12.10	Warner Cartoon
12.20	Grampian Headlines
12.25	Teleflos
12.30	News & Weather
12.55	Emmerdale
1.25	Home and Away
1.55	Shortland Street
2.20	The Other Peak Practice
2.50	Wild West Country
3.20	News
3.25	Grampian Headlines
3.30	The Riddlers
3.40	Wizadora
3.50	Old Bear Stories
4.05	Animanlacs
4.30	Garfield and Friends.
4.40	Just Us
5.10	Chart Bite
5.40	News & Weather
6.00	Teleflos
6.05	Home and Away
6.30	North Tonight: Weather
7.00	Emmerdale
7.30	The Big Story
8.00	**The Bill** - Deakin and Woods have an emotional and desperate mother on their hands when her daughter is kidnapped.
8.30	**Heartbeat** - Nick investigates the case of a missing baby stolen from its pram.
9.30	**Searching** - Carla Lane comedy. Last in the series.
10.00	News & Weather
10.30	The Way It Was
11.00	Grampian Headlines
11.05	Reflections
11.10	Prisoner: Cell Block H
12.15	War of the Worlds
1.10	Shift
2.05	The Beat
3.00	The Album Show
3.50	Profile
4.10	**The Little Picture Show** - with Wendy Lloyd.
5.00	Vanessa
5.30	News

SCOTTISH

10.20 News **10.25** Now You See It **10.55** Samurai Pizza Cats **11.25** Dinosaurs **11.50** Square Meals **12.20** Scotland Today **12.30** News **12.55** Scotland Today **1.20** The Other Peak Practice **1.50** Home and Away **2.20** Highway to Heaven **3.20** News **3.25** Scotland Today **5.10** Emmerdale **5.40** News **6.00** Home and Away **6.30** Scotland Today **7.00** Scottish Passport **10.00** News **10.30** A Game of Two Halves **11.00** Married with Children **11.30** Scotland Today **11.45** Prisoner **12.40** Good Advice **1.10** Memories **2.10** Cinema, Cinema, Cinema **2.40** Noisy Mothers **3.35** The Album Show **4.30** Pop Profile **4.40** America's Top Ten **5.05** Jobfinder **5.25** Scotland Today **5.30** News

Calendar of Events — 1995

DATE	EVENT	CONTACT	
May			
6	**Kielder Reiver orienteering event** An exciting mountain bike challenge.	Forest Enterprise:	01434 220242
13	**Board Sailing event.**	Jack Coates:	01434 681677
14	**Kielder Board Sailing Marathon**	Jack Coates:	01434 681677
12 - 14	**Birds in the Forest** Activity Weekend	Forest Enterprise:	01434 220242
17	**Jack Charlton Fishing Competition** for disabled anglers	Northumbrian Water:	01434 240398
21	**Kielder Wateraid Festival** A variety of walks and entertainment for all the family	Northumbrian Water:	01434 240398
27 - 29	**Flying Fifteen Northern Championships**	Jack Coates:	01434 681677
29 May - 4 June	**RYA Dinghy Sailing** Week course following RYA Certificate syllabus	Hawkhirst Adventure Camp:	01434 250217
June			
3	**Wigfic Fishing Competition** 100 anglers competing at Kielder Water	Northumbrian Water:	01434 240398
9 - 11	**Forest Life** Activity Weekend	Forest Enterprise:	01434 220242
18	**Folk at Falstone**	Northumberland National Park:	01434 605555
July			
1	**Jim Clark Rally**	Forest Enterprise:	01434 220242
22	**Ron Hill/Pertex Mountain Duathlon**	Forest Enterprise:	01434 220242
30	**National Bog Day** Learn about Border mires	Forest Enterprise:	01434 220242
30	**Family Fun Day** - Leaplish Waterside Park Displays, children's entertainment, music	Northumbrian Water:	01434 240398
August			
5	**Kielder Festival and Fell Race** Forest open day, folk music sessions, craft stalls, real ale, falconry, border games and much more!	Forest Enterprise:	01434 220242
5 - 12	**Hawkhirst Activity Week** A week long programme of activities	Hawkhirst Adventure Camp:	01434 250217
13	**Family Fun Day** - Leaplish Waterside Park Displays, children's entertainment, music	Northumbrian Water:	01434 240398
19	**Falstone Show**	Mrs Armstrong:	01434 240228
20	**Family Fun Day** - Leaplish Waterside Park Displays, children's entertainment, music	Northumbrian Water:	01434 240398
26	**Bellingham Show**	Mrs Wyrley-Birch:	0191 4133878

3 a Look at the 'Calendar of Events, 1995' for Kielder Water, then read the notes below. Make any changes necessary.

Notes

Kielder Board Sailing Marathon on May 15.

Northumberland National Park number is 603942.

Bellingham Show contact is Mrs White on 0191 2324297.

National Bog Day cancelled - no interest.

June 18 should be 'Folk Music' at Falstone.

Hawkhirst Activity Week from August 6 to 13.

English National Fishing Competition August 28 and 29. Contact Ramsay White 01661 823946.

---

b You are going to hear 15 questions about the Calendar of Events for Kielder Water. Listen to the cassette and write down the answers. Do **not** write down the questions.

1 _____
2 _____
3 _____
4 _____
5 _____
6 _____
7 _____
8 _____
9 _____
10 _____
11 _____
12 _____
13 _____
14 _____
15 _____

c Listen again and check that you have answered the questions correctly and then compare your answers with your neighbour.

4 a Translate the following.

Vocabulary

Antiques Fair _____   outdoor events _____
painting exhibition _____   crafts events _____
classical music _____   channel _____
parachute jump _____   broadcasts _____
marathon run _____   event _____
treasure hunt _____   contact _____
lecture theatre _____   calendar of events _____
exhibition centre _____   festival _____
charity _____   show _____
fund raising _____   nature _____
nature lovers _____   science fiction _____
public lectures _____

Structures

What's on? _____
What's on at the Central Cinema? _____
Are there any sporting events on this week? _____
Yes, there's a football match on Saturday. _____
What's on Channel 4 at 9.25am? _____
He-Man's on Grampian at 9.25am. _____
When is 'The Big Breakfast' on? _____
It's on Channel 4 at 7am. _____
If you were interested in sport, which programmes would you watch? _____
If I was interested in sport, I would watch the golf. _____
I'd like to watch 'The Beechgrove Garden' at 8pm. _____
That's at the same time as 'The Mind Field'. _____
I wanted to see that. _____
But you watched it last week. _____
Well okay we'll watch... _____
We'll watch 'The Beechgrove Garden' if I can watch the 'Wildlife Showcase'. _____
_____
Is there a cinema in your town? _____
What's on at the moment? _____
I would like to go to the Antiques Fair at the Royal Hotel. _____
Would you like to come too? _____
What about you? _____

UNIT 48

Where did you go on holiday last year?

1 a Look at the pie chart below which shows you where British people went on holiday in 1995. Using the phrases in the box, complete the sentences below (there may be more than one possibility).

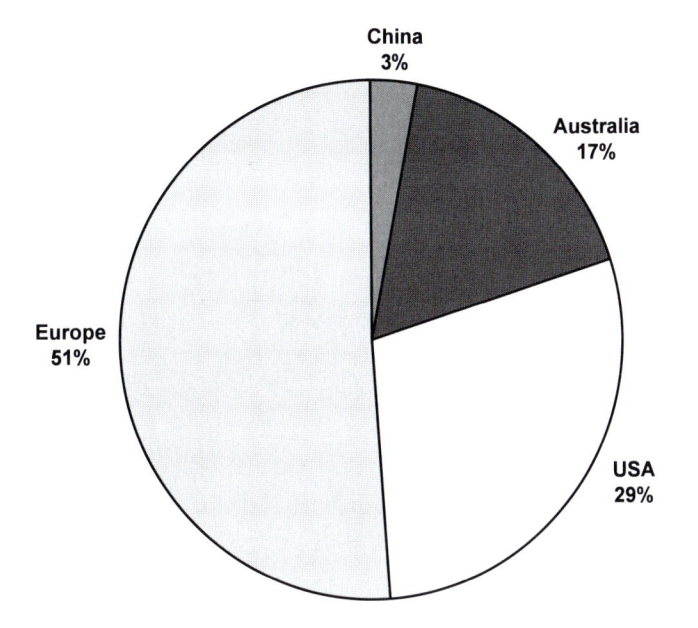

Pie chart:
- China 3%
- Australia 17%
- Europe 51%
- USA 29%

Box of phrases:
- nearly everybody
- some people
- not many
- hardly anybody
- just under 30%
- just over 15%
- more than half
- less than half
- nobody

1 _____ went to China in 1995.
2 Most people went on holiday to _____ in 1995.
3 _____ went to Australia in 1995.
4 _____ went to the USA in 1995.
5 _____ went to Europe in 1995.

b Work in groups of 10. Ask each of the other 9 people where they went on holiday last year. Write the name of the countries in column A and the number of people who went there in column B.

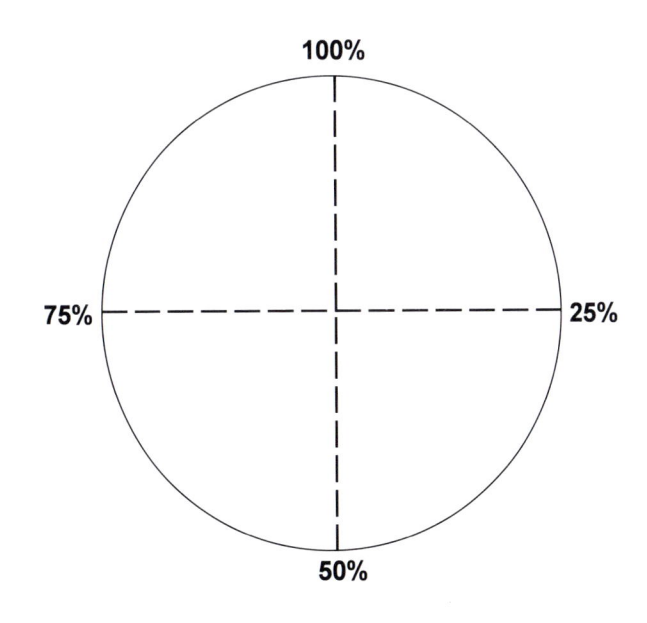

(A) Countries	(B) No of People	%

c Now work out the percentage of your group who visited each country. You can do this by adding a zero to the number in column B. Show this in the pie chart information. When you have finished, make up 5 sentences using the phrases from exercise 1a.

2 a You are on holiday in England. You have just arrived in Nottingham with a group of 12 people. The coach driver is about to give you some useful information. Look at the map below and then listen to the cassette. You will hear it twice and may make notes while you listen.

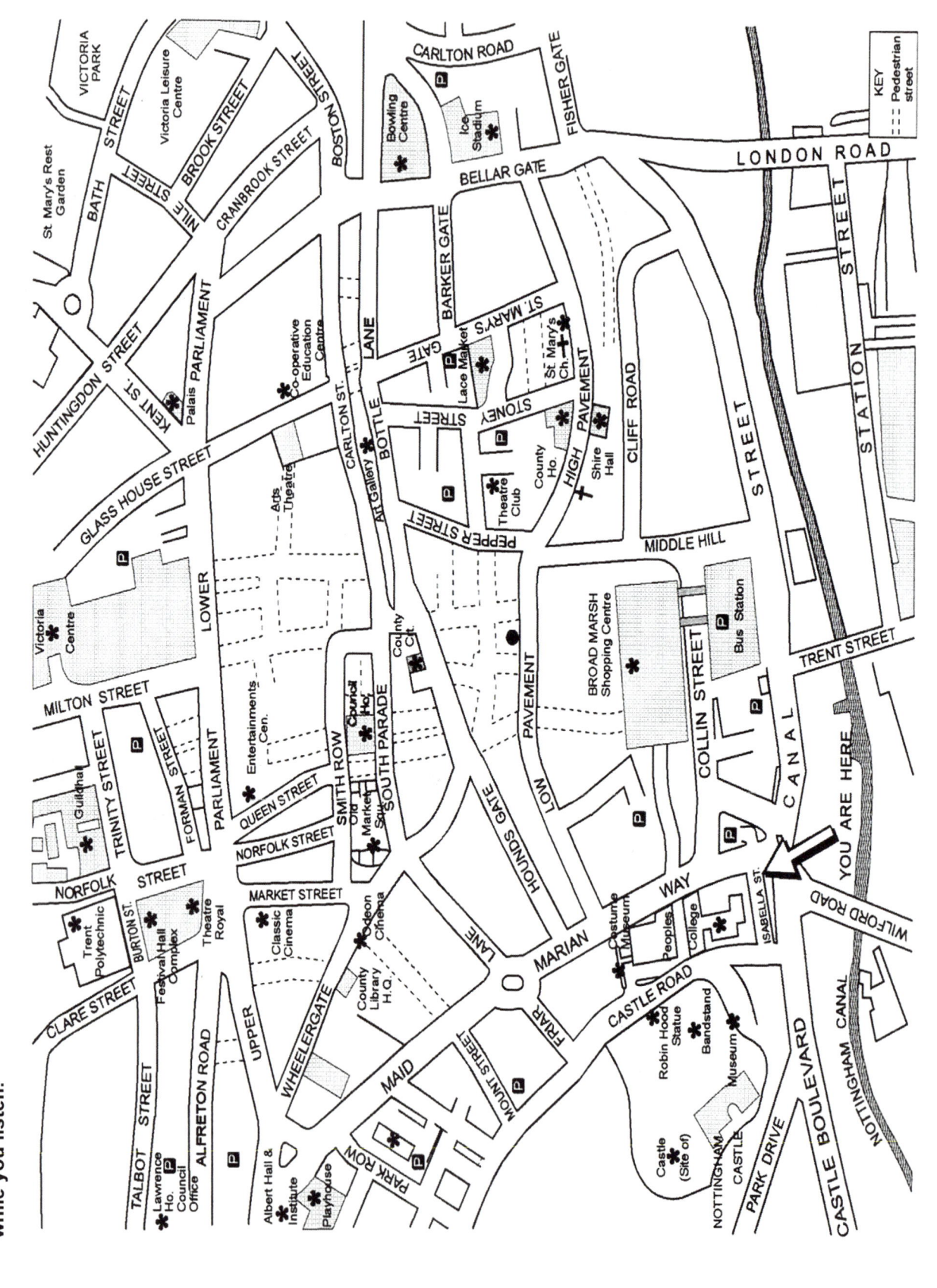

2 b Compare your notes with your neighbour.

eg *I thought he said the castle was open between 9am and 2pm. No, I'm sure he said between 9am and 1pm.*

c Now ask your neighbour the following questions.

1 How much is it to visit the castle?
2 How do you get from the castle to the Victoria Centre?
3 Can I visit the castle at 2pm? Why (not)?
4 Where is the Theatre Royal?
5 How many car parks are there?
6 How do you get from the Victoria Leisure Centre to the Victoria Centre?
7 Can I go to the exhibition in the art gallery if I am 12 years old?
8 What time does the bowling centre open?
9 What is the number of the bus?
10 How do you get from Nottingham Castle to the ice stadium?
11 What is 'the Bell'?
12 What can you find in the Old Market Square?
13 Why would you go to the Ice Stadium?
14 Can I visit St Mary's Church this afternoon?
15 In how many languages do they have information at the Tourist Information Centre?

d Ask your neighbour 5 more questions using the map.

3 a Look at the advert below and answer the questions.

RHINE VALLEY

Dear Reader
Enjoy the delights of the Rhine Valley on this superb value for money tour.

The price includes:
- Return overnight coach travel from Newcastle.
- Return ferry crossings.
- 4 nights accommodation in rooms with hand wash basin at selected family run hotels.
- Breakfast and evening meal each day.
- Services of a tour guide.

Rooms with private bathroom available for a supplement. Single room extra.
Optional excursions to Rudesheim and Rhine Gorge, Bernkastel, Cochem and Koblenz also available.

Deposit £35.00 per person plus insurance of £14.90 per person made payable to Travelscope Promotions.

To request a full colour brochure, complete the coupon below or telephone Reader Holidays

0191 201 6000

Alternatively, call at the Reader Holiday Desk, Front Reception, Thomson House, Groat Market, Newcastle Upon Tyne NE1 1ED

Payment by cheque, credit card or postal order.

5 days FROM £99.00
31st July or 23rd October 1996

RHINE VALLEY - Please send me the brochure on the Rhine Valley tour.
Mr/Mrs/Ms/Miss.................Initials..............Surname..................
Address..
Post Code................................Tel No...............

---

1 What is this an advert for? _____
2 Where would you see an advert like this? _____
3 Is a mid-day meal included? _____
4 If I want a bathroom, do I have to pay more? _____
5 Can I pay for the holiday in cash? _____
6 Who is organising the holiday? _____
7 What costs £14.90? _____
8 What number do I call for more information? _____
9 What is the difference between 'Mr', 'Mrs', 'Ms' and 'Miss'? _____
10 Would you go on a holiday like this? Why (not)? _____

3 b Now ask your neighbour five more questions about the advert.

c Ask your neighbour the following questions.

1. Where was the best place you have ever been on holiday? Why?
2. Where was the worst place you have ever been on holiday? Why?
3. What is important to you on holiday (weather, food, culture, etc)?
4. Why do you go on holiday?
5. If you could go anywhere on holiday, where would you go? Why?

4 a Translate the following.

Vocabulary

pie chart _____
percentage _____
caves _____
shopping centre _____
ice stadium _____
skates _____
bowling centre _____
stained glass window _____
spire _____
controversial _____

artist _____
Rhine Valley _____
from £99.00 _____
return overnight coach _____
ferry crossings _____
hand wash basin _____
family run hotel _____
supplement _____
optional _____
plus _____

Structures

Most people went to... in 1995. _____
Nearly everybody went to... in 1995. _____
More than half went to... in 1995. _____
Less than half went to... in 1995. _____
Some people went to... in 1995. _____
Not many went to... in 1995. _____
Hardly anybody went to... in 1995. _____
Nobody went to... in 1995. _____
30% of people went to... last year. _____
I thought he said the castle was open between 9am and 2pm. _____
I'm sure he said between 9am and 1pm. _____
Where was the best place you have ever been on holiday? _____
The best place I have ever been on holiday was to... _____

UNIT 49

What's the best book you've ever read?

1 a Read the following advert.

✍ .... *Be a Writer*

Earn while you learn and pay your fees.

The Write School, founded in 1952, will show you how to write magazine articles, short stories, novels and TV scripts, which you can sell.

Top professional writers give you expert advice on writing and selling your articles and stories to publishers who are always on the look out for new writers.

Learn At Home

All you need is to spend a few hours each week studying and you can earn an extra income from home.

If you have not recovered the cost of the course by the time you finish, your fees will be refunded.

Please write for our free book:
Learning to Write Successfully
No stamp needed.
Call: Freephone 0800 4287912

**The Write School
Freepost LR1
London W4**

---

b Ask your neighbour the question below.

1 What is this an advertisement for?
2 What is the name of the advertiser?
3 How old is the school?
4 Who can give you advice on writing?
5 What else can they give you advice on?
6 Where is the school located?
7 Do I have to go there if I want to study?
8 Is it possible to get the course fees back? Why (not)?
9 If I phone, will I have to pay for the call?
10 What is the phone number?

c What is the best book you have ever read? Fill in the information you can remember about it.

Title _____

Can you remember who it was by? _____

How many main characters were there? _____

Name(s)? _____

Where was it set (your country, another country)? _____

When was it set (past, present, future)? _____

What was the story about? _____

d Listen to your neighbour and make notes. When he/she is finished, tell him/her about his/her favourite book based on your notes.

eg   You said the best book you have ever read was called...

Here are some phrases to help you.

*You said it was by ...
You said there were 3 main characters, ...
Then you said it was set in ...
I think you said it was set in the past. Is that right?
You said the young girl left home when she was 12
and went to live in a city.*

Unit 49 217

2 a The following paragraphs are from 2 articles which appeared in the newspaper. Read the paragraphs and see if you can find the titles for the stories. Then decide whether the paragraphs belong to Story A or Story B.

Story A	a b
Story B	c

a It's ten years today since the biggest rock concert ever took place.

b And what help did Liveaid give to Africa in facts and figures? Over £40 million was raised to help the situation.

c The boy was taken to Bristol Childrens' Hospital and is now said to be comfortable.

d When he was breathing again I continued talking to her until the ambulance arrived.

e A short report by Bob Geldof will also show the situation in Ethiopia as it is today 10 years after the famine.

f **Toddler 'serious' in hospital after choking on a grape**

g A two year old boy was seriously ill in hospital yesterday after choking on a grape.

h More than 70,000 people were at Wembley Stadium on July 13, 1985 and the concert was watched by 1.4 billion people in over 170 countries.

i So, if you missed it first time around, make sure you don't miss it tonight.

j Phil Donalds, the telephone operator gave Janice first aid instructions over the phone.

k Between 8.30pm and 9.30pm television presenters will be interviewing musicians, fans and backstage staff who were all at the original concert.

l His mother, Janice, 32 of Bristol rang 999 when he stopped breathing yesterday afternoon.

m "I told her to try and remove the grape by hitting her son on the back" said Mr Donalds.

n 'Liveaid' as the concert was know, was broadcast in 1985 by the BBC and tonight you have a second chance to see it.

The concert will be shown in two parts, from 6pm to 8.30pm and from 9.30pm to 1.35am.

o **The Day the World Rocked**

b When you have all the parts to the story, work with your neighbour and put the paragraphs in the order you think is correct.

eg I think g is the first paragraph of Story B. Do you agree?

Story A	o
Story B	f

c Compare your work with other groups.

d Ask your neighbour these questions.

When was the last time you read a newspaper?
Can you remember what any of the articles were about?

3 a You have travelled to Frankfurt International Book Fair with a group of 15 people. Your tour guide gives you the following map of Frankfurt Exhibition Centre. Look at the information and ask your neighbour 5 questions.

eg *What is in Hall 1.1?*

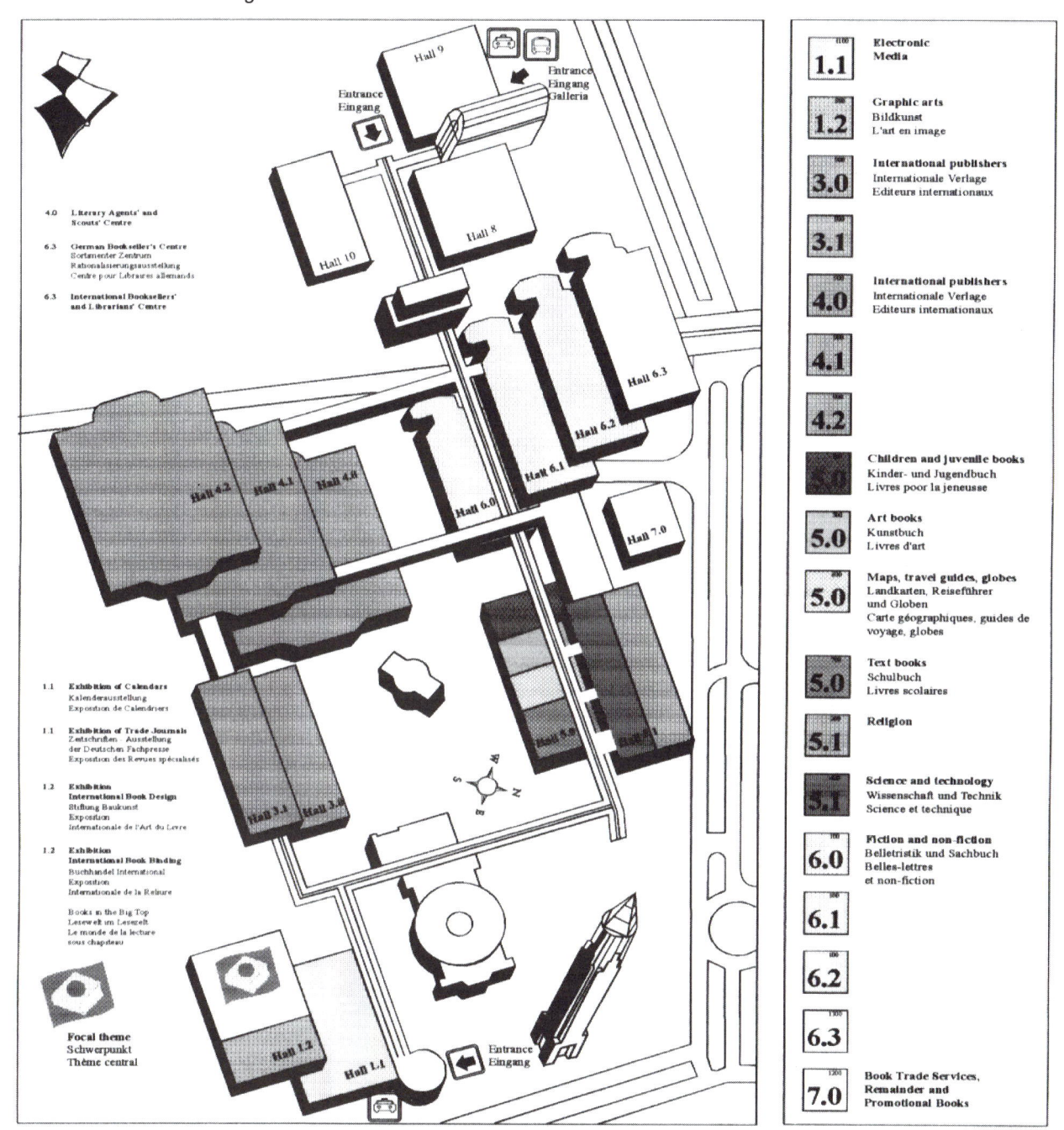

1.1	Electronic Media
1.2	Graphic arts / Bildkunst / L'art en image
3.0	International publishers / Internationale Verlage / Editeurs internationaux
3.1	
4.0	International publishers / Internationale Verlage / Editeurs internationaux
4.1	
4.2	
5.0	Children and juvenile books / Kinder- und Jugendbuch / Livres pour la jeunesse
5.0	Art books / Kunstbuch / Livres d'art
5.0	Maps, travel guides, globes / Landkarten, Reiseführer und Globen / Carte géographiques, guides de voyage, globes
5.0	Text books / Schulbuch / Livres scolaires
5.1	Religion
5.1	Science and technology / Wissenschaft und Technik / Science et technique
6.0	Fiction and non-fiction / Belletristik und Sachbuch / Belles-lettres et non-fiction
6.1	
6.2	
6.3	
7.0	Book Trade Services, Remainder and Promotional Books

Additional map legend:

- 4.0 Literary Agents' and Scouts' Centre
- 6.3 German Booksellers' Centre / Sortimenter Zentrum / Rationalisierungsausstellung / Centre pour Libraires allemands
- 6.3 International Booksellers' and Librarians' Centre
- 1.1 Exhibition of Calendars / Kalenderausstellung / Exposition de Calendriers
- 1.1 Exhibition of Trade Journals / Zeitschriften-Ausstellung der Deutschen Fachpresse / Exposition des Revues spécialisés
- 1.2 Exhibition International Book Design / Stiftung Buchkunst / Exposition Internationale de l'Art du Livre
- 1.2 Exhibition International Book Binding / Buchhandel International Exposition / Exposition Internationale de la Reliure
- Books in the Big Top / Lesezelt im Lesezelt / Le monde de la lecture sous chapiteau
- Focal theme / Schwerpunkt / Thème central

b Now listen to the cassette and make notes. You will hear it twice.

c Ask your neighbour the following questions.

1. How much does it cost to get into the exhibition?
2. What time will your group leave the fair?
3. What time is the presentation on stand G17 in Hall 5.0?
4. How many people will visit the book fair?
5. Where are the toilets?

d Now ask your neighbour 5 more questions about the Frankfurt International Book Fair.

4 a Translate the following.

Vocabulary

to make money _____	backstage staff _____
to earn _____	billion _____
founded _____	facts and figures _____
novels _____	to raise money _____
TV scripts _____	to stop breathing _____
professional writer _____	toddler _____
expert advice _____	serious _____
publishers _____	to choke _____
on the lookout for _____	grape _____
extra income _____	telephone operator _____
to recover the cost _____	first aid instructions _____
to refund _____	seriously ill _____
freephone _____	exhibitors _____
freepost _____	exhibition _____
to take place _____	multimedia _____
to broadcast _____	discuss _____
BBC _____	pros and cons _____
TV presenter _____	photocopying _____
musicians _____	workshop _____
fans _____	

Structures

What was the best book you have ever read? _____

Can you remember who it was by? _____

You said the best book you have ever read was called... _____

You said it was by... _____

You said there were 3 main characters called... _____

Then you said it was set in... _____

I think you said it was set in the present. _____

Is that right? _____

You said a young girl left home when she was 12 and... _____

UNIT 50

Revision

1 a Ask your neighbour these questions about his/her school days.

1. Which was your favourite subject at school? Why?
2. Which was your least favourite subject? Why?
3. Who was the best teacher you've ever had? Why?
4. Who was the worst teacher you've ever had? Why?
5. Do you think that school prepares you for working life? Why (not)?

b Look at these statements and say what you think about them.

1. Exams should not be marked by teachers.
2. Exams are unfair.
3. Teachers should be paid according to pupils results.

c Your neighbour is applying for a job with you. Ask him/her for details to fill in the form below.

Surname _____	**First Name** _____
Address _____	**Date of Birth** _____
_____	**Telephone Number** _____

Education
Name/Address of Institute   From   To   Qualifications

Work Experience
Name/Address of Employer   From   To   Position

Skills and Languages _____
_____

Hobbies and Interests _____
_____

2 a Tell your neighbour about any courses you have been on since you left school. He/she wants to know where they were, when they were, what they were about, and why you did them.

b Ask your neighbour these questions.

1 Have you ever done a work placement? Where? When?
2 Was it useful? Why (not)?
3 Would you like to work in another country? Why (not)?

3 a Read these questions and then tell your neighbour about yourself.

1 Why are you learning English?
2 Which skills do you need the most?
3 How do you practise English between lessons?
4 Do you think you are improving? Why (not)?
5 What do you find most difficult about learning English?

4 a Read the sentences and underline the correct form.

1 I wrote/have written the letter last night.
2 He worked/has worked here for 20 years.
3 She went/has gone to America last year.
4 He started/has started University in 1995.
5 I visited/have visited him last week.

b Read these sentences and put in the correct form.

1 He (work) _____ here since 1992.
2 He (live) _____ in this town for 30 years.
3 She (go) _____ home early yesterday.
4 She (own) _____ that car since she was 18.
5 I (live) _____ here all my life.

c Read these sentences and say the negative form and the question form to your neighbour.

1 He is washing his hair.
2 She goes to work at 8 o'clock.
3 I am wearing a jumper.
4 They watched TV last night.
5 She has lived here for 10 years.

4 d Make up 5 sentences using the following words.

1 yesterday _____

2 already _____

3 tomorrow _____

4 since November _____

5 now _____

e Tell your neighbour 3 things you didn't do yesterday.

f Add 3 more words to each of the lists and then compare with your neighbour. Explain why you chose these words.

1 doctor   _____ _____ _____

2 furniture department   _____ _____ _____

3 CV   _____ _____ _____

4 dog   _____ _____ _____

5 Spring Bank Holiday   _____ _____ _____

5 a Can you name 10 spare time activities? When you have 10, ask your neighbour which one(s) he/she likes doing and say whether you agree or not.

eg *Do you like sailing? Yes, I do. So do I. Do you like sewing? No, I don't. Oh, I do.*

b Now look at your neighbour's list and say if you think the activities are interesting, boring, expensive, etc.

eg *I think that bird watching is very interesting. What do you think? Oh, I agree.*

6 a Ask your neighbour these questions and find out where and when they learnt this skill.

1 Can you swim?
2 Can you type?
3 Can you speak Italian?
4 Can you cook?
5 Can you drive?

7 a Ask your neighbour these questions.

1. How much TV do you watch a day?
2. Is the TV in your house switched on every day?
3. How do you decide what to watch on TV?
4. Do you think that there is a lot of rubbish on TV?
5. Do you think that watching TV is relaxing?

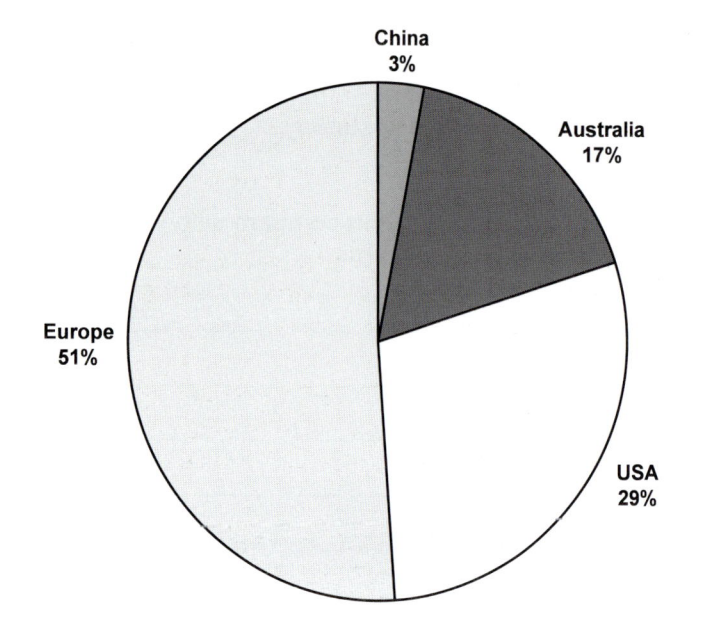

Pie chart:
- China 3%
- Australia 17%
- USA 29%
- Europe 51%

8 a Make up 5 questions about the information in the pie chart.

eg *Where did most people go in 1995?*

1. _____
2. _____
3. _____
4. _____
5. _____

9 a Ask your neighbour these questions.

1. Have you ever been to an exhibition?
2. Where and when was it?
3. Who did you go with?
4. Why did you go?
5. Was it interesting?

10 a You are going to talk about yourself now. Try and keep going for at least 5 minutes. Here are some guidelines.

- your school days
- evening courses you've taken
- why you are learning English
- how you practise your English
- skills which you have
- your opinion about TV

UNIT 51

Which newspaper do you read and why?

1 a Here are some comments. Read them and guess who is speaking. Compare with your neighbour.

1. Elsie Carr, 83, grandmother.
2. Sandra McEwan, 21, student.
3. Ron Barker, 55, banker.
4. George Lawrence, 47, former manager.
5. Mary Adams, 46, teacher.

A "I always buy the Times from the newsagent's in the station. I read it on the train on my way to work. I look at the headlines first to see if there's anything interesting. I'm very interested in politics so I look for anything about that. I played football when I was younger so I usually go to the sports page next and look at the results from last night's games."

B "My daughter lives and works in Rwanda, so I turn to the 'world news' page first. I often buy different newspapers because they report on the situation there from different points of view. She's been out there for 5 years and she's a teacher, like me. I telephone her about once a month and I like to know about the situation there when I speak to her."

C "I was born in this town and I've always lived here. I have 4 children and 9 grandchildren who all live here too. The only newspaper I read is the local paper, the Courier. I'm not interested in what's going on in other places. The paper is delivered every Friday and the first thing I do is look for people I know in the photographs. I read these articles and then go to the births, deaths and marriages column to see if I know anybody there. If there has been something special, like a play in my grandchildren's school, I look for something about that, and then I read the rest of the newspaper."

D "I'm unemployed and I'm looking for a job. The best place to look is in the newspapers. I can't afford to buy newspapers every day so I go to the library in the mornings and look through 2 or 3 different newspapers. I turn to the 'situations vacant' page first and look through the advertisements. If I see a job which I can do I go home and write a letter and a CV. If I can't find anything I read the rest of the newspapers."

E "I always read the Express because I have a friend who is a journalist there. I don't read the headlines or look at the photographs. I look for the name of my friend in the "by" line and if I find her name I read the article. If I don't find her name I don't read any of the articles and throw the newspaper away."

b Now read the following questions and answer them briefly.

eg *How often do you read a newspaper? I read a newspaper once a week, usually on Sunday. Which paper do you normally read, and why? I normally read the Sunday Times because I think it reports events well and is not biased.*

1. How often do you read a newspaper? _____.
2. Which paper do you normally read? _____.
3. When do you read it? _____.
4. Do you read all of it? _____.
5. Do you look at the photographs or text first? _____.
6. Do you turn to a certain page first? _____.
7. Do you look at headlines first? _____.
8. Do you read the first paragraph of the article and then decide if it's interesting? _____
9. Do you look for certain words in the text? _____.
10. Do you look to see who has written the article? _____.

c Discuss your answers with your neighbour and then in small groups. Can you draw any conclusions from your answers?

2 **a** Here are one-line summaries of 6 newspaper articles. Read them and then decide if the news is regional news (R), national news (N), or world news (W). When you've finished, compare your answers with your neighbour.

1. This article is about money raised at a church fete.   R
2. This article is about current unemployment levels in Britain.   ___
3. This article is about the next Grand Prix motor race in Brazil.   ___
4. This article is about new tax increases by the government.   ___
5. This article is about a famous singer who was born in this town.   ___
6. This article is about a meeting of 5 Heads of State to discuss the crisis in Bosnia.   ___
7. This article is about a member of the Royal Family.   ___
8. This article is about a new supermarket which has just opened.   ___
9. This article is about global warming and the greenhouse effect.   ___
10. This article is about a man who has won £20 million.   ___

b Now match the one-line summary and the first sentence of the article.

a | Unemployment figures for the last month are down according to new statistics released by the government today. | 2

b | 3 points separate world champion Michael Schumacher from Damon Hill before this week's Grand Prix in Brazil. |

c | Jed Rover, 29, lead singer of 'Loud and Clear' returned home last night to spend a few days with his parents, Mr and Mrs Harry Rover of 23 Church Avenue, Cirencester. |

d | Despite promises that there would be no new tax increases this year, the Chancellor of the Exchequer yesterday announced an increase in income tax of 1%. |

e | Heads of States from 5 countries are meeting in Dublin on Saturday to discuss the growing crisis in Bosnia-Herzogovina. |

f | At last Saturday's church fete held at St Mungo's church, £4,500 was raised. |

g | The health of the Queen is in question after reports that she has been suffering from severe headaches. |

h | The new Safeways Superstore was officially opened in St George's Square last Thursday by Ted Aspinall, Director of the Superstore chain. |

i | A very happy Mr Nigel Harrison jumped for joy when he received a cheque for £20 million - this week's jackpot in the National Lottery. |

j | "The sea level will rise and submerge London by the year 2003 if nothing is done to prevent global warming" was the clear message at this year's Global Care Conference. |

c Compare your answers with your neighbour.

d Now ask your neighbour these questions.

1. How much money was raised at the church fete?
2. Who won £20 million?
3. How much is the increase in income tax?
4. How old is Jed Rover?
5. Who is Ted Aspinall?

e Discuss with your neighbour which of these articles you would read. Why?

eg I would read the article about the next Grand Prix motor race because I'm very interested in motor racing and I try and watch all of the races.

3 **a** You are going to hear the evening news. Before you start ask your neighbour what these words mean:

injure - planted - stolen - getaway car - exhibitor - decrease - cut

Make notes while you are listening. You will hear the cassette twice.

✎ **Notes**

eg   *Bomb attack - London Underground - Kings Cross - 5.30am.*

---

b Listen again and then compare with your neighbour.

c Now ask your neighbour these questions.

1. How many stories were there?
2. How many people were injured in the bomb attack?
3. What is the registration number of the getaway car?
4. How many exhibitors were at the International Motor Show?
5. How much was a litre of unleaded petrol before the price cut?

d You are going to retell one of the stories. Work with your neighbour and use your notes. When you're ready, tell the rest of the class.

e Now look at the newspaper you brought with you. Find two articles about local news, 2 articles about national news and 2 articles about international news. Cut them out and then on a separate piece of paper, write a one-line summary of the article. Give your articles and your summaries to your neighbour and see how quickly he/she can match the article and the summary.

4 a Translate the following.

Vocabulary

newspaper _____
article _____
raised _____
church fete _____
current _____
unemployment _____
levels _____
motor race _____
tax increases _____
famous _____
to discuss _____
crisis _____
Bosnia _____
Royal Family _____
global warming _____
greenhouse effect _____
won _____
according to _____
statistics _____
released _____
severe _____
lead singer _____

officially _____
Chancellor of the Exchequer _____
increase _____
to jump for joy _____
to receive _____
jackpot _____
National Lottery _____
sea level _____
to rise _____
to submerge _____
to prevent _____
clear message _____
Heads of State _____
growing _____
bomb attack _____
to injure _____
to plant _____
getaway car _____
exhibitor _____
decrease _____
to cut prices _____

Structures

How often do you read a newspaper? _____
I read a newspaper once a week, usually on Sunday. _____
Which paper do you normally read, and why? _____
I normally read the Sunday Times. _____
I read it because I think it reports events well. _____
This article is about money raised at a church fete. _____
The article is about current unemployment levels. _____

UNIT 52

What would you do if you won £20 million?

1 **a** Below is an article about Terry Benson and his wife who won £20 million on the National Lottery. While they were collecting their winnings their house was broken into and lots of things were stolen. Read the questions 1 - 10 through, and then find the answers as quickly as possible in the article.

1. How old is Mr Benson?
2. How did the burglars break in?
3. Where was the family when the house was burgled?
4. What did Terry buy Brenda for their 30th wedding anniversary?
5. How old was Brenda when her mother died?
6. Who is John Benson?
7. How many children do Terry and Brenda have?
8. How much money will their children get?
9. How much does Mr Benson earn a week?
10. Will he continue to work?

£20 million lottery couple's home is burgled.

Lottery multi-millionaire Terry Benson yesterday asked burglars to return jewellery stolen from his home while his family were collecting their £20 million jackpot prize.

Mr Benson (61) said thieves had taken items of sentimental value belonging to his wife Brenda and he would pay a reward to get them back.

The jewellery was stolen between 8pm and midnight from their home in Valentine Street on the Boothferry Estate in Hull while the family was in London at a news conference.

Mr Benson said "I will offer a reward of £1,000 for the pearl necklace I bought Brenda for our 30th wedding anniversary and for the bracelet which Brenda received from her mother for her 21st birthday."

Brenda, whose mother died when she was aged 15, said "This has certainly spoilt our celebrations."

Burglars, who broke in through the back door were disturbed by a relative who was looking after the house. John Benson, Mr Benson's cousin, said "I heard a noise so I got up and put the lights on. By the time I had gone downstairs, they had run away."

When asked about the £20 million win, Terry Benson added, "This is a lot of money, but it won't change our lives." He and his wife Brenda will keep half of the money and the rest will be split between their four children. Mr Benson said he will continue to work at his present £200 a week job.

b Now read the article again and answer the following questions.

1. What kind of things had been stolen from the house? _____
2. What will Mr Benson do to try and get the stolen goods back? _____
3. When was the jewellery stolen? _____
4. Did the burglars leave suddenly? Why? _____
5. Are the family upset? _____

c Do you feel sorry for the family? Why (not)? Discuss with your neighbour.

eg I don't feel sorry for the Benson family. Mr Benson has just won £20 million and can afford to buy lots of new things. I think it's unfair that one person can win so much money.

I don't agree with you. I think he's very lucky to win £20 million, but I don't think that £20 million can replace items of sentimental value. Wouldn't you like to win £20 million? I certainly would.

2 a Here is an information sheet from the National Lottery explaining how to play. Look at the information and then answer the questions below.

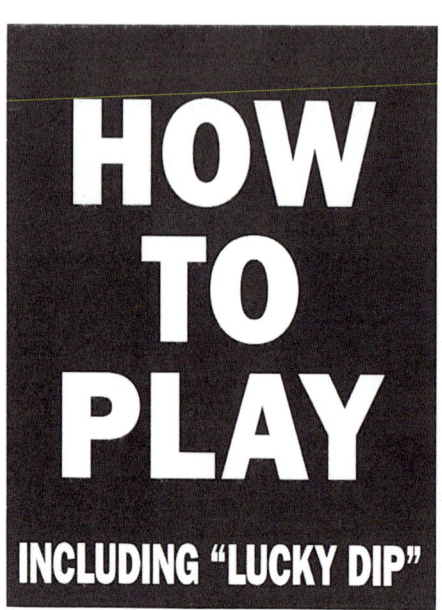

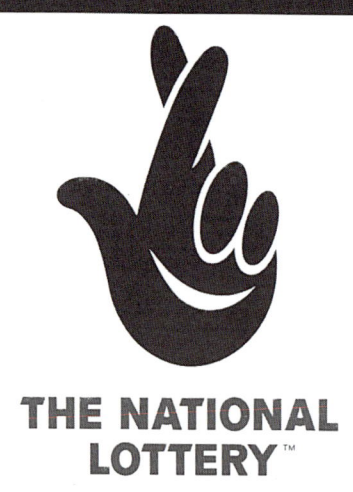

HOW TO PLAY
INCLUDING "LUCKY DIP"

THE NATIONAL LOTTERY

PLAYING THE NATIONAL LOTTERY

1 CHOOSE YOUR NUMBERS.

The National Lottery playslip has a number of boxes on it. These boxes are called "boards".

You select your six numbers by marking them on a board.

If you want to pick another six numbers use another board.

Only use a pencil or a blue or black pen. Put a clear, bold, vertical line through each number you've chosen. If you make a mistake, mark the void box and use another board.

2 LUCKY DIP – THE EASY WAY TO PLAY.

With Lucky Dip the terminal randomly selects a set of six random numbers for you. All you have to do is:

- Simply ask your National Lottery retailer for a "Lucky Dip". (You can have as many Lucky Dip selections as you like).
  OR
- Mark the Lucky Dip (L. Dip) box on each of those boards on which you wish to play Lucky Dip. (Note: you should not select a set of numbers and mark the Lucky Dip box on the same board.)

3 PAY THE RETAILER.

Next, give your playslip to the sales assistant and pay £1 for every set of six numbers and Lucky Dip selections you have chosen.

4 GET YOUR TICKET.

When you've paid, the retailer will enter your selections into the terminal and give you a National Lottery ticket. It will have your chosen numbers (including any Lucky Dip selections) and the draw date(s) printed on it. **You must check** that the numbers you have selected, the number of selections and the draw date(s) are correct and that the barcoded serial number is clearly readable. Then write your name and address on the back. Keep your ticket safe, you'll need it to check off your numbers in the draw. Don't lose it! You'll need it to claim your prize, as it is the **only proof** that you are a winner.

5 LOOK OUT FOR THE WINNING NUMBERS.

If six numbers on one of your printed selections match the six main numbers that are drawn – in any order – you are a jackpot winner. You also win a prize by matching five, four or even three out of the six.

There will also be a seventh 'bonus number' drawn. If you already have five matching numbers, look out for it. The bonus number gives you the chance to win the second highest prize.

As well as the televised draw, you'll find the winning numbers in national newspapers and clearly displayed in all National Lottery retailers.

© Camelot Group plc. The National Lottery logo is the property of the Secretary of State for National Heritage and is produced with the permission of Camelot Group plc who are the exclusive licensees of the logo.

b Now ask your neighbour these questions.

1 I am 14 years old. Can I play the National Lottery?
2 How many numbers do I choose?
3 Where can I buy a payslip?
4 What should I use to mark the pay slip?
5 How many numbers can I choose for £2.00?
6 What 3 things do I have to check?
7 Why do I have to keep my ticket safe?
8 When are the numbers drawn?
9 How many numbers do I have to match to win a prize?
10 How many numbers are drawn?

2 **c** **Explain to your neighbour how to play the National Lottery.**

eg *First you take a payslip. After you have taken a payslip, you choose 6 numbers. After you have chosen 6 numbers, you mark your numbers on the board. After you have marked your numbers on the board, you give your payslip to the sales assistant.*

d **If you have a National Lottery in your country and you have played it, explain to your neighbour how to play.**

e **You work for a regional newspaper and have just heard that somebody in your town has won £5,000 on the National Lottery. You are going to interview them, but before you do, think about what questions you are going to ask. Here are some ideas to start you off.**

- Where did they buy their winning ticket? How many times have they played?
- What are they going to do with the money?
- Would they have liked to have won more?
- Are they going to continue buying tickets?
- Will they buy them from the same shop?

When you are ready, start the interview with your neighbour.

3 **a** **Do you think you're lucky? Look at the following sets of numbers and in each set, mark 4 numbers. When you are finished, you will hear the drawn numbers on the cassette. Listen and see if you have the same numbers.**

```
          LOTTERY
1.  1 2 3 4 5 6 7 8 9 10
2.  1 2 3 4 5 6 7 8 9 10
3.  1 2 3 4 5 6 7 8 9 10
4.  1 2 3 4 5 6 7 8 9 10
5.  1 2 3 4 5 6 7 8 9 10
6.  1 2 3 4 5 6 7 8 9 10
```

b **How many times did you have...**

1 no numbers the same as the draw?
2 one number the same as the draw?
3 two numbers the same as the draw?
4 three numbers the same as the draw?
5 all four numbers the same as the draw?

Did anybody get all the numbers drawn?

c **Look at the numbers you chose and then discuss the following questions with your neighbour.**

Was there a particular reason why you chose these numbers? Did you choose the same number more than once? How many times did you choose each number? Which number did you choose the most? What do you associate with this number?

d **Discuss the following with your neighbour.**

1 Do you have a National Lottery in your country?
2 Have you ever played it?
3 Have you ever won anything on the lottery?
4 What would you do if you won £20 million?
5 What wouldn't you do if you won £20 million?

4 a Translate the following.

Vocabulary

multi-millionaire _____	split _____
burglars _____	present _____
stolen _____	to choose _____
thieves _____	to draw numbers _____
sentimental value _____	to mark _____
reward _____	outlets _____
news conference _____	sign _____
pearl _____	to claim _____
wedding anniversary _____	proof _____
to spoil _____	bold _____
celebrations _____	vertical _____
to break in _____	sales assistant _____
to disturb _____	retailer _____
cousin _____	randomly _____
downstairs _____	winner _____
added _____	guaranteed _____

Structures

I don't feel sorry for the Benson family. _____

Mr Benson has just won £20 million. _____

He can afford to buy lots of new things. _____

I think it's unfair that one person can win so much money. _____

I don't agree with you. _____

I think he's very lucky to win £20 million. _____

I don't think £20 million can replace items of sentimental value. _____

Wouldn't you like to win £20 million? _____

I certainly would. _____

First you take a payslip. _____

After you have taken a payslip you choose 6 numbers. _____

After you have chosen six numbers you mark your numbers on the board. _____

After you have marked your numbers on the board, you give your payslip to the sales assistant. _____
_____

What would you do if you won £20 million? _____

If I won £20 million, I would buy a house. _____

If I won £20 million, I wouldn't give any of it away. _____

UNIT 53

What was on the news last night?

1   a   Read the following questions and then discuss your answers with your neighbour.

1   How often do you watch the news on TV?
2   What time do you normally watch the news? Why?
3   Which channel do you normally watch it on?
4   Why do you watch the news on this channel?
5   How many TV newsreaders can you name?
6   How often do you listen to the news on the radio?
7   Where do you normally listen to the news on the radio?
8   How many radio newsreaders can you name?
9   Why do you listen to the news on this radio station?
10 Do you prefer listening to news on TV or radio? Why?

b   Now work in groups of 5 and answer the following questions.

1   Do most people watch/listen to news at the same time every day?
2   Do most people prefer listening to news on radio or TV?
3   Could people name more newsreaders on TV or on radio?

c   When was the last time you heard the news? Think about one of the news items you heard. See what you can remember about it and make notes below. When you're ready, tell your class as much as you can about it. Did anybody else hear the same news item?

eg   *I heard an interesting story on the news last night. It happened in Japan the day before yesterday. It was about a bomb attack in Tokyo.*

✎ **Notes**

When I heard it:

Where it happened:

When it happened:

What it was about:

---

2 **a** Newspaper headlines have to summarise an article and make you want to read it in a maximum of 7 or 8 words. Look through an English newspaper and see how many words there are in the longest headline. What kind of words are left out? Are the headlines sentences or not? How many words are there in the shortest headline?

b Here are 5 headlines. Try and match the headline and the first sentence of the article. See how many you can match without using a dictionary.

1 Breakthrough on sheep dip-formula.
2 Big cat purrs like a kitten.
3 Graf back at her most graphic.
4 Germans take over UK Car Company.
5 Labour's local choice.

☐ **a** The German Car Company, BMW, yesterday announced its plans to take over the British car manufacturer Rover.

☐ **b** Perth constituency Labour party has chosen its candidate for the next general election.

☐ **c** The most remarkable aspect of the Jaguar XJ6 is how little it has changed over the years.

☐ **d** An Agricultural Supplies company is claiming a breakthrough with a new environmentally friendly formula for its sheep dip.

☐ **e** Steffi Graf fought her way to the Wimbledon singles title and took the plate after winning 4-6, 6-1, 7-5.

c We already know that we can classify news items into regional news, national news and world news, but there are many more ways of classifying news items.

Newspapers divide news into 'sections' Look at the 5 sections below and decide which section you would find the articles from exercise 2b in.

Sport ☐   Farming ☐
Business ☐   Motoring ☐
Politics ☐

d Look through an English newspaper and see how many sections it is divided into and what these sections are. Make a list of the sections below.

Date _____	Newspaper _____
Section	**Page**

e Now find 3 articles which you find interesting. Give them to your neighbour to read and then ask him/her about them.

eg *What do you think of the article on page 45 in the sports section?*
Well I'm not really interested in sport so I didn't really find it very interesting.
And what about the article on fashion?
Oh yes, I thought that was very interesting.

3 a Newspapers don't just have news articles in them, they also have a lot of other information. Here are some items you find in newspapers. Can you think of any more?

1. crosswords
2. horoscopes
3. letters to the editor
4. births, marriages and deaths
5. public notices

b Discuss with your neighbour which of these you read and why?

eg I always read the headlines and then do the crossword while I'm having my morning coffee. I like reading the horoscopes too, but I don't read them until the evening.

c Now try the crossword below. Some of the letters are already given to help you.

Across

1. You keep your car here at night. (6)
4. This means of transport will take you where you want to go, but it might be expensive. (4)
6. Would you like _ and sugar in your coffee? (4)
7. In the evening, I don't like watching TV. I like reading a good _. (4)
11. When I buy something, I give the cashier some money and she gives me the goods, my change, and a _. (7)
13. Excuse me, can you tell me how to get _ the station please? (2)
14. There are 12 inches (or 30 cm) in a _. (4)
15. My _ are paid into my bank account. (5)
17. They fly in the sky. (5)
18. I come home from work and I ... my evening meal. (3)
19. _ you like the colour blue? (2)

Down

1. You go here to keep fit. (3)
2. You use this to draw a straight line. (5)
3. Every morning I get up and I _ to the bathroom. (2)
4. One plus one. (3)
5. I'm sitting on a chair _ a classroom. (2)
7. You may use one of these to carry your papers to work. (9)
8. You need a pair of these to cut paper. (8)
9. It's a beautiful day. The _ is shining in the sky. (3)
10. I'll meet you _ 7.30pm outside the cinema. (2)
12. When I go shopping in the supermarket, I put my groceries in a _. (7)
15. This is where patients in hospital stay. (4)
16. The opposite of early. (4)

4 a Translate the following.

Vocabulary

news _____
newsreader _____
sport _____
business _____
farming _____
motoring _____
crosswords _____
horoscopes _____
editor _____
births _____
marriages _____
deaths _____
public notices _____
market _____

Structures

What was on the news last night? _____
I heard an interesting story on the news last night. _____
It happened in Japan the day before yesterday. _____
It was about a bomb attack in Tokyo. _____
What do you think of the article on page 45 in the sports section? _____
Well I'm not really interested in sport. _____
I didn't really find it very interesting. _____
And what about the article on fashion? _____
Oh yes. I thought that was very interesting. _____
I always read the headlines. _____
I do the crossword while I'm having my morning coffee. _____
I like reading the horoscopes... _____
... but I don't read them until the evening. _____

UNIT 54

Young French student requires rented accommodation.

1 a Look at these questions and discuss your answers with your neighbour.

eg   *If I wanted to buy a second-hand car, I would look in our local newspaper or on the noticeboard of our local supermarket.*

1   If you wanted to buy a second-hand car, where would you look?
2   If you wanted to sell your TV, where would you advertise?
3   If you wanted to rent a flat, where would you look?
4   If you wanted to learn a language, where would you go?
5   If you wanted a part time job, where would you look? Where would you advertise?

b In many countries you can find all kinds of advertisements in the 'classified ads' section of a newspaper. Here are some headings from the classified ads section. See if you can put the advert in the correct column.

CLASSIFIED ADS						
Cars	Pets	Accommodation Wanted	Tuition	Situations Wanted	Situations Vacant	To Let

1   Beautiful kittens, house trained, await loving homes at Willows Cat Shelter. Donations requested. Tel 5366221.
2   House, 3 bedrooms, required for professional family. Medium to long let preferred. Tel 684033. Mobile (0421) 511346.
3   Experienced gardener required two days per week. Tel Mrs Stanton on 843661, after 6pm.
4   English as a foreign language, tuition with experienced EFL teacher, in groups, or one-to-one. Tel 632018.
5   Bedsit, central Haydon Bridge, shared bathroom, kitchen, £32 per week. Tel 684571.
6   GCSE French. Like help? Experienced teacher. Tel 604286.
7   Ford Escort 1.8 Diesel van - G registered. Taxed and tested. Good condition. Long MOT - £900 or nearest offer. Tel 322496.
8   Labrador puppies (3) black, 7 weeks old, 1 dog, 2 bitches, beautiful temperaments, free to a good home. Tel 684256.
9   Young French student, female, requires rented accommodation. Anything considered. Write Box P988.
10 Stone farm house, unfurnished, 3 bedrooms, fitted kitchen, living room, bathroom, central heating, coal fire, double glazing, garage. £350/£400 per calendar month. Tel 229429 business hours.
11 Student, 19, requires gardening/general outdoor work, up to 5 days per week. July to early September. Corbridge area. Tel 673030.
12 Mini 1000, T registered, 4 months MOT, alarm, sun roof, 55,000 miles - £375. Tel 682562.

c Ask your neighbour the following questions.

1   How much is the bedsit in Haydon Bridge?
2   Why would you ring 604286?
3   How much do the Labrador puppies cost?
4   How old is the student looking for gardening work?
5   Why would you ring the mobile phone number?
6   Does the young French student have a telephone?
7   What number would you call if you want to improve your French?
8   Who would you ring after 6pm?
9   When would you ring 229429?
10 What number would you call if you wanted a pet cat?

d Here are some abbreviations which are used in newspaper advertisements. See if you can find what these abbreviations are for. All the answers are contained in the adverts above.

1 pcm   2 pw   3 ch   4 ono   5 wks

2 a Your editor has given you the following adverts back because they contain several mistakes. Listen to the cassette and make the necessary corrections. You will hear the cassette twice.

Articles for SALE

TV, black/white, £250, nearly new, Tel (01327) 913249

Bicycle, girl's, 3 gears, blue, with basket, 3 years old, Tel (01375) 29929

Fridge, new, unwanted wedding present, £120, Tel (01325) 912634

3-piece suite, yellow, excellent condition, £325 ono, Tel (01444) 400650

Dining table, solid wood, for 8 people, antique, £350, Tel (01325) 742151

Wardrobe, wood, very good condition, £65, Tel (01375) 422313

Tent, 2-man, lightweight, never used, £80, Tel Mike (01421) 29477

Washing machine, good condition, 10 months old, under guarantee, £245 ono, Tel (01833) 27419

---

b Read this dialogue and practise with your neighbour.

A 422313. Hello.
B Hello. I saw your advertisement for the wardrobe in the paper last night. Do you still have it?
A Yes.
B What's it like?
A Well, it's solid wood and it's quite big. It's in very good condition, you see, I bought it for my son, but he doesn't like it.
B That sounds all right. How much do you want for it?
A £65, but I'll take £60. At the moment it's in the living room.
B Well I can come and see it at 12 o'clock if that's all right with you?
A Yes that's fine.
B How do I get there?
A Do you know St John's Church?
B Yes.
A Well coming from town you turn left at St John's then take the first right and then second left. I'm at number 14 - it's the second house on your left and there's an orange Ford Escort packed outside.
B Okay, see you then. Bye.
A Bye.

c Now telephone your neighbour and ask about some of the other items which are for sale.

d Ask your neighbour these questions.

1 Have you ever looked through the classified adverts section of a newspaper?
2 Have you ever bought anything through a classified advert?
3 What are the advantages and disadvantages of buying something from a classified advert?
4 What are the advantages and disadvantages of selling something through a classified advert?
5 If you were selling the items in 2a, how would you do it?

e Tell your teacher about your neighbour.

3 a Here is a guide to placing an advert in the classified ads section of a newspaper. Look at the information and then answer the questions below.

Your guide to placing an advert in the classifieds.

This guide gives you details of how to get the best results from our classified ads section.

How do I place an advert?

There are a number of ways in which to place an advert and it's so easy.

By Telephone (0114) 2300800.
Our classified line is open from 9am - 5.30pm Mon & Tues and from 9am - 5pm Wed, Thur & Fri.

By Fax (0114) 2300888
Our fax is available at all times during the day and night, 7 days a week.

By Post
Simply post your advert to:

**Sheffield Herald
Rotherham Road
Sheffield   S31
2LL**

In Person
Our front counter will be pleased to receive your advert at our Rotherham Road Office, Sheffield. Office hours are: Mon - Fri, 9am - 5pm.

How do I pay?

Our staff will be happy to advise you on payment. You can either pay by cheque - made payable to Sheffield Herald, or you can pay by Mastercard or Visa.

Deadlines
The deadline for advertising is   Tuesday evening, for the following Friday's publication.

---

1 If you want to place an advert, what number would you ring? _____
2 When can I ring on a Wednesday? _____
3 What is the fax number? _____
4 Can I fax this number at 8.30am on a Wednesday? _____
5 What is the address of the Sheffield Herald? _____
6 When can I deliver my advert in person? _____
7 Can I pay for the advert by credit card? _____
8 Who do I make the cheque payable to? _____
9 If I want my advert in next Friday's paper, when does the Herald have to receive it? _____
10 Where is the office of the Sheffield Herald? _____

4 a Translate the following.

Vocabulary

bedsit _____	shared bathroom _____
long let _____	taxed and tested _____
second-hand _____	condition _____
to advertise _____	MOT _____
to learn _____	or nearest offer _____
part time job _____	puppy _____
pets _____	dog _____
wanted _____	bitch _____
tuition _____	temperament _____
situations vacant _____	female _____
beautiful _____	unfurnished _____
kittens _____	business hours _____
house trained _____	calendar month _____
cat shelter _____	alarm _____
donations _____	sunroof _____
requested _____	to place an advert _____
professional _____	classified ads section _____
medium let _____	front counter _____
mobile _____	to advise _____
experienced _____	payable to _____
gardener _____	deadline _____
English as a Foreign Language _____	

Structures

If I wanted to buy a second hand car, I would look in the local newspaper. _____
I would look on the noticeboard of our local supermarket. _____
Hello, I saw your advert for the wardrobe in the paper last night. _____
What's it like? _____
Well, it's solid wood and it's quite big. _____
It's in very good condition. _____
You see, I bought it for my son, but he doesn't like it. _____
That sounds all right. _____
How much do you want for it? _____
£65, but I'll take £60. _____
Well I can come and see it at 12 o'clock if that's all right with you? _____
Yes that's fine. _____
How do I get there? _____
Coming from town you turn left at St John's Church. _____
Then take first right and then the second left. _____
I'm at number 14. _____
It's the second house on your left. _____
There's an orange Ford Escort parked outside. _____
Okay, see you then. Bye. _____

UNIT 55

Are you free on Tuesday afternoon?

1 a Listen to the cassette and write the appointments in the diary. Brian Hawthorne is telling you about his appointments during the month of October. You will hear the cassette twice.

October

1	Tue	_____	18	Fri	_____
2	Wed	_____	19	Sat	_____
3	Thu	_____	20	Sun	_____
4	Fri	_____	21	Mon	_____
5	Sat	_____	22	Tue	_____
6	Sun	_____	23	Wed	_____
7	Mon	_____	24	Thu	_____
8	Tue	_____	25	Fri	_____
9	Wed	_____	26	Sat	_____
10	Thu	_____	27	Sun	_____
11	Fri	_____	28	Mon	_____
12	Sat	_____	29	Tue	_____
13	Sun	_____	30	Wed	_____
14	Mon	_____	31	Thu	_____
15	Tue	_____			
16	Wed	_____			
17	Thu	_____			

b Compare your work with your neighbour.

c Look at your diary and tell your neighbour about your appointments.

eg On the first I had a meeting at our Head Office in Lyon. I had a week's holiday from 7 - 11. I had a meeting this morning with David Prescott and next Tuesday I'm meeting Frances Latour at 3 o'clock.

d Roleplay arranging an appointment. Look at the information below. You work in the purchasing department of Psi Computers. Your neighbour is one of Psi's suppliers - Sigma Supplies. You are selling a lot of computers at the moment and you want to arrange an appointment to discuss a larger discount for your company. Ring Sigma and arrange an appointment. You'll need to sort out when, where, what time and how to get there.

Here are some phrases to help you.

Hello, this is...
Can I speak to...?
I'd like to arrange a meeting to discuss...
Are you free on ...?
Can you make it a bit earlier?
Do you know how to find us?
I look forward to seeing you then.

2

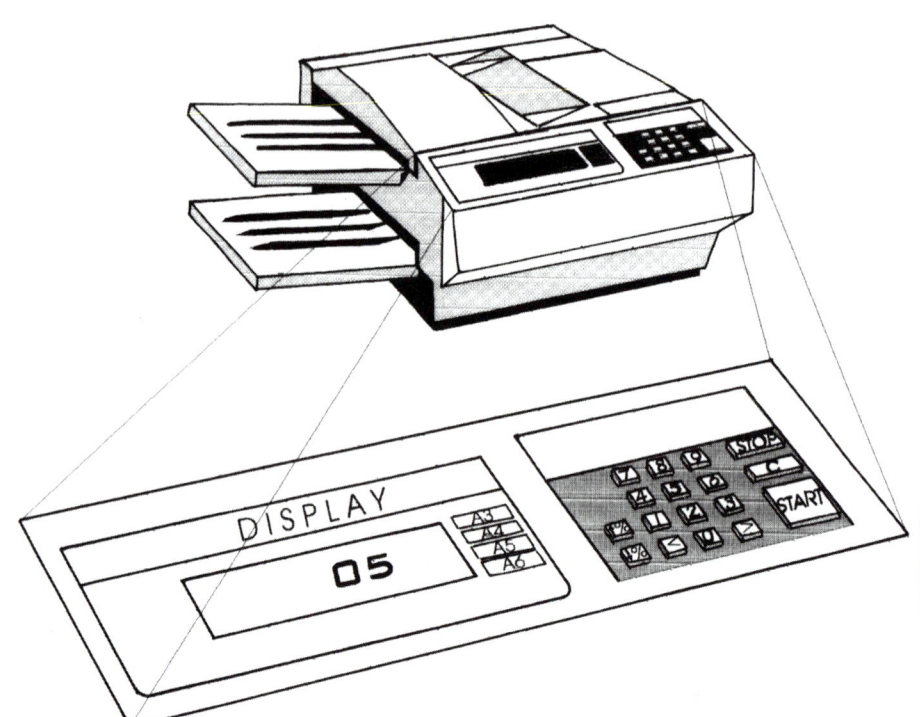

Instructions for Use

1. Lift lid and place the text/diagram face down on the glass surface.
2. Close lid.
3. Select paper size (A4 or A3).
4. Select the number of copies required.
5. Press the green start button.
6. If you require double-sided copies, select the double-sided button before selecting the number of copies required. Press the green start button. When the first side is done, open the lid and place the second side face down on the glass surface. Press the green start button.

Note: The photocopier requires a 5 minute warm-up period before operation. If a red light comes on, check that there is enough paper in the copier.

a   **Look at the information and ask your neighbour these questions, then make up some more.**

1. If you want to make a single copy of one side, what do you have to do?
2. Which button do you select first?
3. What colour is the start button?
4. If a red light comes on what should you check?
5. What size paper can you photocopy?

b   **Now explain to your neighbour how to do the following:**

1. You have a single A4 sheet which you need to copy 4 times.
2. You have 2 A4 sheets which you need to copy onto 1 double-sided A4 sheet.
3. You have an A3 sheet which you need to copy 10 times.
4. You have 2 A4 sheets which you need to copy 20 times onto single-sided A3.
5. You have 4 A4 sheets which you need to copy 10 times onto double-sided A3.

c   **Now ask your neighbour these questions.**

eg   *Have you ever used a photocopier? Yes I have. I often use a photocopier to copy documents.*

1. Have you ever used a photocopier? Where? When? Why?
2. Do you think photocopiers are useful?
3. Do you think photocopying is a waste of paper?
4. Have you ever had any problems with photocopiers?
5. Can you think of 3 advantages and 3 disadvantages of photocopiers?

d   **List 5 other pieces of equipment you have in your office and then explain to your neighbour how to use them.**

3 a Here is a diagram of Sandhouses Trading Estate. There are several companies on this estate and the buildings they rent are called 'units'. This is so that visitors can find the company which they are looking for more easily. Below is a list of who is renting each unit. Ask your neighbour how to get from one unit to another.

eg   Excuse me. Can you tell me how to get to MacMillan's Dog Foods - all it says on the business card is MacMillan's Dog Food, Unit 13, Sandhouses Trading Estate.

How To Find Us

Unit 1	Storey's Discount Carpet Warehouse	Unit 8	R & B T-Shirts
Unit 2	Martin White Car Repairs	Unit 9	Z1 Reprographics Ltd
Unit 3	M & S Factory Shop	Unit 10	Computer World
Unit 4	Squire's Mountain Bike Centre	Unit 11	Discount Jeans Centre
Unit 5	The Fylde DIY Store	Unit 12	The Furniture Store
Unit 6	Johnson's Garden Furniture	Unit 13	Macmillan's Dog Food
Unit 7	Da Roma's Pizza Delivery	Unit 14	Paul Richard's Printers

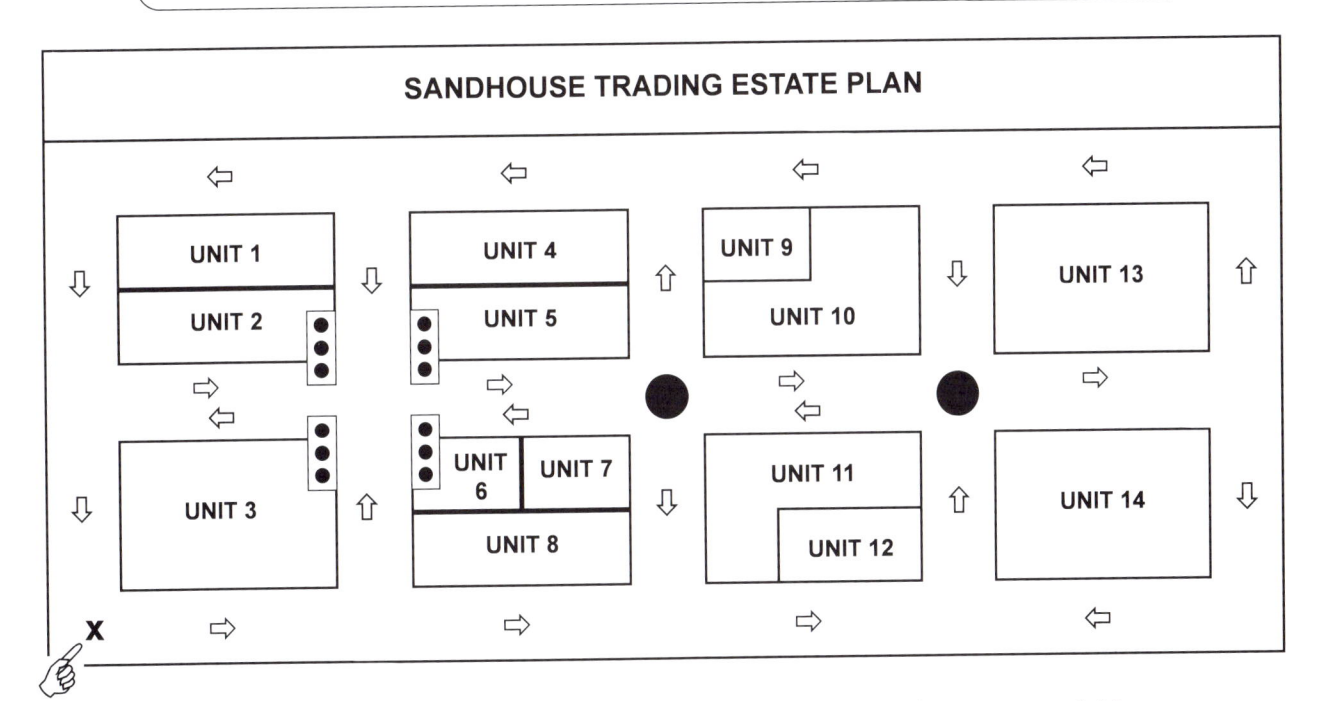

SANDHOUSE TRADING ESTATE PLAN

[Map showing Units 1-14 arranged on the trading estate with directional arrows. X marks "you are here" at bottom left.]

b Read the following situations and then telephone your neighbour.

1 You want to know what the opening hours for Squire's Mountain Bike Centre are. Ring them and ask.

2 You are hungry and decide to order a pizza. Ring Da Roma's Pizza Delivery and tell them what you want and where to deliver it.

3 Somebody crashed into your car yesterday. It is not badly damaged but needs some bodywork. Ring Martin White Car Repairs and arrange a time when you can take your car in.

4 You need some toner for your Hewlett-Packard 4L printer. Ring Computer World and see if they have any. Find out how much it costs and how to get there.

5 You want a bird table. Ring Johnson's Garden Furniture. Find out if they have any in stock, how much they are and if they can deliver.

c Tell your teacher what you have arranged.

4 a Translate the following.

Vocabulary

meeting _____
head office _____
project _____
to arrange _____
purchasing department _____
supplier _____
to increase _____
trading estate _____
companies _____
single-sided _____
double-sided _____
to copy _____
10 times _____
sheet of paper _____
units _____
visitors _____
carpet _____
warehouse _____
car repairs _____
factory shop _____
DIY store _____
garden furniture _____
printer _____
photocopier _____
to lift _____
face down _____
to select _____

Structures

On the first I had a meeting at our Head Office in Lyon. _____
I had a week's holiday from 7 - 11. _____
I had a meeting this morning with David Prescott. _____
Next Tuesday I'm meeting Frances Latour at 3 o'clock. _____
Hello, this is... _____
Can I speak to...? _____
I'd like to arrange a meeting to discuss... _____
Are you free on...? _____
Can you make it a bit earlier? _____
Do you know how to find us? _____
I look forward to seeing you then. _____
Have you ever used a photocopier? _____
I often use a photocopier to copy documents. _____
Excuse me. Can you tell me how to get to...? _____
All it says on the business card is... _____

UNIT 56

She's going to type a letter.

1 a Look at photograph sequence 11 'Typing a Letter' on the next pages and discuss with your neighbour what the sequence is about.

b Describe the woman to your neighbour.

eg *She's tall and thin with short, dark hair. She's wearing a blouse and...*

c Ask your neighbour these questions,

1. What is the lady going to do? What is her job?
2. What is she holding in her left hand?
3. What is she going to do with the paper?
4. What has she done with the paper in the second picture?
5. What has she done with the chair?
6. Why will she need to use the pencil?
7. What has she placed on the desk?
8. What will she do before signing the letter?
9. What has she done before using the pencil?
10. How did she correct her mistake?
11. Before checking the letter, what did she have to do?
12. What did she do after rolling the paper into the typewriter?
13. What was she doing before she sat down to type?
14. How did she check the letter?
15. What will she do after signing the letter?
16. What sort of an office is this?
17. How is the typewriter marked to identify it?
18. How was the office heated?
19. How would you type a letter?
20. Do you think anybody still types in this way? Who?

d Now ask your neighbour these questions.

1. Can you type? When/Where/How did you learn?
2. Have you ever used a typewriter like this?
3. Do you think everybody should learn to type?
4. Should children learn to type at school?
5. What are the advantages/disadvantages of typing on a typewriter or on a computer?

Typing a Letter (Photograph Sequence 11)

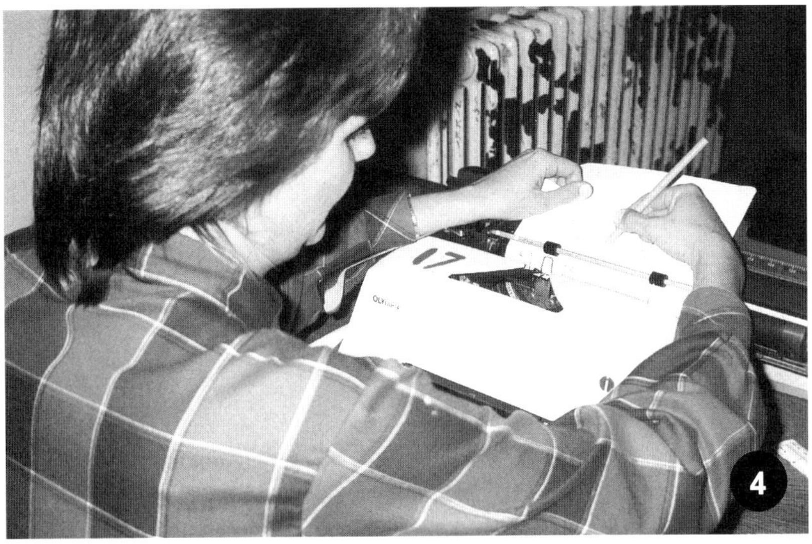
4

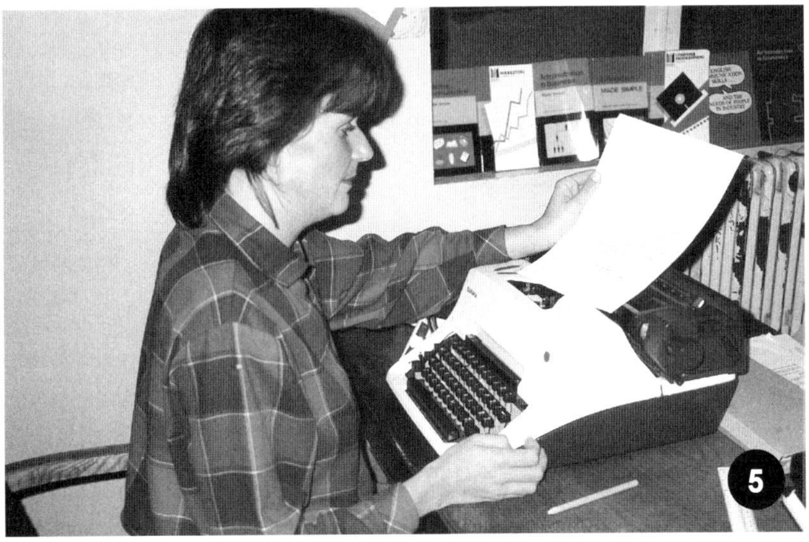
5

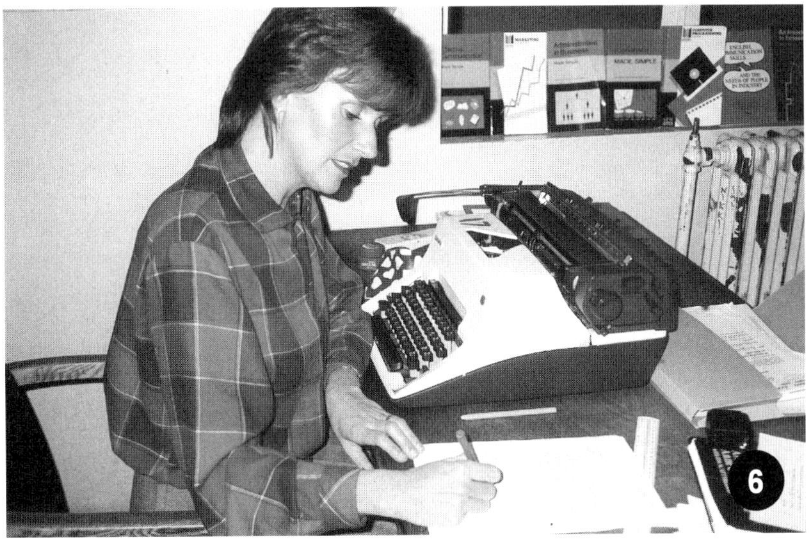
6

2 **a** Jennifer MacLean works in the Personnel Department of "Urgent Office Supplies". She is working on the holiday plan for July, August and September. Listen to the cassette and mark on the sheet when the employees are taking holiday. You'll hear the cassette twice.

Name	Payroll No	HOLIDAY CHART											
		July					August				September		
		3	10	17	24	31	7	14	21	28	4	11	18	25
Elaine Robertson	95													
David Walker	79													
Michael Craig	17													
Natalie Kerr	32													
Sarah Marshall	34													
Deborah Atkinson	15													
Patricia Oliver	91													
Mark Campbell	12													
Howard Mills	37													
Jennifer MacLean	33													

b **Ask your neighbour about the people.**

eg *When is Elaine Robertson taking her holiday? How long is Michael going on holiday for? Who is taking holiday in the first week of August?*

c **Now ask your neighbour these questions.**

1 How many days holiday do you get per year?
2 Do you get more or less holiday per year as you get older?
3 Who decides when you can take your holiday - you or the company?
4 Have you ever taken unpaid leave? When? Why?
5 Would you prefer to have more days holiday per year? Why (not)?

d **Read these statements and discuss them with your neighbour.**

1 I think the company should let me take holiday when I like, not when the company closes.
2 There is always a lot to do before going on holiday.
3 I think the amount of holiday should increase with age.
4 If I work overtime I should get more holiday.
5 The company is more important than the individual.

e **Now read these statements and discuss them with your neighbour.**

1 If employees are ill, the days should be deducted from their holiday entitlement.
2 Employees should not go on holiday during busy periods.
3 Holiday entitlement should decrease with age.
4 If public holidays fall on Sundays, Mondays should be free.
5 The individuals are more important than the company.

The Comptuer Store

☆ LHT 7150 Multimedia
☆ Intel pentium processor
☆ 8Mb RAM
☆ 540 Mb hard disk
☆ 14" SVGA Monitor
☆ Quad speed CD-ROM drive
☆ Stereo sound card and speakers
☆ Internal fax modem facility
☆ Windows 95
☆ Many software and CD titles

£1349 ex VAT
£1585.08 incl VAT

Specialist Business Centre at every store

- dedicated sales people
- business leasing
- account facilities
- telephone ordering

Where to find us:

Birmingham: Axletree Way, Wednesbury
Tel 0121 505 7950 / Fax 0121 505 7951

Manchester: 750 Chester Road
Tel 0161 877 2120 / Fax 0161 877 2103

Reading: South Park, Rose Kiln Lane
Tel 01325 591265 / Fax 01325 591766

3 a Ask your neighbour the following questions.

eg *What is this advertisement for? It's an advertisement for a new computer.*

1   What is the name of the company?
2   How big is the hard disk?
3   How much is the price including VAT?
4   What size is the monitor?
5   Can I send a fax from the computer?
6   How many branches does the company have?
7   What is the fax number of the branch in Manchester?
8   What is the address of the branch in Birmingham?
9   What is the code for Reading?
10 Can my company arrange to lease the computer?

b Now ask your neighbour these questions.

eg *Have you ever used a computer? Yes I have. I use one every day at work.*

1   Have you ever used a computer?
2   How often do you use a computer?
3   Do you know what make it is?
4   Do you know what the processor speed is?
5   Which applications do you use most? Why?
6   Which software packages do you use most? Why?
7   Do you ever use CD's? If so, which? Why?
8   When did you first use a computer?
9   What are the advantages of computers?
10 What are the disadvantages of computers?

4 a Translate the following.

Vocabulary

typewriter _____

Personnel Department _____

to work on _____

holiday plan _____

to take holiday _____

payroll no _____

processor _____

monitor _____

sales people _____

business leasing _____

documents _____

fax _____

modem _____

software _____

application _____

software package _____

Structures

She's going to type a letter. _____

She's tall and thin, with short, dark hair. _____

She's wearing a blouse and... _____

When is Elaine Robertson taking her holiday? _____

How long is Michael going on holiday for? _____

Who is taking holiday in the first week of August? _____

What is this an advertisement for? _____

It's an advertisement for a new computer. _____

Have you ever used a computer? _____

Yes I have. _____

I use one every day at work. _____

UNIT 57

Exam Practice 1

1 a   Tell your neighbour about yourself. Use the following points as a guide.

- personal details   -   name, address, tel no
  date of birth, place of birth, nationality
  marital status

- parents   -   names, ages, occupations, hobbies

- children   -   names, ages, birthdays, appearance

- brothers and sisters   -   names, ages, wives/husbands, relationships

2 a   Look at photograph sequence 12 'Buying a Car' on the next pages and discuss with your neighbour what the sequence is about.

b   Ask your neighbour these questions. Read the questions carefully.

1   Why have this man and woman parked their car?
2   What is the man doing with his right hand?
3   What have the man and woman done after locking the car door?
4   Why do they lock the car door?
5   What do you think they will do next?
6   What is the salesman trying to do?
7   Why is the salesman sitting at a desk with a pen in his hand?
8   What is the older man going to do?
9   What was the lady doing while her husband was talking to the salesman?
10 What will he do with his old car?

c   Now ask your neighbour these questions.

1   Have you ever bought a second-hand car?
2   Have you ever bought a new car?
3   What are the advantages and disadvantages of buying a second-hand car?
4   What are the advantages and disadvantages of buying a new car?
5   Have you ever had any problems with second-hand/new cars?

Buying a Car (Photograph Sequence 12)

253

3 a You are going to hear a taped announcement. Before you listen, look at the map of Cambridge. You will hear the cassette twice and you may make notes if you wish.

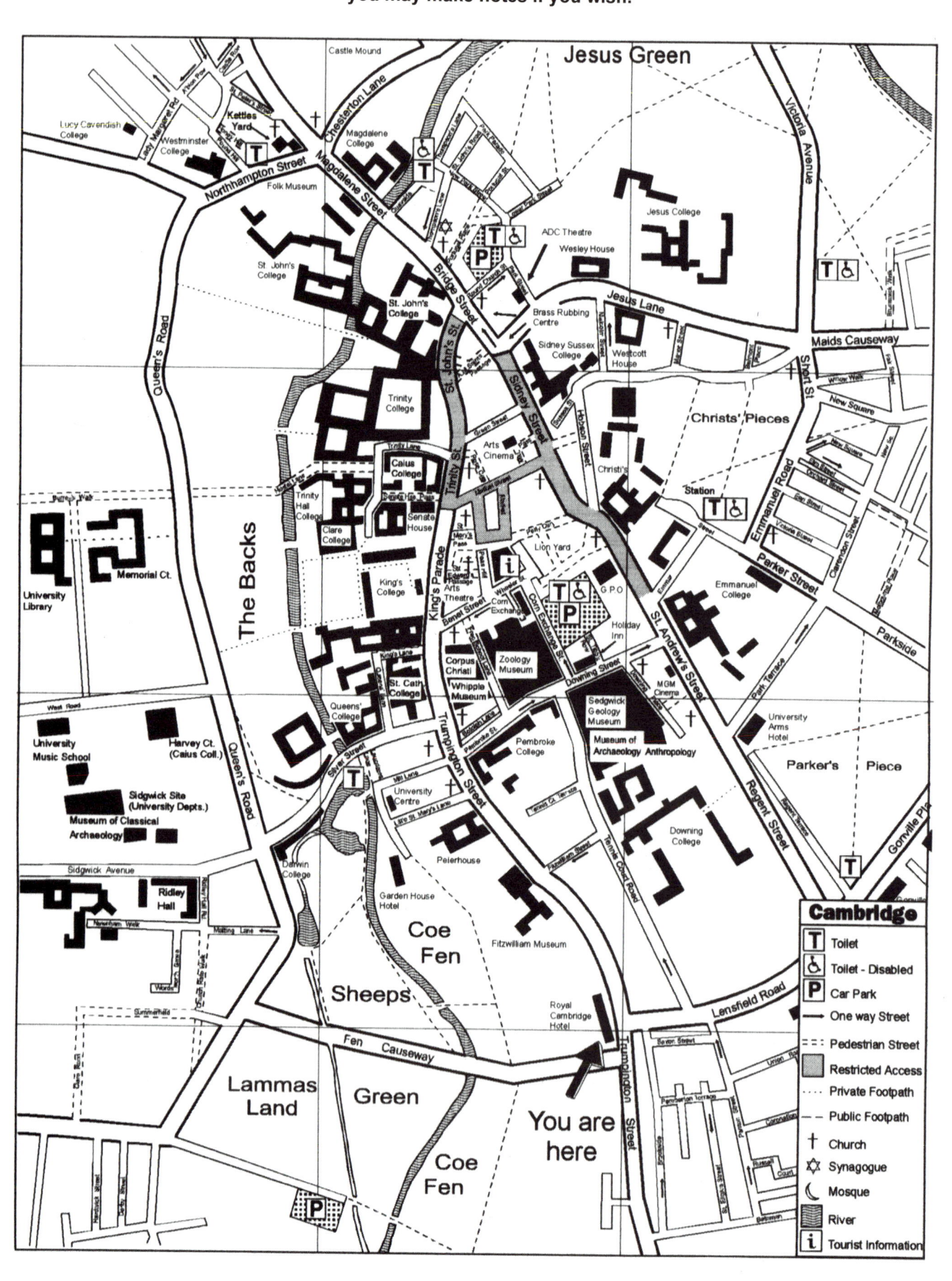

3 b Here are 15 questions about the trip to Cambridge. Ask your neighbour and when you've finished, make up 5 more question of your own.

1 Will you go and visit the Fitzwilliam Museum straight away? Why not?
2 Coming out of the hotel on to Trumpington Street, which way would you turn to visit the colleges?
3 From the Fitzwilliam Museum, how would you get to Emmanuel College?
4 From Sidney Sussex College, how would you get to the nearest toilet?
5 How would you get from Clare College to Queen's Road? Would you cross the river?
6 If you wanted to visit two museums in the afternoon after lunch, which would you choose and which direction would you take?
7 If you were at St John's College and needed some tourist information, how would you find it?
8 Supposing it rains, what will happen to the river trip?
9 What are the Backs? Will you see them in the afternoon?
10 Could you walk from Queen's College back to the hotel? How?
11 If you are at Jesus College and want to go to church, where might you go?
12 How long will you have in the Zoology Museum if you arrive at 3.45pm and spend the rest of the visit there?
13 Would you expect to find traffic on King's Parade?
14 If you got a taxi at Magdalen College in a rush back to the hotel at 5.50pm, what route would the taxi take?
15 Supposing you were having a drink at the University Arms Hotel and needed to get back to the coach quickly, how would you go?

4 a Ask your neighbour these 15 questions about the advertisement on the next page. When you've finished, make up 5 more questions.

1 What is this an advertisement for?
2 What is the address of the vineyard?
3 How would you get there?
4 What is the nearest town or village?
5 What roads are nearest to the vineyard?
6 Is the vineyard open every day?
7 Is the visit free?
8 What is the winter season for the vineyard?
9 How long is the vineyard open (a) in summer, (b) in winter?
10 Could you take a group to visit?
11 What are Bank Holidays?
12 How much does a conducted tour cost?
13 Can you eat and drink on such a tour?
14 How could you arrange a conducted group tour?
15 Are children admitted?

5 a Read the following statements and say whether you agree with them or not. Discuss your reasons with your neighbour.

1 Tax on alcohol should be much higher.
2 People who drive the most should pay more car tax.
3 Medical care should be provided by the state.
4 Everyone has the right to work.
5 Unemployment benefit is far too high.

Come and drink English Wine at an English Vineyard

How to find us...

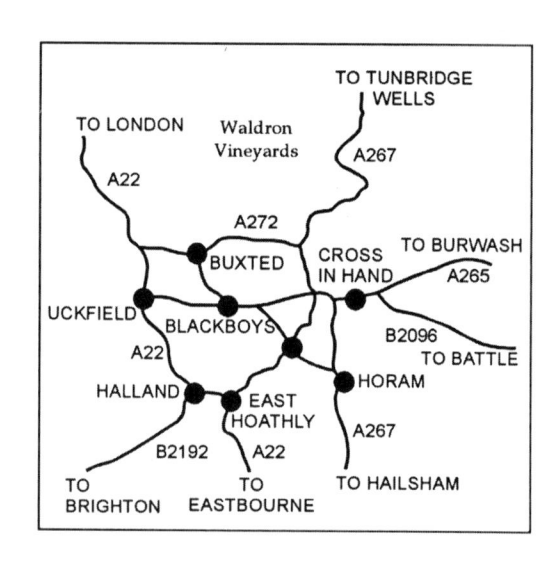

St George's English Wines
Waldron Vineyards
Heathfield East Sussex
Telephone: Horam
(014353) 2156

Conducted Tours (by appointment)

Includes talk, colourslide presentation, vineyard tour, tasting and a selection of optional buffets. Ideal for groups and clubs. Daytime, evenings and weekends. £2 - £4.50

Light lunches and cream teas are served on certain days. Ample free parking.

Our Summer season starts on St George's Day, April 23 and from then to September 30 we are open daily 11am to 5pm, including Sundays and Bank Holidays.

During winter, October 1 - April 22, our vineyard shop is open every Thursday, Friday, Saturday and Sunday 1pm - 4pm.

Vineyard Walkabout

Walk at your leisure through the vineyards followed by a tasting of St George's English Wine £1.25
Children Free

UNIT 58

Exam Practice 2

1 a   Tell your neighbour about yourself. Use the following points as a guide.

- personal details   - name, address, tel no
  - date of birth, place of birth, nationality
  - marital status

- family   - parents, children, brothers and sisters

- work   - work experience (where, when, what, how long)
  - current occupation (what, where)
  - ambitions

2 a   Look at photograph sequence 13 'A Rep Calls' on the next pages and discuss with your neighbour what the sequence is about.

b   Ask your neighbour these questions.

1. Why has the man arrived with 2 small cases?
2. Why do you think the receptionist took the rep's calling card?
3. Where will the rep go after the receptionist's phone call?
4. Who is the lady in the light coloured dress? What is she doing?
5. Describe the room where the three people are. What are they doing?
6. What do you think the Director was doing before the rep arrived?
7. What will the Director say to the rep?
8. Describe the sales techniques of the rep. What do you think of them?
9. What is the lady in the light coloured dress bringing in for the two people? What is on the tray?
10. What is the man writing?
11. Why are they shaking hands?
12. After visiting the company, what will the rep do?
13. In which season is this visit taking place?
14. How is the rep dressed?
15. In your opinion, what sort of company is this?

c   Now ask your neighbour these questions.

1. What do you think about Sales Reps?
2. Would you like to work as a Sales Rep? Why (not)?
3. What do you understand by 'sales technique'?
4. What do you think is important for a successful Sales Rep?
5. Do you think languages are important for Sales Reps?

A Rep Calls (Photograph Sequence 13)

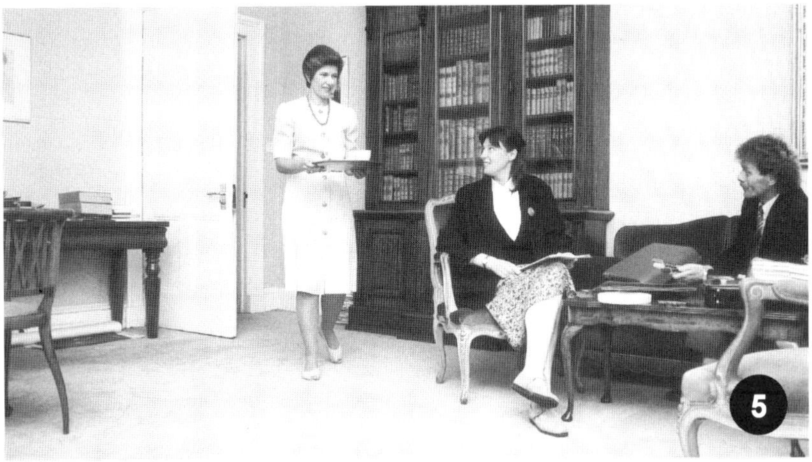
5

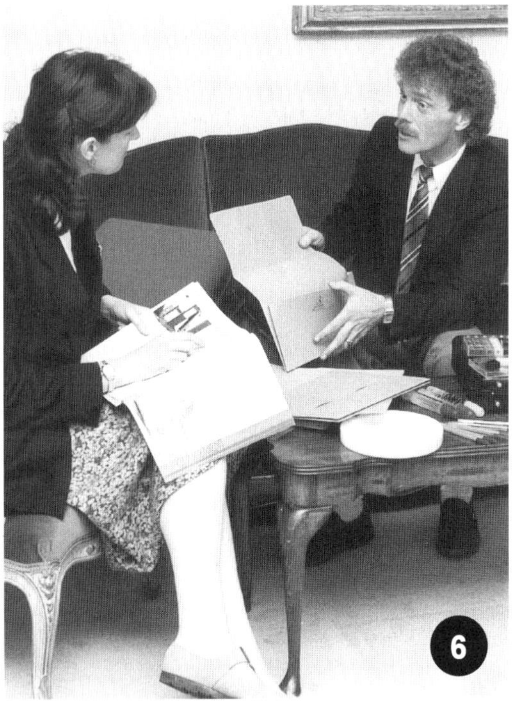
6

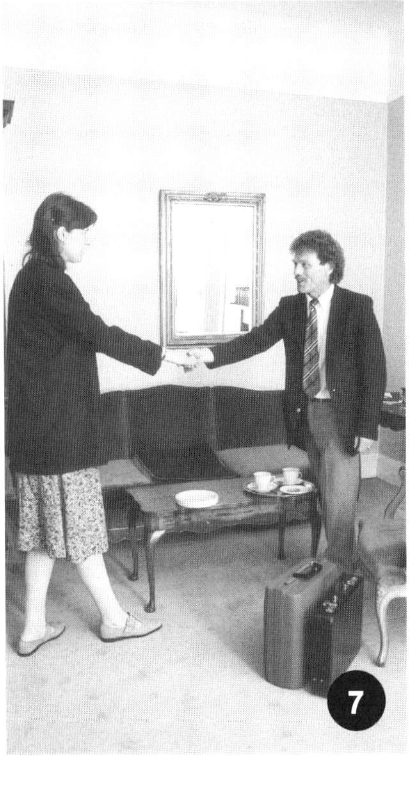
7

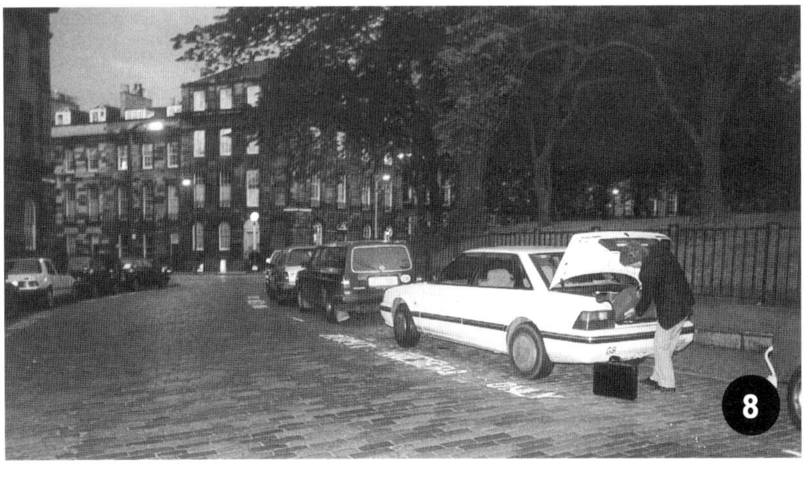
8

3 **a** You are going to hear a taped announcement. Before you listen, look at the diagram of the Winchester Conference Building. You will hear the cassette twice and you may make notes if you wish.

FIRST FLOOR

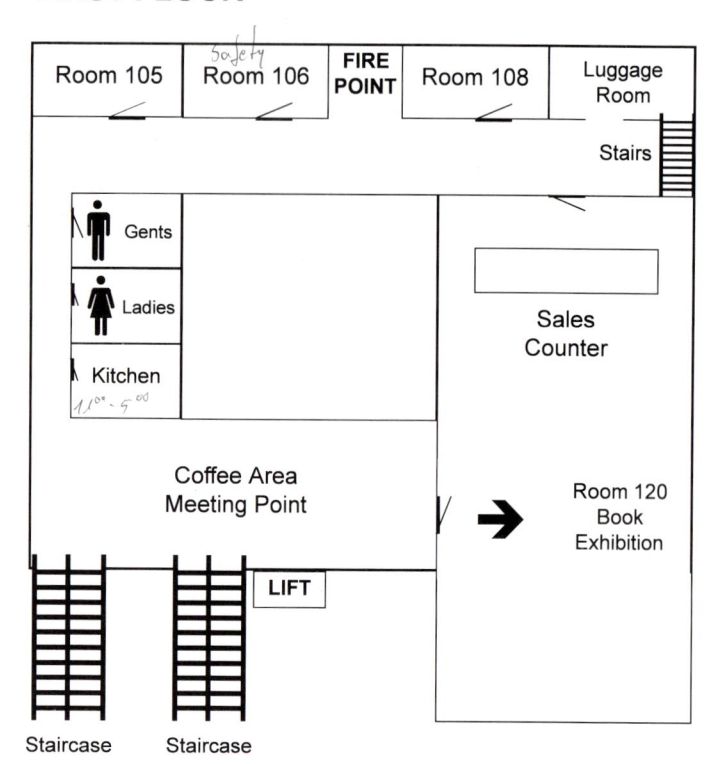

| Room 105 | Room 106 | FIRE POINT | Room 108 | Luggage Room |

Gents / Ladies / Kitchen

Sales Counter

Coffee Area Meeting Point

Room 120 Book Exhibition

LIFT

Staircase   Staircase

Stairs

GROUND FLOOR

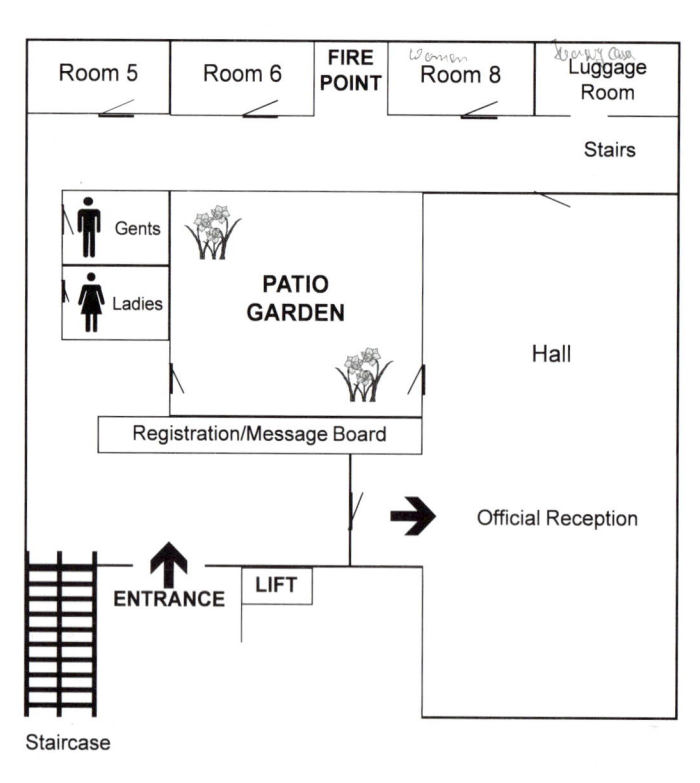

| Room 5 | Room 6 | FIRE POINT | Room 8 | Luggage Room |

Gents / Ladies

PATIO GARDEN

Hall

Registration/Message Board

Official Reception

ENTRANCE   LIFT

Stairs

Staircase

↙ Main Gate and Road   ↘ To Residential Blocks

3 b   Now ask your neighbour these questions.

1   From the kitchen, how would you reach the official reception?
2   After registration you want to store a heavy box of leaflets. Where would you go?
3   Will the weather affect the official reception? How?
4   From the first floor lift, you want to attend the lecture on 'Safety standards'. How would you go?
5   After attending the women's discussion group on Monday afternoon, how would you get coffee?
6   If you want a snack at 4 o'clock in the afternoon, where should you go?
7   After registration you want to buy some books. Where would you go?
8   After hearing a talk in Room 108 you want to go to your residential block. How do you get there.
9   If you were in Room 108 and the fire alarm rang, what would you do?
10 You want to leave a message for a friend who is also at the conference. How would you do it?
11 If you went into the hall at 8pm this evening, what would you find? Why?
12 Could you get tea or Coca Cola at the kitchen? When?
13 Can you buy books at the book exhibition?
14 At the reception you find the Hall very hot and smoky. What could you do?
15 How would get from the patio garden to Room 105?

4 a   Ask your neighbour these questions about the advertisement on the next page.

1   If you were an employer, would you be interested in this scheme?
2   Why (not)? Is it simple?
3   How much would you get for each new worker?
4   How much should you pay each new worker?
5   Which people are eligible?
6   Can you benefit if you take on new workers part time?
7   How can you find out more about the scheme?
8   Can you find out information on a Sunday? How?
9   What kinds of businesses can take advantage of this scheme?
10 Why should this attract small businesses?
11 Do you have to pay for telephone calls to find out more?
12 If you were out of a job, could you make use of this scheme? How? Why not?
13 Where has this advertisement come from?
14 Do you think it is a good idea?
15 What other schemes do you know for creating jobs in your country?

5 a   Read the following statements and say whether you agree with them or not. Discuss your reasons with your neighbour.

1   School education does not prepare people for the real world.
2   There is no point in training people for jobs which don't exist.
3   Unemployment is increasing because of cheap foreign labour.
4   Working people should pay more tax to support the unemployed.
5   Factories are being closed down and replaced by supermarkets and retail parks.

Now you can give young people a job and get paid for it.

There's a new scheme which allows you to take on young workers at realistic wages, and be paid £15 a week for each one.

It's as simple as that. No administrative problems. No complicated red tape.

Jobcentres and Careers Offices will be glad to tell you about eligible young people. You'll be helping out young people, and helping yourself expand, without getting involved in unrealistic labour costs.

It's called the New Workers Scheme. Ideal for small and medium-sized businesses, but still attractive to large businesses.

The jobs must be full time for one year. The wages must be no more than £55 (under 20), or £65 (aged 20).

You can take on as many workers as you like.

The people must be under 21 and in their first year of employment.

ACTION FOR JOBS

For more information dial 100 and ask for FREEFONE NEW WORKERS. (Lines are open from 9.00 am to 9.00 pm, seven days a week). Or send in the coupon below.

To: New Workers Scheme, FREEPOST, Curzon House, 20-24 Lonsdale Road, London NW6 4YP. Please send me details of the New Workers Scheme.

Name: _____ DE2
Company: _____
Position: _____
Address: _____

New Workers Scheme
Department of Employment DE

UNIT 59

Exam Practice 3

1 **a** Tell your neighbour about yourself. Use the following points as a guide.

- personal details
  - name, address, tel no
  - date of birth, place of birth, nationality
  - marital status

- family
  - parents, children, brothers and sisters

- work
  - work experience (where, when, what, how long)
  - current occupation (what, where)
  - ambitions

- hobbies and interests
  - what/how often/when/how much travelling/what equipment you need
  - how it started/training
  - ambitions

2 **a** Look at photograph sequence 14 'Buying a Dress' on the next pages and discuss with your neighbour what the sequence is about.

b Ask your neighbour these questions.

1 What was the lady wearing when she went into the clothes shop?
2 Why do you think she is going into the clothes shop?
3 What did the shop assistant do first?
4 What is she doing in the third photograph?
5 How did she pay for the dress?
6 Why do you think she paid by credit card?
7 What did the shop assistant do with the dress after the customer had paid?
8 Why do you think she bought the dress?
9 Where do you think she will go now?
10 Describe the shop.
11 What did the lady do before trying on the dress?
12 Describe the shop assistant.
13 What kind of clothes shop is this?
14 Would you go to this kind of shop to buy your clothes? Why (not)?
15 When was the last time you bought a new suit or dress?

Buying a Dress (Photograph Sequence 14)

264

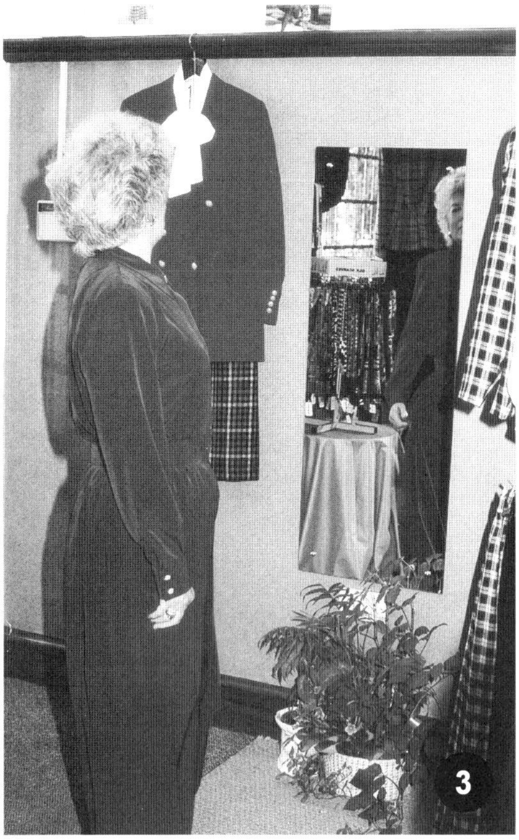
3

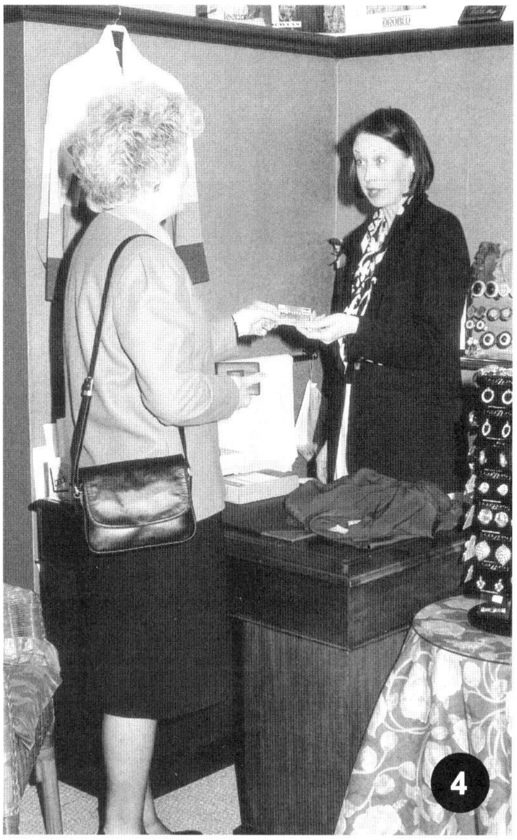
4

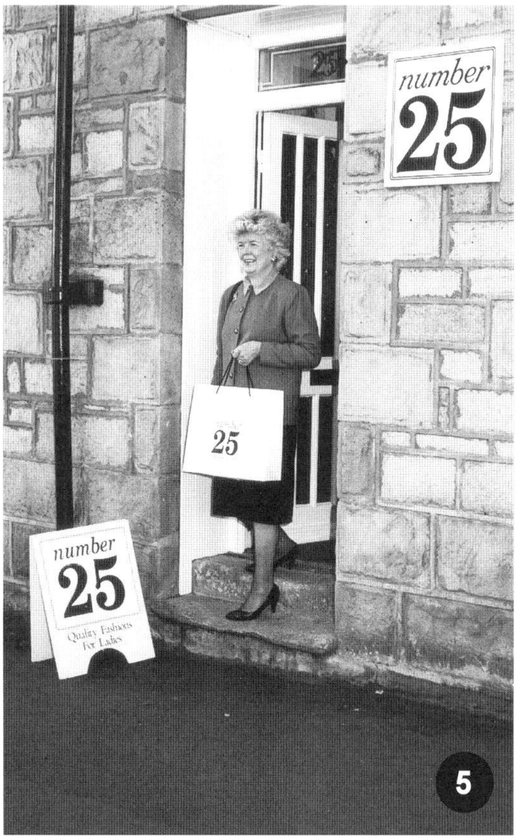
number
25
25
number
25
Quality Fashions
For Ladies
5

3 a You are going to hear a taped announcement. Before you listen, look at the floor plan. You will hear this cassette twice and you may make notes if you wish.

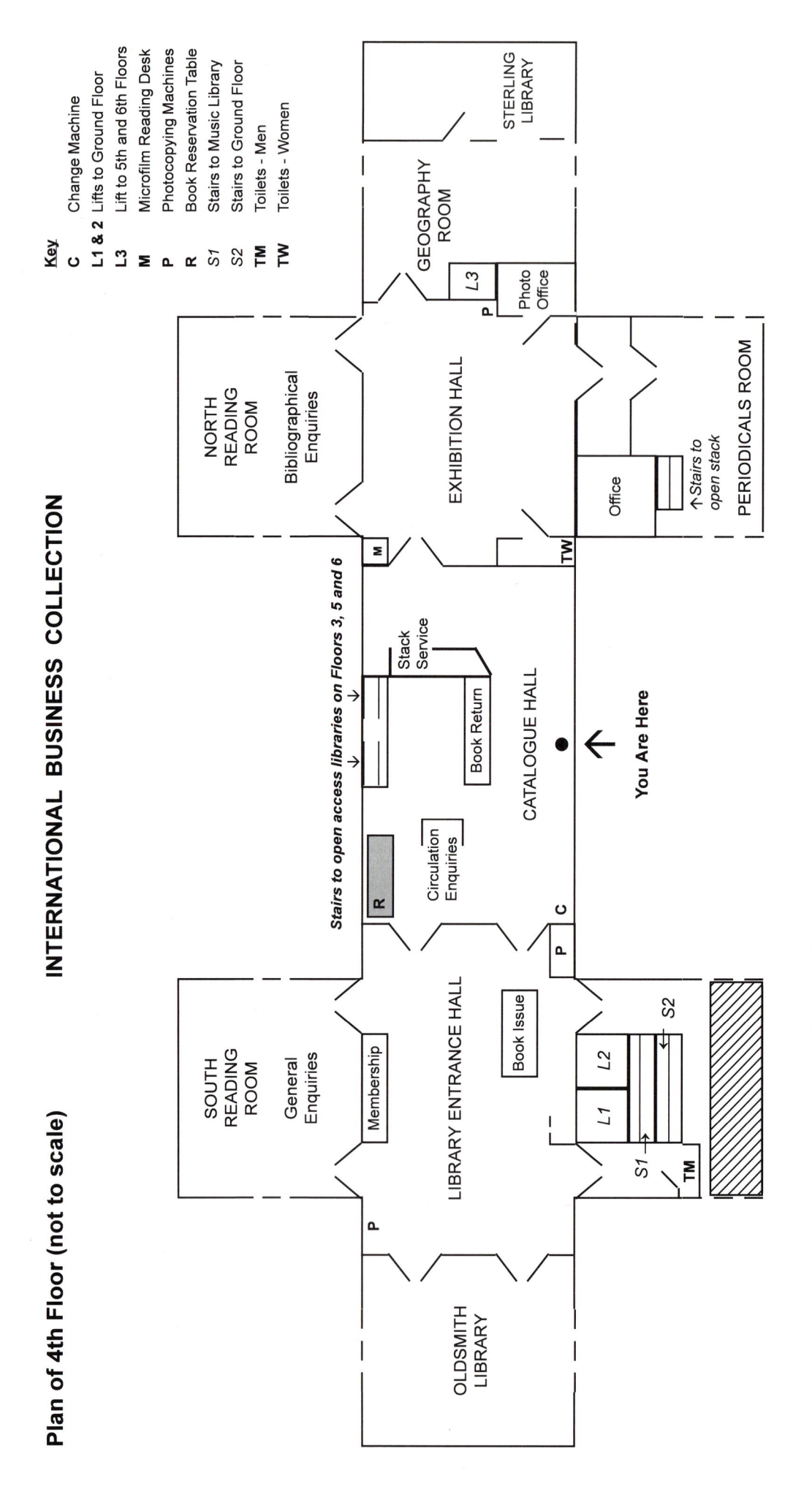

INTERNATIONAL BUSINESS COLLECTION

Plan of 4th Floor (not to scale)

Key
- **C**   Change Machine
- **L1 & 2** Lifts to Ground Floor
- **L3**   Lift to 5th and 6th Floors
- **M**   Microfilm Reading Desk
- **P**   Photocopying Machines
- **R**   Book Reservation Table
- *S1*   Stairs to Music Library
- *S2*   Stairs to Ground Floor
- **TM**   Toilets - Men
- **TW**   Toilets - Women

PETERSTONE BUSINESS COLLEGE - THE LIBRARY

3 b Now ask your neighbour these questions.

1. When will the group reassemble? And where?
2. Supposing you are in the South Reading Room at 2.55pm, what must you do?
3. Why must you keep your voices down?
4. If you want to make a bibliographical enquiry, that is, about a particular book, what will you do?
5. Supposing you are in the Geography Room and wish to reserve a book, what should you do?
6. Supposing you wanted to photocopy something in Japanese, what would you do?
7. How would you get to the parts of the library on other floors?
8. If you wanted to visit Singapore on a business trip, what might you do?
9. You have been looking at a display of Italian business documents and need to go to the toilet. What would you do?
10. When you take out your Membership Card, where will you get it? Will it be free?
11. You want to look at the latest issue of The Economist and Management Today. Where would you find them and how would you get there from the Sterling Library?
12. After reserving a book you go to the nearest lift. How do you get there?
13. You find something in the South Reading Room which you would like to photocopy but you first need change for the machine. What would you do?
14. After you reassemble, how much longer will the library stay open?
15. Where would you look up details of a book in the catalogue?

4 a Ask your neighbour some of these questions about the advertisement on the next page.

1. What is the object of this advertisement?
2. If you come home and smell gas, what should you do first?
3. If you come home at night and the house is dark, what should you remember?
4. Where would you find the telephone number of the Gas Emergency Service?
5. Where can you write it?
6. What two things should you do after opening doors and windows?
7. If you ring the Gas Emergency Service at midnight will someone be there?
8. What if you are a smoker?
9. If the lights are on, should you switch them off?
10. How do you turn the gas off at the meter?
11. How would you recognize the meter main outlet?
12. What would the most common cause of a gas problem be?
13. Do you use gas in your home? From a bottle or mains supply?
14. What are the dangers and advantages of gas?
15. Who are British Gas?

5 a Read the following statements and say whether you agree with them or not. Discuss your reasons with your neighbour.

1. Testing of nuclear weapons is necessary.
2. Credit cards are dangerous.
3. People should spend their holiday in their own country to support the economy.
4. Thin people are unhappy.
5. Children should be seen and not heard.

DO'S AND DON'TS THAT COULD HELP YOU SURVIVE A GAS LEAK

DO'S

DO OPEN DOORS AND WINDOWS TO GET RID OF THE GAS

DO CHECK TO SEE IF THE GAS HAS BEEN LEFT ON UNLIT OR IF A PILOT LIGHT HAS GONE OUT

DO TURN OFF THE GAS SUPPLY AT THE METER

DO CALL THE GAS EMERGENCY SERVICE - WE'RE IN THE PHONE BOOK UNDER GAS, AND WE'RE ON CALL 24 HOURS A DAY EVERY DAY (MAKE SURE SOMEONE'S THERE WHEN WE ARRIVE!)

USE THIS SPACE TO NOTE DOWN YOUR GAS EMERGENCY SERVICE PHONE NUMBER - LOOK IT UP NOW!

DON'TS

DON'T OPERATE ELECTRICAL SWITCHES - ON OR OFF

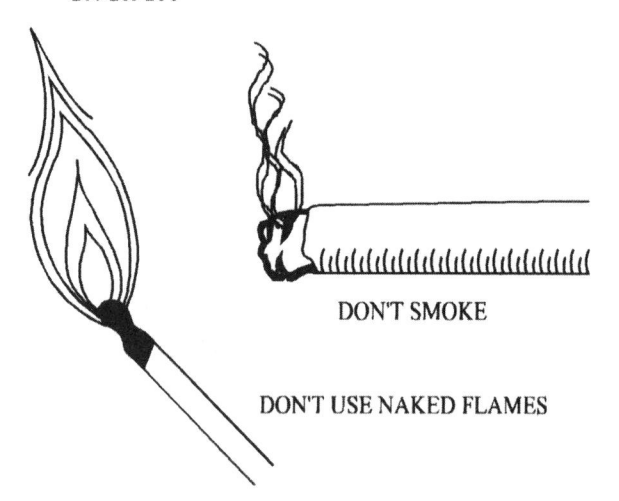

DON'T SMOKE

DON'T USE NAKED FLAMES

DON'T LEAVE IT TO SOMEONE ELSE - CALL THE EMERGENCY SERVICE.

British Gas
CARING FOR YOUR SAFETY

CUT THIS ADVERTISEMENT OUT AND KEEP IT SOMEWHERE HANDY. IT COULD SAVE YOUR LIFE.

UNIT 60

Exam Practice 4

1 a Tell your neighbour about yourself. Use the following points as a guideline.

- personal details - name, address, tel no
  date of birth, place of birth, nationality
  marital status

- family - parents, children, brothers and sisters

- work - work experience (where, when, what, how long)
  - current occupation (what, where)
  - ambitions

- hobbies/interests - equipment, training, ambitions

- town - how big/where
  - tourist attractions
  - industry
  - unemployment levels

2 a Look at photograph sequence 15 'A Business Trip' on the next pages and discuss with your neighbour what the sequence is about.

b Describe the people to your neighbour.

c Ask your neighbour some of these questions.

1 What did the businessman do before leaving on his trip?
2 What is he going to take with him?
3 After packing his suitcase, where did he go and why?
4 What did the secretary have ready for her boss?
5 Describe the woman's office.
6 What does the man have to do first at the airport?
7 How did the businessman get to the airport?
8 Describe the woman at the airport.
9 What will the businessman do when he arrives at his destination?
10 Who do you think he spoke to before going to his meeting?
11 At the hotel, what did he do before making a phone call?
12 What do you imagine the two men said to each other when they met?
13 How many people attend the meeting? Who do you think they are?
14 What do you think the person presenting the businessman says?
15 What will the businessman do after the speech of the man on his right?

A Business Trip (Photograph Sequence 15)

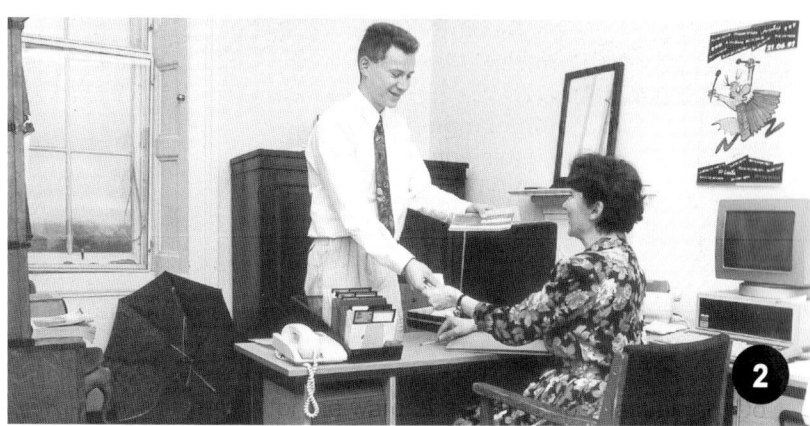

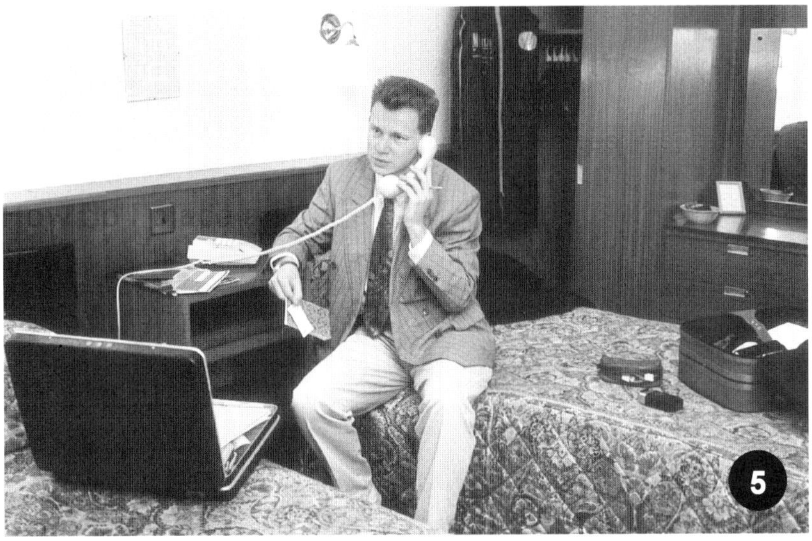

5

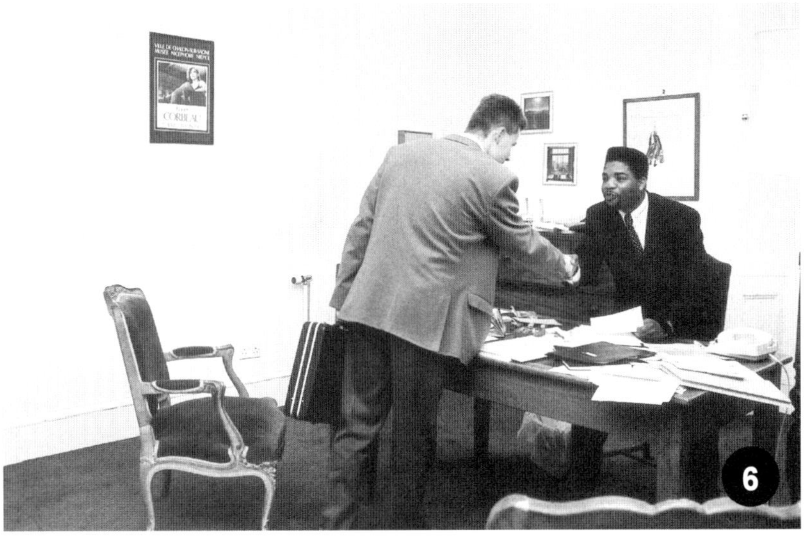

6

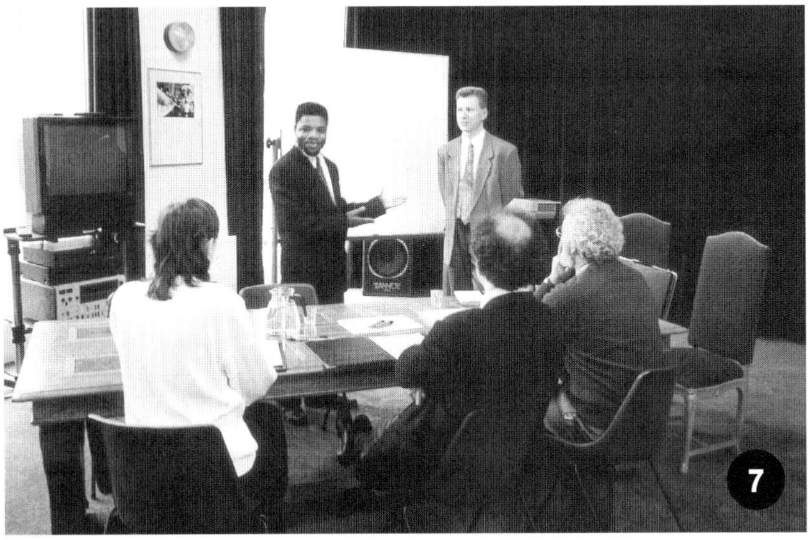

7

3 a You are going to hear a taped announcement. Before you listen, look at the diagram. You will hear the cassette twice and you may make notes if you wish.

THE GOLD SHOPPING CENTRE - LOWER MALL

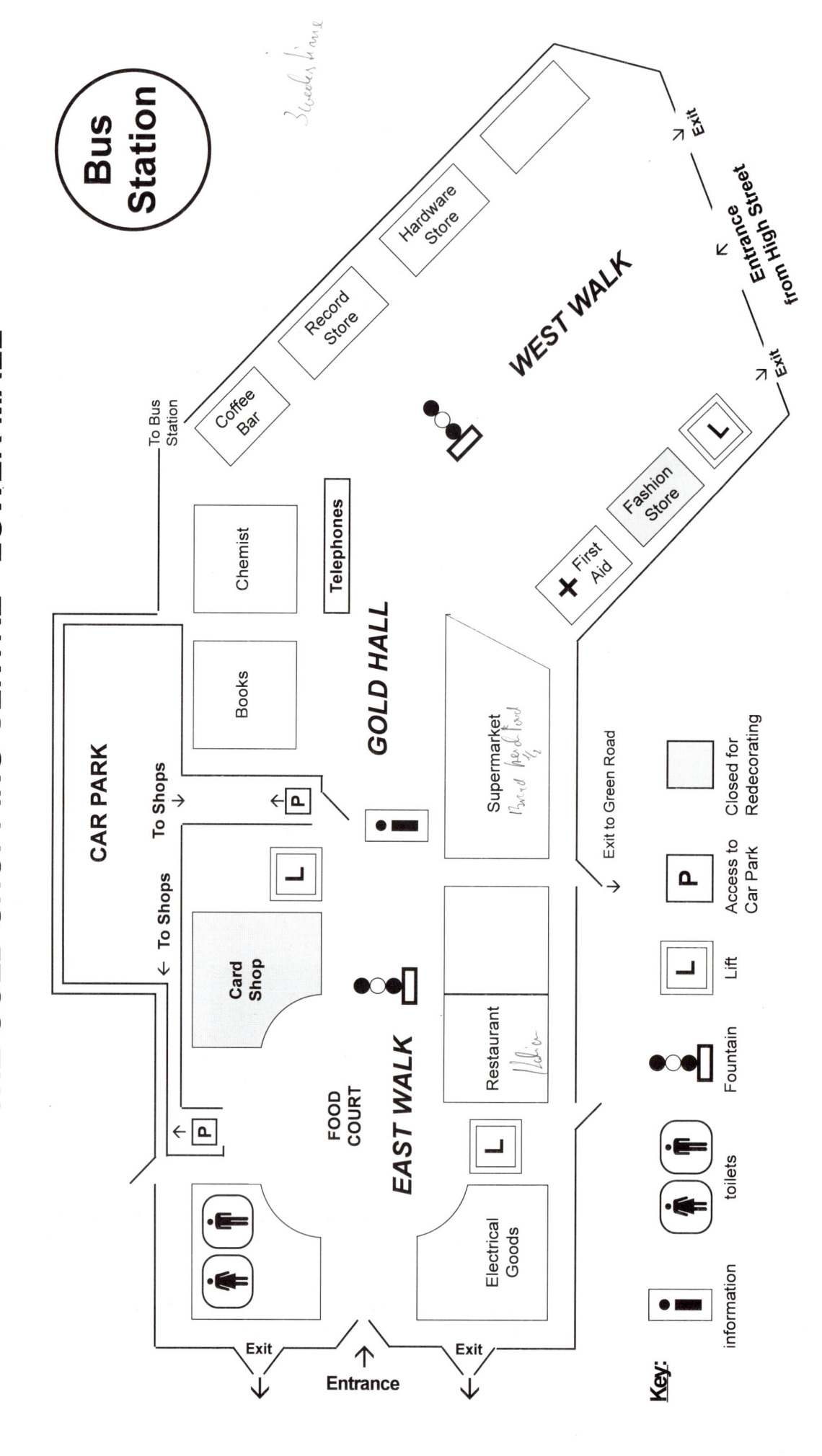

3 b   Now ask your neighbour these questions.

1   At what time of day do you hear this announcement?
2   Why is this called 'late night shopping'?
3   Until when are the shops open? Could you get coffee after they close?
4   Supposing you are Peter's mother, where would you find him? How would you get there from the High Street entrance?
5   Will you be able to have dinner or supper in the Mall? Where?
6   Could you buy some reduced-price records next week? Why not?
7   Suppose you had been buying some cheap records, how would you go to get some Italian food?
8   Which shops are not open? Why?
9   If you are in the restaurant and want to go to the car park, how could you go?
10 You have been buying a video recorder and want to go to the next floor up. How would you get there?
11 You enter the shopping centre from the High Street and want to go directly to the top floor. How would you go?
12 What will you find if you come out of the coffee shop when it closes and go to the toilet?
13 You would like to buy some apples and oranges. Where would be the best place to go?
14 Your friend has an accident and needs urgent medical attention - where would you go?
15 Can you get 30 per cent off music cassettes?

4 a   Ask your neighbour these questions about the advertisement on the next page.

1   Who lived in this house?
2   How long did he live here?
3   Who was Keats?
4   Can I visit Keats' house on a Sunday morning?
5   Is it open on public holidays?
6   Can I go by car?
7   Where can I park?
8   If I arrive, hot and tired, can I get tea at the house?
9   Can I take a group of visitors to the house?
10 Do I have to make any special arrangements for taking a group of visitors?
11 How much does it cost to go in?
12 Is the house near Hampstead Heath?
13 Where is the nearest underground station?
14 Could I walk from Belsize Park? How far is it?
15 Would you like to visit Keats' house? Why (not)?

5 a   Read the following statements and say whether you agree with them or not. Discuss your reasons with your neighbour.

1   People who don't exercise should not get medical care.
2   Young people have no respect for their parents.
3   All murderers should be executed.
4   Television is the best source of information.
5   Intelligence is inherited.

KEATS HOUSE

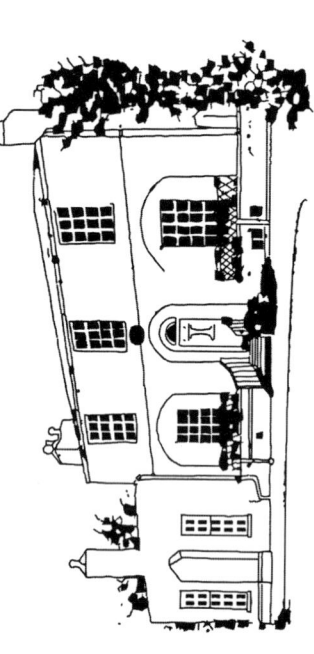

John Keats, the poet, lived here 1818 - 1820. The house contains relics, books and manuscripts relating to Keats, his family, friends and fiancée, Fanny Brawne.

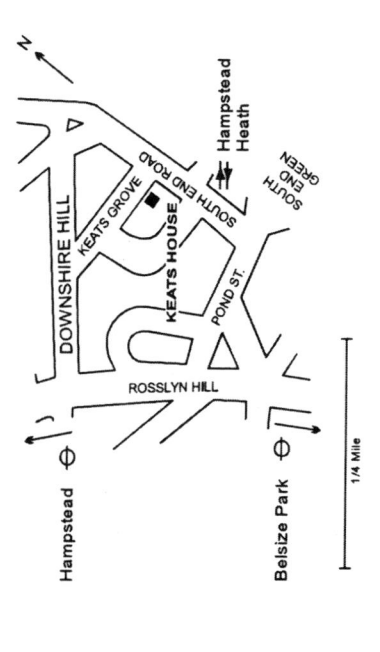

Φ Underground Station
⇌ British Rail

Information

OPENING HOURS	Monday to Saturday 10 - 1 and 2 - 6. Sunday 2 - 5. Easter, Spring and Late Summer Bank Holidays 2 - 5. Closed Christmas Day, Boxing Day, New Year's Day, Good Friday and May Day.
PARKING	Hampstead Heath 200 yards.
MUSEUM SHOP	Publications, souvenirs.
REFRESHMENTS	No catering, nearby tea shops.
PARTIES	Guided parties (limited to 25 persons) by arrangement with the Curator.
DISABLED	Not suitable for wheelchairs.
ADMISSION	Free

HOW TO GET THERE

BUSES	268 to Rosslyn Hill; 24, 46 and C11 to Hampstead Heath.
UNDERGROUND	Northern Line (Edgware branch) to Hampstead or Belsize Park
BRITISH RAIL	North London Line to Hampstead Heath.

Other Books in this Series

How to Pass Spoken English for Industry and Commerce Preliminary Level Students' Book ISBN 3-922514-33-2

How to Pass Spoken English for Industry and Commerce Preliminary Level Teachers' Book ISBN 3-922514-37-5

How to Pass Spoken English for Industry and Commerce Preliminary Level Students' Cassette ISBN 3-922514-38-3

How to Pass Spoken English for Industry and Commerce Preliminary Level Picture Book ISBN 3-922514-39-1

How to Pass Spoken English for Industry and Commerce Intermediate Level Students' Book ISBN 3-922514-35-9

How to Pass Spoken English for Industry and Commerce Intermediate Level Teachers' Book ISBN 3-922514-43-x

How to Pass Spoken English for Industry and Commerce Intermediate Level Students' Cassette ISBN 3-922514-44-8

How to Pass Spoken English for Industry and Commerce Advanced Level Students' Book ISBN 3-922514-36-7

How to Pass Spoken English for Industry and Commerce Advanced Level Teachers' Book ISBN 3-922514-45-6

How to Pass Spoken English for Industry and Commerce Advanced Level Students' Cassette ISBN 3-922514-46-4

Other Examination Preparation Books:

How to Pass English for Business First Level
ISBN 3-922514-30-8

How to Pass English for Business Second Level
ISBN 3-922514-31-6

How to Pass English for Business Third Level
ISBN 3-922514-32-4

Zeiten sind wichtig!

Ido - Ft does!

Berufbezeichnung

Berufskolleg Rheine
Frankenburg Str. 5